T0162693

Dare To Struggle

The History and Society of Greece

Richard M. Berthold

iUniverse, Inc.
New York   Bloomington

Dare To Struggle
The History and Society of Greece

The views expressed in this work are solely those of the author and do not necessarily reflect the views of the publisher, and the publisher hereby disclaims any responsibility for them.

iUniverse books may be ordered through booksellers or by contacting:

iUniverse
1663 Liberty Drive
Bloomington, IN 47403
www.iuniverse.com
1-800-Authors (1-800-288-4677)

Because of the dynamic nature of the Internet, any Web addresses or links contained in this book may have changed since publication and may no longer be valid.

ISBN: 978-1-4401-6395-1 (sc)
ISBN: 978-1-4401-6394-4 (ebk)

Printed in the United States of America

iUniverse rev. date: 10/2/2009

For
the Acquire Boys, the Gamers and the Weirdos,
none of whom had anything to do with this book

CONTENTS

Table of Maps

Chart

PREFACE

One might question the need for another Greek history, particularly at a time when regard for the western tradition, at which the Greeks are at the root, is less than fashionable in some intellectual circles. Indeed, there are dozens of Greek histories readily available, most far more detailed than this volume, and it might seem unnecessary to tell the story yet again.

In fact it is very necessary. It is a traditional proposition in the west, one to which most intelligent people will pay immediate lip service, that ancient Greece was great and vitally important to the history of the human race. But why? Few, including many in classical studies, it seems, can provide any sort of substantial answer to this question. Vaguely gesturing towards the Parthenon and mentioning such things as democracy and Euripides and Plato, as most would do, barely hints at the reason for the greatness of Greece. Other cultures have after all created beauty and nurtured great intellects. Other peoples have exercised far more power over far wider areas than the Greeks. In terms of extent and longevity Roman society, which ultimately captured Greece, must certainly be deemed greater. What is it about the Greeks?

Virtually all Greek histories and the Greek sections of Western Civilization texts only imply answers to this question, content to detail the achievements of ancient Greece and let the reader make inferences from that. The basic questions behind the truly staggering discoveries of the Greeks are never asked, let alone answered. General histories will, for example, offer the ideas of the Presocratics or detail the workings of the Athenian democracy, but they will not attempt to explain *why* after two and a half millennia of urban civilization the Greeks should be the first to express such incredibly novel ideas and develop such unprecedented political systems. Behind the philosophy of Aristotle, the plays of Sophocles and the democracy of Pericles are more fundamental ideas, which are only infrequently mentioned in Greek histories and rarely explained. These are the most important discoveries of the Greeks, the vital concepts that permit the flowering of their spectacular culture and are at the core of the whole western tradition: constitutionalism, rationalism, humanism and the idea of the individual. These ideas simply do not exist in all the societies before Greece, and given their importance to the Greeks, to us and to the world, their discovery and evolution need to be understood. This volume, unlike any other introduction to Greek history and society, attempts to provide that understanding.

It also attempts to provide, through an examination of the Greeks, a greater understanding of ourselves. Perhaps the prime purpose of the study of history is to illuminate the present, especially when dealing with a society that is so key in the cultural evolution of the human race. Consequently, many references are made to the present, especially to the history and society of post-World War II America, since many of the ideas and problems faced by our country in these years were first raised and confronted by the Greeks. Consider for example the parallels between Athens during the Peloponnesian War and our own agony in Vietnam; history may not repeat itself, but it is surely sometimes hauntingly familiar. Drawing these connections between past and present should make both Greek history and our recent past more meaningful.

This book is written in a perhaps more vernacular style than is typically encountered in standard histories. A soporific formality and stuffed-shirt seriousness are certainly not the requirements of a good history, especially one written for the non-specialist. But rest assured: this is a perfectly serious book, from which you may garner, I believe, a better understanding of the Greeks than you might from a more extensive history. I am, on occasion, a real live scholar and can cover the pages with arguments and footnotes with the best of them; try getting through my *Rhodes in the Hellenistic Age* without dozing off. This book of course is not a scholarly work and lacks the attendant argumentation and documentation, but I assure you my observations are for the most part in the mainstream and there is no more subjectivity than can be expected in any good history. And while I am extremely enthusiastic about the Greeks and their achievement, I also recognize their shortcomings and foolishness. The Greeks found in this book are neither the flawless, white Aryan supermen of nineteenth century German classicists, nor the contemporary revisionists' intellectually fraudulent progenitors of all that is racist and sexist in western society.

This history makes no attempt to cover every aspect of Greek society. My emphasis is on the social and political development of Greek civilization and its relevance to contemporary society and values. With the exception of the Persian wars and Alexander's conquests the historical narrative – this happened, then that happened – is kept to a minimum, but it is nevertheless sufficient to provide a sound understanding of the course of Greek history and to support an examination of Greek ideas. Literature is extensively referred to, but not in terms of its aesthetic value. Rather, the poetry, plays, histories and philosophical works are used as a window on Greek society, examples of the Greeks speaking about themselves. There is very little on the most obvious legacy of the ancient world: art. This is after all a history.

Finally, as is quite clear from this book, I believe that societies, like individuals, can be evaluated according to objective standards upon which reasonable people can agree. To assert that all cultures are equal and that all values are relative is in my opinion an absolutely absurd notion. And measured in terms of the importance of its ideas and their impact upon others I am ready to judge ancient Greece the most important society in the history of the planet. Yet while the very precious – and dangerous – gifts the Greeks bear are certainly a tribute to the vitality and creativity of their particular society, they are equally a measure of the potential residing in all human beings, a potential that indeed can only be fully realized with the acceptance of the constitutionalism, rationalism and humanism discovered by the Greeks.

The Suggested Readings at the end of each chapter are intended to steer the interested reader towards further information and more in-depth coverage of the topics in the chapter. The prime directive in selecting titles was readability, but some works of a less than compelling nature are included because of their coverage of the subject. I have endeavored to supply dates for every individual mentioned in the text, but this was not always possible; the dates following the names of kings and tyrants are for their reigns. Because the Greek year typically began in the early summer or fall, some dates are expressed as two of our years; e.g., 480/79. With regard to the inevitable problem of transliterating Greek names, I follow a policy of enlightened inconsistency: the Latinized version is used except when the Greek form appears more natural (e.g., Delos). Unless otherwise noted all dates are B.C.

Because of the cost, I was unable to produce my own maps for this history and was thus compelled to use historical maps in the public domain. These were originally printed in a much larger format and are consequently very difficult to read in the smaller format of this book. The maps were also originally printed in color, and the color keys to various territories have virtually disappeared in grey scale. I might suggest finding a commercially published Greek history in the library and xeroxing a map or maps. And of course my thanks to John King Lord (1848-1926); your maps live on.

I would like to thank Barbara Jello Haines for her cover design, and I must of course acknowledge the primary guidance of our mistress Clio, Muse of History, in writing this book: *Domina Clio, Dominare Nos.*

Richard M. Berthold
Albuquerque, NM

\#\#\#\#\#\#\#\#\#\#\#\#\#\#\#\#\#\#\#

INTRODUCTION

WHY BOTHER WITH THIS STUFF?

History is bunk.

- Henry Ford

Obviously, if you are reading this introduction, you have presumably already found good reasons to bother with this stuff, but read on if you have ever wondered about the need to study history and want the historian's pitch. Curiosity and interest probably prompted you to pick up this book, and these are perfectly valid motivations. It was curiosity and interest that drew me to the study of ancient history, and I actually make a living off this stuff (which means of course that I have a vested interest in selling you the goods). But there must be more to it than that, you think, or else this guy and people like him would not have jobs. True enough. There is something more, and that something more involves the search for truth.

History, like fiction, is interesting and amusing because it is vicarious experience, and it is as vicarious experience that history is ultimately valuable to us. Experience is how we learn. Through experience we add to the stock of knowledge upon which we base our judgments and decisions. The child sticks his hand in the fire and has an exciting experience, from which he may conclude certain things about the nature of fire and its relationship to human flesh. Learning is the natural issue of experience, of finding out what's behind Door No. 1, Door No. 2 and Door No. 3.

But our direct experience of the world is sorely limited by the brief span of our lives and the narrowness of our physical and cultural environments. Three score and ten is not a hell of a lot of time to do that many things, especially when you must spend a large part of it making a living, and until recently most of the human race never got beyond a few miles of their birthplace.

Even today most people never directly experience a seriously different culture, and as far as I know no one has ever personally experienced a different time.

Here is where the study of history comes in. It allows us to break out of these limits. In the words of Lord Acton "It liberates us from the tyranny of our environment." Through history we can step outside of our time and place and learn indirectly, through the experiences of other peoples in other times and other places. This is hardly something strange; most of our learning is founded on vicarious experience. The child generally avoids the painful encounter with fire because his mother presents him with the experience indirectly by describing what happens.

Fine, but how valid are these experiences to twenty-first century man, you may be wondering. After all, the Greeks didn't have to worry about nuclear weapons or the price of gas or global warming. Or to put it in the words so feared by academics in the sixties: "Is this stuff relevant?"

It sure is. Because while the shape of society and its technology and values may change, men and women remain men and women. The basic motivations and emotions of human beings are constants, and ancient Greeks and medieval Japanese and modern Americans are all driven by essentially the same needs, desires and fears. The Athenian man in the street basically wanted the same things as his American counterpart - a good job, security for himself and his family, the respect of his fellows and so on. The details may change, but the basics do not. We are all, whatever time and place we may be born into, faced with a similar set of problems, questions that are an immutable part of the human condition. How do I stay alive and provide for my offspring? How do I order my society and relate to my fellow humans? How do I relate to the universe as a whole? Every society in the history of the planet has had to find answers to these questions.

There are also the unchanging impersonal forces of history, the general social and economic laws that have held true throughout time. For example, you can't fool Mother Marketplace: debase your currency and inflation will result. This will happen whether the context is Late Imperial Rome or contemporary America, whether the mechanism is the reduction of precious metal in the coins or spending financed by big deficits. But such forces are in a sense "human," since they do not exist apart from human beings and thus by their constancy demonstrate the constancy of humans. Inflation results because the man selling his goods wants his due or more, a human trait that has never changed and that has in the twentieth century contributed to the collapse of the Marxist societies.

All societies, no matter how seemingly bizarre, have a basic relevance to us, but some are more meaningful than others, and Greece may be counted among these. Why the Greeks in particular are an important source of vicarious experience and a valid field of study should be fairly obvious. The roots of our western civilization lie deep in the society of ancient Greece, which has contributed countless important ideas and institutions to the development of our society. Indeed, the most important and distinctive elements of western civilization were born in Greece: constitutionalism, rationalism, humanism, the idea of the individual.

The result of all this vicarious experience picked up through history? Very simply, a better understanding of man and society and thus of ourselves and our society. Of course history cannot supply any pat solutions or blueprints for the future, but the more you know about other societies, the better you can understand your own, and the better you understand your own, the greater the chance of solving its problems and wisely determining its policies. Unfortunately, human beings have not shown themselves to be very good at this sort of thing. We seem to be doomed to make the same mistakes and do the same silly things over and over. Your reading this book will hardly change that, but you have to start somewhere, right?

It seems appropriate, before skipping off to the Balkan Peninsula, to provide a spot definition of exactly what "history" is. Most broadly and simply it is everything that has happened, all the facts. This is obviously an unworkable definition, however, since it includes an overwhelming amount of totally trivial and unimportant information. The fact that the President brushed his teeth this morning is technically history, but who cares? Now, if in the course of that dental routine the tooth paste tube exploded, removing him from office, we could all agree that we had an historical event on our hands. Clearly, it is necessary to consider the impact of the event upon its environment in order to determine its historical importance. What kind of ripple does it produce in the space-time continuum?

Enter the historian. It is his task to weigh the facts and consider their importance in the scheme of things. It is not only his task, but also something he can hardly avoid. In the nineteenth century there emerged in reaction to the romantic excesses of the previous age a school of "scientific" history, which maintained that the historian, like the scientist, must detach himself from his work and be totally objective. No more coloring the facts to fit or create your own vision of the past, just the straight poop. The goal of the historian was to record history, in the words of Leopold Ranke, "wie es eigentlich gewesen ist" – "as it actually was."

Well, objectivity is an admirable goal, but total objectivity is impossible. The simple selection of a topic and relevant facts is an injection of oneself into the material, a statement that you consider that bit of history important enough to examine. Further, the mere listing of events, the bare recording of data, is the work of a chronicler, not an historian. The historian's job requires a dose of subjectivity.

Now, I am not espousing the outright distortion of facts and the Joe Stalin school of history. The data must be presented as accurately and objectively as possible, but there must be something more. The historian must make some attempt at interpretation of his material, at understanding what he records. There must be an evaluation of events, an examination of causes, a delineation of trends and so forth. History must be something more than recording what happened; it must be, as E.H. Carr puts it, "an interaction between the historian and his facts, an unending dialogue between the present and the past." And that's exactly what you get in this book.

Enough of this. Ladies and gentlemen, Club Hellas is proud to present - the Greeks!

# # # # # # # # # # # # # # # # # # # #

I. GIVE US YOUR INDO-EUROPEANS, YEARNING TO BE GREEK

The Minoans and Mycenaeans

One pair of wheels, bound with bronze, unfit for service.

- Linear B tablet[1]

The taproots of our western civilization go back beyond the Balkan Peninsula and the Greeks, back ultimately to the river valleys of the Nile and the Tigris and Euphrates. There, near the end of the fourth millennium, Egypt and Sumer (southernmost Iraq) reached a level of agricultural technique and political organization that allowed them to build the world's first cities, and civilization was born. From these communities emerged the basic discoveries and developments of human society: irrigation, smelting and refining of ores, bricks, wheeled vehicles, basic mathematics, monumental architecture, the sailboat and of course those seemingly eternal hallmarks of civilization – bureaucracy and organized warfare. And most important, those industrious Sumerians came up with the invention that marks the actual beginning of history – writing.

But despite these achievements the influence of ancient Near Eastern society on the evolution of western civilization is minimal. True, there was an "east-west drift" of the basic technological developments; bronze, for example, was brought to Greece by settlers from Anatolia (Asia Minor or modern Turkey) in the third millennium. There was also some cultural influence, but apart from artistic techniques and motifs this was severely limited and mostly indirect, with one exception. That one exception is Hebrew monotheism,

1

which through its offspring Christianity has had a tremendous impact on the west. But the transformation of the Semitic tribal god into the universal deity of western society came too late to affect the Greeks during their time on center stage. Further, Greece was most susceptible to serious culture-shaping influences from the east during the Mycenaean period, and as we shall see, there is a clean break between the Mycenaean world and the city-state society of the Archaic and Classical Ages. The Greeks would later certainly borrow a great deal from the east, such as the Phoenician alphabet, but by then the basic character of their society would be too firmly rooted to be significantly influenced by eastern cultural patterns. And that society would represent something completely new on the face of the earth. In its underlying character it would be not just different, but profoundly different from all the eastern palace-centered autocracies that preceded it, and it would dramatically affect the societies that followed. What might be considered the essential and distinctive elements of western civilization – constitutionalism, rationalism, humanism and the idea of the individual – were all homegrown by the Greeks. They did not exist in any of the dozens of pre-classical societies in the Near East.

Before moving on to the Greeks, it is necessary first to say a few things about Minoan Crete, even though during its days of power and glory the island was manifestly not Greek. Minoan society (named after the legendary Cretan king Minos) was, however, the first European civilization, and more important, it dramatically influenced the first wave of Greeks to arrive in the Balkan Peninsula. In more ways than one the prehistory of the Aegean is admittedly opening act material, but a brief look at the Minoan world will not only set the stage for the story of the Greeks, but also provide an idea of the kinds of problems faced by the historian of this very early period.

Crete was settled in the seventh millennium by Neolithic immigrants, probably from Anatolia. As might be expected for a Stone Age society, events move at a glacial pace for about the next four thousand years, but life was then stirred up by new waves of Anatolians looking for better pickings in the southwest. They settled in Crete and the Cyclades (the south Aegean islands) and brought with them a new material for making tools and weapons – bronze, an alloy of copper and tin. Consequently, the beginning of the third millennium roughly marks the advent of the Bronze Age in the Aegean basin, and this period is called "Minoan" on Crete and "Helladic" on the Greek mainland.

Minoan civilization really got rolling around 2000, when an urban revolution of sorts occurred on the island. In place of small farming communities actual cities began to appear and grow, and sometime around 1700 Cnossus, a city of perhaps 10-15,000 inhabitants on the north coast of the island, appears to have established some sort of loose control over all Crete. The victory of Cnossus stimulated further economic and social growth, and Crete soon reached the height of her prosperity and cultural achievement, rivaling her oriental contemporaries, New Kingdom Egypt, the Hittite Empire in Anatolia and the Babylonian Empire in Mesopotamia (modern Iraq). For three centuries Minoan civilization would blossom, and then it would suddenly be destroyed, virtually overnight.

Agriculture, especially cultivation of those Mediterranean staples, the vine and olive, appears to have been the occupation of most of the island's inhabitants, but then, until fairly recently the majority of the population of every society has been directly involved in the production of food. It was not farming that made Crete wealthy and supported her cities, however, but trade. Her excellent location allowed her merchants to act as middlemen for products flowing to and from the Near East, Aegean and far west, and while she exported the occasional lot of domestic wine or olive oil, the serious money came from the carrying trade.

The Minoan trade network stretched two thousand miles from the Levant to the Iberian Peninsula, but it was most extensive in the Aegean. The Minoan script cannot be read, but their economic activity is clearly revealed by archaeology, especially the study of the humblest but most important of ancient remains, potsherds. The foreign pottery fragments found in the Levantine ports for this period are mostly Minoan, and since amphorae, large ceramic pots, were the packing crates of antiquity, this can only mean Crete dominated the trade in this region. In the Aegean the remains from the Cyclades for these centuries are overwhelmingly Minoan in character, while those from the eastern and southern parts of mainland Greece show strong Minoan influence. Further, the survival of "Minoa" as a common place name in the region strongly suggests the existence at one time of numerous Minoan trading stations.

On the basis of such evidence Sir Arthur Evans, the excavator of Cnossus, postulated the existence of a Minoan thalassocracy or sea empire. In addition to the archaeological remains he pointed to the literary tradition: to judge from passages in Herodotus, Thucydides and Aristotle among others, it is clear the classical Greeks believed that the Cretans, under their king Minos, once held an Aegean empire. And there is the tale of Theseus and the Minotaur. Legends are rarely created out of thin air and usually have a core of truth, and Evans argued that a story about an Athenian youth sent to Crete as tribute was a memory of Minoan control of the mainland. So the Cretans ruled the waves and parts of the mainland. Others disagreed with Evans, however, and argued that Minoan society was never strong enough economically or militarily to control any part of the mainland, since that would require a

substantial military force. Indeed, the military tradition is virtually nonexistent in Minoan art, which would seem a bit strange for any serious military power. A further consideration: during the Late Minoan period – after about 1500 – Minoan ceramic ware in Egypt and the Levant was rapidly displaced by Helladic (Greek) ware, which can only mean that Minoan merchants lost the lucrative eastern trade to the Greeks. Since Crete was hardly likely to voluntarily surrender such a prop of her wealth and power, this must in turn mean that she had lost control of the sea-lanes. Any Minoan Empire must consequently predate 1500.

What is the answer? The archaeological and literary evidence for a thalassocracy of some sort is too strong to abandon the idea altogether, and it also makes fine sense (though making fine sense is of course not always characteristic of human affairs). We know from the remains that Crete had an extensive trading network, which meant a large merchant marine. Since piracy was endemic in these times, the merchantmen must have been armed and/or protected by a Minoan navy. Further, because of these same aquatic predators, the sea was always a source of danger, since piracy was not limited

4

to capturing merchant vessels, but included Viking style raids on coastal settlements. The easily beached ships of these Aegean Bluebeards were a constant menace to the inhabitants of the Aegean shore, and thus virtually all towns of any size had walls. But none of the cities on Crete was walled, which suggests very strongly that they were protected instead by a navy. On the other hand, it is difficult to see how Crete could ever be strong enough to control directly any part of the mainland, though there is clear evidence of cultural impact and domination. Consequently, the Minoans probably controlled the Aegean Sea and the islands, while exerting a great deal of economic influence on the mainland. Their thalassocracy was probably at its peak in the seventeenth century and on the wane in the late sixteenth, since the Minoans lost control of the trade network after 1500. This seems the most reasonable understanding of the meager evidence, but historical certainty is very elusive in the Bronze Age world and many a "reasonable understanding" has been toppled by new discoveries.

As you might expect, our knowledge of Minoan society, deriving almost exclusively from archaeology, is slight. Society centered on the palace, especially the great palace at Cnossus. From there the king held sway over the rest of the island, perhaps through some sort of vassalage, and his rule was facilitated by a developed palace bureaucracy. As in the Near Eastern monarchies, he was the head religious figure in the state, and he may have directly controlled part of the island's commercial enterprises, which would make him the head businessman as well. Minoan society as a whole might be characterized as a paternal semi-theocratic monarchy ruling over a large lower class, which had no political rights, but which does not seem to have been overly oppressed. There must have been a small commercial class that carried on the business of the island and struggled to enter the upper class of wealthy merchants and landowners. Social stratification does not appear to have been rigid, and there was probably upward mobility for the rare individual who was talented and lucky.

Little can or need be said about Minoan religion, which appears to have been pretty much standard issue for the period. The gods were conceived of in anthropomorphic terms and seem to have been mostly female and connected with fertility and the earth, though evidence for any sort of primal Mother Goddess is completely lacking. Women played a major role in cult practices, and figured in bull-leaping, a practice in which a young man or woman grabbed the horns of a charging bull and somersaulted over his back. This might seem an improbable activity (and rodeo stars have claimed it is impossible), but it is the only way to understand the frescoes that explicitly depict it. Given the participation of females and the importance of the bull in Minoan religion, this was undoubtedly not so much sport as some sort of religious ritual. The tremendous number of cult artifacts and sites found on the island demonstrate the importance of religion, but there does not appear to have been the overwhelming concern for the afterlife found in Egypt or the grinding pessimism found in Mesopotamia. If their art is any indication, the Minoans found a great joy in life and in nature, which is the most frequent subject of their graphic endeavors. The portrayal of war, so abundant in Greek art, is extremely rare, and even human figures are uncommon. Perhaps the highest (and certainly the most obvious) expression of Minoan culture is the palace complex at Cnossus, with its maze of living quarters, audience halls, storerooms, hallways and the first running water bathrooms in European history. Looking around at just the ruins, one can easily see how the Theseus legend might get started. To the average peasant, who had rarely visited a building with more than a couple of rooms, the palace complex would seem like a labyrinth, and in his awe and fear of anything strange the bumpkin might well imagine a menacing guardian. Since the bull played such an important role in religion and was depicted everywhere, it was only natural the guardian creature should be half man and half bull – the Minotaur. The word labyrinth (Greek: *labyrinthos*) itself may derive from the palace, since the walls of this maze-like structure were covered with images of the *labrys*, the sacred double ax.

But Cnossus also reveals something strange. Sometime in the fifteenth century the capital developed a separate culture, one that did not extend to the rest of the island. The palace, for example, was rebuilt in a distinctive mainland style, which included a throne room. All of a sudden militaristic motifs show up strongly in the art, and a great deal of Helladic pottery is found. And most significantly, Linear A script, the as yet undeciphered writing found on clay tablets in several sites on Crete, is replaced by a different script, Linear B. Linear B tablets are found all over the mainland, but on Crete for the most part only in Cnossus and only after the middle of the fifteenth century. In the 1950s Linear B was deciphered by the cryptographer and amateur Hellenist Michael Ventris, and it is quite definitely Greek. Cnossus had apparently gone Greek. What had happened to the capital of the once powerful Minoan Empire? In order to answer that question it is necessary to take a look at developments on the mainland.

Before the third millennium Greece was inhabited by a Neolithic people about whom we know little, and not much was happening. Around 3000 or so, waves of immigrants rolled into the Balkan Peninsula, probably from Anatolia and seemingly overwhelmed the locals with the latest technology, bronze. Thus, the Bronze (or Helladic) Age was under way in Greece. Only one important item was missing: the Greeks.

Sometime in the course of the first half of the second millennium a new wave of invaders surged into the peninsula. Unlike any before them, these people definitely came from the north. In fact, they were completely different from all the Semitic and Hamitic peoples who had been busy building and destroying civilizations in the Mediterranean and Near East. They were Indo-European. Like Semitic or Asianic, Indo-European (or Indo-Aryan, the original name, for obvious reasons now in disfavor) is a linguistic grouping, designating a family of languages that can all trace their roots back to a common tongue, called Indo-European. Hittite, Tocharian, Illyrian (Albanian), Thraco-Phyrgian (Armenian), Greek, all the Italic (including Latin and its Romance derivatives), Germanic, Celtic, Slavic, Baltic (except Estonian), Iranian (Persian, Kurdish, etc.) and Indic (Hindi/Urdu, Punjabi, Assamese, etc.) languages are descendants of Indo-European, and the core of the people who spoke and spread these languages were likewise descended from one original group.

Where exactly the Indo-Europeans hailed from is a matter of great debate, though eastern Anatolia and the plains of southern Russia are two prime candidates. Precisely when they entered the Balkan Peninsula is also in dispute: the traditional view favors the period around 2000, but many now believe the arrival of these strangers should be dated closer to the middle of the millennium. And why they decided to move at this particular time is unclear as well: traditionally the movement has been seen as a folk migration, like the later Germanic invasions of the Roman Empire, but some now think it consisted of smaller groups, bent on conquest and fully aware of exactly where they were heading. But whatever the precise cause, sometime in the first half of the second millennium an Indo-European wave washed west, south and southeast, carrying these barbarians into Western Europe, the Italian and Balkan Peninsulas, Anatolia, the northern tier of the Middle East and (much later) northwestern India. By the time of the migrations Indo-European had already begun fragmenting into its daughter tongues, and we know now that the groups that moved into the Balkan Peninsula spoke an early form of Greek. The Greeks had arrived.

Deciding that this was the place, these first Greeks abandoned their wandering and adopted a settled way of life, forsaking hunting and gathering for agriculture. From the local inhabitants they learned the cultivation of the olive and the vine, and they discovered sailing, probably with help from the Minoans. In return they brought with them a strong tradition of male sky gods, a language seemingly better suited for precise analysis and communication (at any rate the local tongues disappeared) and the horse. This last provided the motive power for a formidable new military technology, the chariot, which explains why, despite their apparently small numbers, the

Indo-Europeans had a dramatic impact wherever they went. In the Balkans they stimulated the existing culture, and by about 1600 a distinctive Greek civilization had emerged in the central and southern peninsula in urban centers such as Tiryns, Pylos and Mycenae. From the last of these this first Greek society takes its name – Mycenaean.

Mycenaean society, like Minoan, centered on the palace complex, but in the Greek case the palace was also a fortress, indicating that inter-city relations in Greece were somewhat more wild and woolly than on Crete. The Linear B tablets show that each urban center was ruled by a king, who was supported by an elaborate bureaucracy and by subordinates who appear to have been vassals or retainers of some sort. From their fortress-palaces, whose ruins remain impressive to this day, these petty kings dominated the food-producing plains with semi-professional chariot corps and amassed concentrations of wealth previously unheard of in the region. Much more cannot be said, however, since the tablets, though numerous, only record transactions, inventories and other data beloved by the bureaucrat. They are the red tape of the Mycenaean world, demonstrating a high degree of social specialization and complexity, but revealing few clues about structure and ideas.

We are pretty much in the dark concerning relations among the Mycenaean kingdoms. The fortress-palaces suggest that political unity, if it ever existed, was tenuous at best. Mycenae, seemingly the strongest, might have held a loose overlordship, but it was certainly never powerful enough to control directly the entire Peloponnesus (the southernmost part of Greece). There was clearly a cultural unity, and it would appear that the east was aware of the Mycenaean Greeks as a single people. Hittite (Indo-European cousins in Anatolia) texts have references to the "Ahhiyava," who are likely the "Achaeans," the most common Homeric name for the Mycenaeans. The Greeks, incidentally, later called themselves "Hellenes" and their country "Hellas," taking the names from an obscure tribe in east central Greece. This area was the original center of the confederacy that later controlled Delphi, and the spread of the names might be connected with the growing influence of the Delphic oracle. Further, participating in the foundation of Cumae (near Naples) were colonists from Graia, an obscure district in central Greece, and for some strange reason the Latins and other locals began referring to all the local Greek colonists as "Graii," from which was derived "Graeci" – Greeks.

To judge from the artistic remains, Mycenaean society seems have been lively and happy, though in its way a bit more barbaric than Minoan. Mycenaean religion was similar to and influenced by Minoan, but there was also a tradition of male, sky gods, such as Zeus. Such deities are characteristic of a wandering and hunting people, and Zeus, who will become the chief god of the Greeks, is definitely Indo-European in origin. There was in fact a kind of cultural duality in Mycenaean civilization: the upper layers were heavily influenced by Crete, especially in art, but out in the villages among the common folk there was a continuing Greek (Helladic) tradition.

The Greeks learned sailing and mastery of the sea, and if they learned it from the Minoans, they promptly showed their gratitude by taking over the Minoan trade network. Then around the middle of the fifteenth century Cnossus apparently goes Greek, which can only be due to the installation of a Mycenaean prince, presumably through a raid from the mainland. Such would fit with the decline of Minoan sea power: without the protection of a navy the unwalled cities of Crete would be comparatively easy pickings. How far into the island the rule of this usurper extended is completely unclear, but the Mycenaean influences were limited to Cnossus and its immediate environs. Evans believed that Cnossus itself was destroyed in the early fourteenth century, shortly after the Greek take-over, but more and more scholars now accept a much later date for the final destruction, one closer to the Catastrophe of the twelfth century.

But how did once mighty Crete come to this pass? Presumably for the same sorts of political, economic and social reasons that all high civilizations ultimately go into decline. Unfortunately, the extreme dearth of information makes it virtually impossible to consider specific causes, as we can for better documented societies like Rome or Britain, and one can only speak vaguely about the aging society falling prey to the young and aggressive mainland civilization. Very probably contributing to Crete's problems, however, was the eruption of Thera (now Santorini), a volcanic island about seventy miles north of Cnossus. Sometime in the sixteenth century Thera blew up with a violence that dwarfs the A.D. 1883 explosion of Krakatoa and the smaller destruction of Mt. St. Helens in A.D. 1980; it was as if a hydrogen bomb had been detonated in the waters just north of Crete. Thousands of tons of ash and pumice spewed miles into the air, and parts of Crete's farmlands would have been carpeted with debris, though whether enough fell to seriously effect the vegetation is not at all clear. More devastating, an aquatic shock wave (a tsunami) sped outward from the remains of Thera, creating in shallow coastal areas a wall of water as much as a hundred feet high. Ships at sea would not have been unduly troubled, but vessels that were beached, in port or sailing close to the coast, as well as towns in low-lying coastal regions, would have been overwhelmed, as with the great tsunami of A.D. 2005. The smaller Krakatoa explosion caused damage thousands of miles away, so it is very likely the Thera event has a serious impact, particularly on the Minoan navy and trade.

There is, incidentally, a mystery associated with Thera: why did it not leave a bigger dent in the Greek tradition? The effects of what amounted to a thermonuclear device going off in the middle of the Aegean are something people in the area are not likely to forget, yet Greek oral tradition (see Chapter II) contains no recollection of one of the most impressive natural events in history. The legend of Atlantis immediately springs to mind, but there is no Greek evidence for the tale before Plato in the fourth century, none of the details supplied by Plato fit the circumstances of Thera and elements of the legend can in any case be traced back to North Africa. The Greeks remembered all sorts of things from the Bronze Age; why not this?

With the end of Minoan greatness came the ascension and prosperity of Mycenaean society, and during the fourteenth and thirteenth centuries Greece was more united and wealthy than she would be again for more than half a millennium. But the days of brightness were numbered, and within about three hundred years of the Greek capture of Cnossus all of the Minoan and Mycenaean world would go under, the cities sacked and burnt. This was the Catastrophe, but before it arrived, there was one great adventure – at least one we know of – the expedition to Troy.

It used to be thought that the Trojan War, like pretty much everything else in the *Iliad* and *Odyssey*, was just fiction, and then late in the nineteenth century the German businessman Heinrich Schliemann, equipped with his trusty edition of Homer, went to northwestern Turkey and dug up the city of Troy. Schliemann was what we might call a "colorful character," and like many others in the nineteenth century he got a little carried away with the Greeks. When during his later excavations at Mycenae he unearthed the spectacular gold death mask now in the National Museum in Athens, he immediately assumed (quite wrongly) that it had belonged to king Agamemnon (of *Iliad* fame) and promptly sent off a telegram to king George I of Greece, telling the king that he had gazed upon the face of his ancestor. George was a Dane.

The remains discovered by Schliemann and his successors revealed that Troy was already wealthy and strong in the early years of the second millennium, long before Agamemnon and his band of brothers began poking their noses into that corner of the Aegean. The prosperity was doubtless due to Troy's location at the entrance of the Hellespont (the Dardanelles), which gave the Trojans control over the rich trade between the Aegean and the Black Sea. The presence of much Greek ware from after 1400 demonstrates the development of a brisk commerce with the Mycenaean world during its heyday. Troy was definitely a fat city, and all that loot finally attracted the attention of the Greeks.

According to the chronology worked out by the Greeks themselves centuries later, the expedition to Troy took place about 1183. As it happens, level VIIa of the mound of Troy reveals a phase of the city that was destroyed by fire and human violence c. 1190, though level VI, destroyed c. 1270, might also be a candidate. There is no archaeological evidence that it was Greeks who did the deed in either of these cases, but were they not involved in one of the destructions, it is difficult to see why the story would be invented and play such an overwhelming role in the Greek oral tradition. Homer's details cannot of course be trusted. Greed, rather than Helen's face, almost certainly launched those ships, and a ten year siege is clearly out of the question. The war was most likely a raid for booty, carried out perhaps by a coalition of Mycenaean princes, and it may be that it was remembered and celebrated while others were forgotten simply because it was the last big adventure before the Mycenaean world came apart at the seams.

The late thirteenth and twelfth centuries were a period of dissolution in the eastern Mediterranean, as new barbarian invaders and changes in weaponry brought down the chariot-based empires of the high Bronze Age. Movements of peoples in the northern Balkans and in the Danube basin pushed new groups into Asia Minor, where they caused trouble for everyone in sight. During the last decades of the thirteenth century the Hittite Empire, already weakened from a long struggle with Egypt, made its last stand, and by the beginning of the next century the Hittites had been so thoroughly obliterated that their very existence was forgotten until the nineteenth century A.D. The invasions and destruction dislodged whole groups, some now known as the "Sea Peoples," who spread the troubles south into Syria and Palestine and west into the Aegean. The Egyptian Empire collapsed, and king Ramses III (1198-1166) was barely able to defend the Nile delta against massive attacks in the opening years of the twelfth century. The entire power structure of the Near East lay in ruins. This was the Catastrophe.

The Mycenaeans were meanwhile too busy to enjoy this spectacle of destruction to the east. In addition to raiders from the east there were new waves of Greek speakers, moving south from the northern Balkans, and by the middle of the eleventh century most all the Mycenaean centers had either already been sacked and burnt or soon would be. This new gaggle of Greeks, called the Dorians, ultimately swept through the Peloponnesus and on into Crete, where the last vestiges of Minoan civilization were finally eradicated. The Dorian unpleasantness also sent streams of Greek refugees flowing across the Aegean to Anatolia, where the recently created power vacuum allowed them to settle the entire western coastline, which became known as Ionia.

Like their cousins who entered Greece centuries earlier, the Dorians were a rude people and had little with which to replace the high civilization of the Mycenaean world. The standards of civilized life collapsed completely, and Greece reverted to a collection of isolated, crude and illiterate farming communities. A Dark Age settled over the Balkan Peninsula – dark both in its contrast to the brilliance of Mycenaean society and in our almost total lack of knowledge of it. The Minoan-Mycenaean world was utterly destroyed, and its legacy to later Greeks was confined to a few tales and some curious ruins. Dark Age bards sang of Mycenae and Agamemnon and recalled the Dorian migration as the "Return of the Heraclidae" – the return of the sons of Heracles to claim the Peloponnesus – but basically the Mycenaean world was forgotten. For all our ignorance, we today know far more about this first Greek civilization than did the Greeks of Pericles' day.

# # # # # # # # # # # # # # # # # # # #

SUGGESTED READING

For an excellent introduction to the Indo-European problem see Robert Drews, *The Coming of the Greeks* (1988); his *The End of the Bronze Age* (1993) is an equally readable study of the Catastrophe, which he believes was primarily the result of new weaponry rather than massive migrations. R.W. Hutchinson, *Prehistoric Crete* (1962), John Chadwick, *The Mycenaean World* (1976) and especially A.R. Burn, *Minoans, Philistines and Greeks B.C. 1400-900* (1970) are readable introductions, though now out of date in many respects; far more detailed and current is Oliver Dickinson, *The Aegean Bronze Age* (1994), but your eyes will be drooping after a few pages. Christos Doumas, *Thera. Pompeii of the ancient Aegean* (1983) is a well illustrated examination of the island, though heavy on the archaeology. Leonard Cottrell, *The Bull of Minos* (1982) presents an amusing account of the original excavations of Cnossus and Mycenae, and for a really different view of Bronze Age Greece try Larry Gonick, *The Cartoon History of the Universe. Vol. 5: Brains and Bronze* (1980). If you're into that sort of thing, John Chadwick, *The Decipherment of Linear B* (1958) is very entertaining. And of course the best thing to read on the Trojan War is the bard himself; I recommend the Richmond Lattimore translation of the *Iliad*. I also recommend the superb historical novels of Mary Renault, *The King Must Die* (1958) and *The Bull from the Sea* (1962), both of which deal with the Theseus legend. And for a wonderful example of how ideology and mountains of trivial data can lead to hilarious and nonsensical conclusions take a peek at Martin Bernal, *Black Athena: the Afro-Asiatic Roots of Greece* (1987).

################################

II. BLIND HOMER AND THE DARK AGE BLUES

The Birth of the Polis

Therefore let no man be urgent to take the way homeward
until after he has lain in bed with the wife of a Trojan
to avenge Helen's longing to escape and her lamentations.

- Homer *Iliad* 2.354-56[2]

The lights had gone out all over the Aegean world. The Catastrophe and
the arrival of the Dorians had plunged Greece into semi-barbarism, into a
Dark Age. But the new society of this Dark Age, squalid though it might
be when compared to the Mycenaean world, had a grand future and would
produce ideas and institutions unlike any before. For several centuries the
Greeks would be left completely alone, free of serious outside influences and
threats. Unlike their predecessors who had built the Mycenaean world, they
would be able to spread their cultural wings unhampered. In particular they
could now explore a single, but all-important idea brought from their Indo-
European past.

That idea had to do with the nature of authority in the community.
Perhaps because we have had no real experience with them, we are accustomed
to think of all kings as essentially alike. But in fact there are kings and there
are kings, and not all fit the shoes of Louis XIV. In the ancient Near East the
operative idea behind the kingship – and thus behind the whole concept of
authority in the state – was that the power exercised by the king came from
above, from the gods. So long as you have this notion - that the power exercised
by the state derives from heaven - you will never get beyond monarchy in
your political development. Individual rulers might be challenged and even

15

removed, but not the kingship itself, which was by definition part of the order of things, ordained by god. One might as well challenge the law of gravity. And given this conception of the political order, your kingship will almost inevitably have theocratic overtones, as is most obvious in the case of Egypt, where the king was also literally a god manifest, an extrusion of heaven onto the earth.

What the Greeks inherited from their barbarian ancestors was precisely the opposite notion of authority. They understood the power wielded by their early petty kings to come from below, from the community, upon whose behalf, at least in theory, the king ruled. This is the root idea of constitutionalism, the basic concept underpinning our own system of government: the authority exercised by the state, whatever form the state takes, derives from the people. Any government that subscribes to this idea is in theory constitutional, even if the regime is narrow and oppressive and practice does not match theory. Such might be labeled an immature constitutional state; mechanisms allowing the people, the source of authority, to influence and direct the government are necessary for the mature constitutional society. But it is the basic idea that is utterly important, even in its more primitive guises. It is a simple idea, but one fat with political possibilities.

Now, this idea is hardly unique to the Indo-European peoples. Rather, it is common to primitive and especially hunting-gathering tribal societies, and it is easy to see how this notion and the weak kingship (or chiefdom) associated with it might arise within the basically egalitarian tribal organization. The group with an effective hunter-warrior leader will perform more efficiently and thrive, so there is a strong motivation for the hunter-warrior host to invest a talented member with authority, creating a sort of primitive elective kingship. Humans (or at least human males) being hard-wired the way they are, that initially informal arrangement will tend to become more permanent and ultimately hereditary. The hereditary principle will not, however, be completely secure, since the food supply of the hunting-gathering society is so precarious that it cannot long tolerate incompetent leadership, a luxury enjoyed by much more economically sophisticated communities, like imperial Rome or America. So, a weak kingship, intolerant of ineffective leadership, but more important, one in which the king's authority is understood to be derived from the people, even if the people in this instance are narrowly defined as the hunter-warrior host.

Ironically, this idea of authority from below, so important to truly sophisticated political systems, is in fact not that uncommon among very unsophisticated societies. It just seems to get lost as those societies become agricultural and urban, and in only two places does the idea survive and mature and influence other societies: Greece and Italy. It is hardly surprising that the constitutional histories of early Greece and Rome are so similar; both start with the same basic Indo-European institution of a weak warrior kingship whose authority comes from the group. Everywhere else the idea is never developed, either because the society itself does not mature, as with the German tribes, or the idea itself is smothered by more sophisticated cultures, as in the case of the Mycenaean Greeks and Minoan Crete or the Persians, overwhelmed by the power-from-above kingship of neighboring Babylonian society.

But it is a long way from the Indo-European warrior chief to the radical democracy of fifth century Athens, and the first and most important steps on that way were taken very early on, during the Dark Age. Unfortunately, this is a period for which information is extremely scarce, and what was perhaps the most momentous step in the political history of the human race can thus be seen only dimly. Archaeology reveals next to nothing about such developments, and our sole source of direct illumination is the Homeric epics.

The *Iliad* and the *Odyssey* are the earliest examples of Greek literature, since the data recorded on the Linear B tablets have as much literary value as an interdepartmental memo. They used to be regarded as the oldest examples of epic literature in the world, until the decipherment of cuneiform, the script of Mesopotamia, revealed the epic of *Gilgamesh*, which in its written form antedates Homer by a millennium. Of course, although older, *Gilgamesh* is a primitive, though vigorous scrawl compared to the crafted masterpieces of Homer. The Homeric epics as we have them are literary transcriptions of an oral tradition, like the early books of the Old Testament. They are the surviving examples of tales that were sung by illiterate bards to equally illiterate audiences in smoky halls and dusty village squares. And they were not recited from memory, but rather composed and sung on the spot. Each day the bard would create extemporaneously another installment of an epic of 15,000 or so lines, maintaining a complicated narrative and perfect metrical form, a seemingly impossible feat. How could this be done?

Part of the trick is that the bard's basic units of composition are not individual words, but phrases, many of which are stock formulas he has learned as part of his trade. He also knows many clever devices that allow him to fit these phrases into metrical patterns without pausing to think about it. For example, agent nouns such as characters' names tend to come at the ends of lines, so that when the action of the line has been dealt with the bard can easily fill in the remaining metrical feet by choosing from a store of standard epithets the one of appropriate poetic length – "shining Achilles," "swift-footed Achilles," "many-counseled Achilles," etc. Repetition is another device; fully a third of each poem is composed of lines or blocks of lines that are repeated at least once. At the beginning of Book II of the *Iliad*, for example, Zeus sends a dream to Agamemnon, first giving the message to a dream carrier, who then repeats the same five lines to the sleeping king, who then speaks the exact same lines to the heroes. This makes reading the epics a little tedious sometimes, but keep in mind that they were intended for an audience that listened, and probably not too attentively. The skills of the oral poet are like those of the improvisational musician. He knows the general story line (structure of the tune), which can be manipulated only to a certain degree, and he knows the pieces (musical phrases, riffs, embellishments) that can be assembled to create that story. The story and the individual bits that make it up are not new, but the bard's assembly of those bits may be, and the stories consequently evolve as they pass from generation to generation. It is here, in what M.I. Finley calls the "stitching," that the poet shows his genius. And there is genius in Homer – this is why the *Iliad* and *Odyssey* survived out of the dozens of oral epics produced during the Dark Age.

They obviously also survived because they were written down, an accomplishment made possible by one of the grand achievements of the Dark Age: the adoption of an alphabetic script. The cumbersome syllabic script of Linear B had been swept away in the destruction of the Mycenaean world, and sometime towards the end of the Dark Age Greek merchants, increasingly active and requiring some way to keep records, borrowed a script from their Phoenician trading partners in the Levant. When it came to writing, the Phoenicians definitely had a better idea: an alphabetic script based on a relative handful of characters rather than the hundreds and hundreds of signs of earlier systems. The Greeks added the vowels missing from the Semitic version of the alphabet and thus created an easily learnable means of precisely and completely recording their language. Literacy, which had previously been confined to a small group of professional scribes, now became more widely available, and Greece would become a literate society. At any given time only a small minority of Greeks could read and write, mostly members of the middle and especially upper income groups, but that was sufficient to make Greece culturally very different from its Near Eastern predecessors. Incidentally, the Latin script you are at this very moment reading is an offshoot of that Greek alphabet, borrowed by early Rome from the Greeks living in southern Italy.

Since literacy is fatal to oral tradition, the bard had to be illiterate (hence the tradition that Homer was blind), which means a scribe had to take down the lines as they were sung, no mean achievement given the fluid nature of oral composition. It is traditional and convenient to call the poet under whose auspices the epics were recorded Homer, but in fact there were probably two "Homers." The *Odyssey* is very different from the *Iliad*, less purely heroic and more modern, suggesting that it had a bit more time to evolve in its oral form before it was frozen forever by being committed to parchment. As we shall see, things will be changing so rapidly during the Archaic Age (c. 750 – 479) that the difference of a generation or two could easily account for the differing characters of the poems. Consequently, "Homer" is generally dated to the period 750 – 650, with the *Iliad* closer to the 750 end and the *Odyssey* to 650.

Clearly the world depicted in the epics is not that of Homer's time. The poem appears to hark back to the Mycenaean world, despite the presence of many anachronisms, such as the use of iron (by the end of the Dark Age Greece was moving into the Iron Age or more correctly, the Cast Iron Age). Such anachronisms are perfectly understandable. Oral tradition is like a dirty snowball, picking up debris as it rolls along. As the material is passed down through the years the original environment of the tale becomes dimmer, and each bard naturally inserts elements contemporary to his own society. Since, for example, chariots were obsolete as fighting instruments by Homer's day, he has only the foggiest notion of their true use, and his heroes employ them for the most part simply as convenient battlefield rapid transit.

It appears, especially from the place names and the widespread use of bronze, that the original material was Mycenaean, and the natural conclusion is that the two poems are essentially a reflection of life in the Bronze Age. But since the decipherment of Linear B we know that the Mycenaean world was much more complex, more bureaucratic and generally on a larger scale than that found in the *Iliad* and *Odyssey*. Further, none of the names of the characters in the epics are found among the thousands of Linear B tablets. Elements in the epics obviously go back to Mycenaean days, but the society described by Homer, insofar as it has an historical counterpart at all, very probably approximates – in a very idealized way – the simpler, smaller scaled world of the eleventh and tenth centuries. If this proposition is accepted, the poems are then our primary source of information for the society of the early Dark Age.

The heroic world of the *Iliad* and *Odyssey* may be termed a "shame culture." The most important thing, perhaps the only important thing, to a hero is his image among his peers, their estimation of his honor. Honor is the essential aim of the hero's life, the end to which all his actions are directed. He will sacrifice his life, if necessary, for the definition of that honor. Achilles' classic choice between the long, comfortable and unknown life and the short glorious one was really no choice. To be unknown is to have no honor, because there is no one to define it, and for the hero a life without honor is a life without meaning. This is a warrior society, and it is consequently fighting that defines honor. The ultimate achievement of the hero, the attainment of his peak of honor and excellence – his *aretē* – comes in battle at that moment when he is exerting himself to the utmost and thus either killing his opponent or himself being killed. In battle the hero finds his ultimate worth and the meaning of his life, which is why the *Iliad* is filled with mayhem. Now, a great deal of this mayhem appears somewhat counterproductive in terms of taking the city of Troy, but that is because the Greek army is composed of heroes, not soldiers. Winning the war would be grand, but it is a relatively trivial issue when compared to winning individual honor. As Achilles demonstrates, the hero is very deficient in any sense of responsibility or obligation to the group, though ironically the group is absolutely necessary to him as mirror for his honor. Though entertaining feelings of comradeship, these warriors are pretty much interested only in Number One.

Even in the individual battle winning is the least important aspect. Of far greater concern is whom you fight and how you fight. If you are knocking over some lightweight, no one is likely to care. But take on a warrior with a big reputation, like Hector or Ajax, and you move quickly up the ladder of honor, even if you are doomed, like Patroclus, to turn up dead as a result. This is why these characters will stop in the middle of the battlefield and launch into lengthy discourses on their family trees; you need to know the identity (and thus the expected haul of glory) of the man you are attempting to slaughter. And you need to fight fair. No spears in the back, no bushwhacking and no distance weapons, which do not permit a man to fight back. Achilles is killed by an arrow from the bow of cowardly Paris because no hero could possibly defeat him in a fair combat. Even Odysseus, major hero though he be, is held in some suspicion because he occasionally advocates the use of stealth and planning. This is a society in which brawn clearly trumps brains in importance.

The material manifestation of a hero's honor is his prize or trophy. Greek warriors collected armor and tripods instead of heads or scalps, but the underlying concept is the same. This booty is a physical representation of the hero's prowess and worth, providing, especially to strangers, a ready approximation of his status. When you walk into Diomedes' living room and see on display dozens of fine panoplies, you can immediately conclude that you have encountered a hero. Many of the prizes in the epics even have lineages, since the character of the former owners - were they pushovers or serious contenders? - contributes to the value of an item as a trophy. It is over a prize that the conflict in the *Iliad* arises. In order to stop the god Apollo from ravaging the Greek army with disease Agamemnon must free one of his female captives, and to compensate himself he takes another, Briseis, from the booty of Achilles. The superhero storms off in anger, and while he sits sulking in his tent, his Trojan counterpart, Hector, rages unchecked, cutting down the Greeks. A desperate Agamemnon offers Achilles a magnificent collection of gifts, including the return of Briseis, but the hero refuses and returns to the fray only after the slaughter of his beloved companion, Patroclus.

To us Achilles may seem to be acting in a selfish and petty manner, but in terms of his own society his behavior is perfectly understandable. Briseis is a trophy, and to lose her is to lose a symbol of honor and thus honor itself. Achilles says as much: "Now the son of Atreus, powerful Agamemnon,/ has dishonoured me, since he has taken away my prize and keeps it." (*Iliad* 1.355-56) That his buddies are dropping like flies while he refuses to fight cuts little ice with Achilles, since whatever rudimentary sense of social responsibility he has is completely overshadowed by the question of his honor. Though he goes too far in refusing Agamemnon's entirely adequate gifts of reconciliation (and therein lies his tragedy), that refusal demonstrates just how utterly important honor is to the hero.

The most obvious institution in the political structure of this heroic society is the kingship. The primary qualification for the job is power, but not the personal heroic kind, since in this respect Achilles is clearly greater than Agamemnon, the commander-in-chief and overall king (all the first rank heroes in this army are kings back home). Rather, it is the sort of power founded on the allegiance and support of men; Agamemnon brings the most ships and followers to Troy. Nestor says to Achilles: "Nor, son of Peleus, think to match your strength with/ the king, since never equal with the rest is the portion of honour/ of the sceptred king to whom Zeus gives magnificence. Even/ though you are the stronger man, and the mother who bore you was immortal,/ yet is this man greater who is lord over more than you rule." (*Iliad* 1.277-81) The kingship is hereditary, but not securely so, and the new king must secure his rule through his own power. Thus, while Odysseus is away, the nobles of Ithaca intend to raise a new king, against the claim of his son, Telemachus, who is as yet too inexperienced (and in that sense too "young") to take the post on his own. He rules who can rule – there are no child or idiot kings in Homeric society.

The only other apparent political institution is the assembly of warriors, seen in action at the very beginning of the *Iliad*. In this gathering the society of heroes voices its opinions and approves or disapproves of the policies of the king. It is in no sense a legislative body – there is no concept of law - but simply an informal advising and consenting group. And its opinions have absolutely no binding force on Agamemnon, who may go his own way, as long as thinks he can get away with it. The king's authority is in theory absolute, but in practice limited by custom and the need to avoid completely alienating the warrior host. It all comes down to the play of power between the king and his men.

The warriors and their warrior king – they are the aristocracy and all that counts. The rest of society is unimportant and goes pretty much unnoticed. We do, however, catch a glimpse in the *Iliad* of a non-hero, Thersites, who rises to speak at the assembly. He offers what seems a perfectly reasonable opinion on the dispute, but is clubbed into silence by Odysseus with the approval of the warriors. We may find this unfair, but by daring to debate with the heroes Thersites violates the social hierarchy, and by whacking him on the head Odysseus is merely restoring that social order. Significantly, Thersites is the only human to receive more than a stock description, which serves to underline his non-heroic status. The heroes need not be specifically described, because they are uniformly perfect and beautiful, but Thersites must be depicted as lame and ugly, much to the disgust of the warriors. The heroic world, with its emphasis on the physical, has no compassion for ugliness and imperfection.

How does this heroic world correspond to the actual society of the Dark Age? Bear in mind that what you are about to read involves a great deal of speculation and generalization, but it is not fringe material. This is a generally accepted view of the development of the Dark Age world, based on the information derived from the Homeric epics and from descriptions of analogous societies, such as the Germans. When the Roman historian Tacitus wrote at the end of the first century A.D. about the Germanic tribes north of the imperial frontiers, they had apparently not progressed socially much beyond their Dorian Greek cousins of a thousand years earlier. And the institutions and attitudes described by Tacitus roughly match those found in Homer, suggesting strongly that they were part of the common cultural baggage of all Indo-Europeans.

Even more compelling is an historic survival of the old Homeric Indo-European warrior kingship into Greece's classical period. It is found in the north, in Macedon, where the Temenid kings were the true heirs of Agamemnon. The Macedonian monarchy was hereditary, but like the Homeric, not securely so. When king Perdiccas III was killed in 359, his son Amyntas was an infant, so his brother Philip established himself as regent. In the course of the following year Philip did such a smashing job as leader that the warrior host, the Macedonian army, set Amyntas aside and proclaimed Philip the legitimate king. Likewise, Philip's son Alexander had to step lightly in the opening years of his reign because his father's old generals had more influence in the army than he and could have him deposed. Therein lies the old Indo-European idea: Alexander's authority as king of Macedon derived from the assembly of warriors, that is, the Macedonians under arms, which made him a far different king from his Persian opponent, whose authority came from heaven. (See Chapters XIV and XV.)

Finally, the story you are about to be told all makes sense, though this is hardly an unerring guide to history.

Picture Greece in the immediate wake of the Catastrophe: the Mycenaean cities are in ruins, and society is now made up of crude, isolated agricultural communities, the largest probably containing no more than a few thousand inhabitants, if that. The typical community is ruled by a chief or petty king, whose rule is based on personal power and hereditary only to the extent that he who inherits can rule. He might seem a crude barbarian compared to the splendid monarchs in Babylon and Egypt, but his little kingship carries within it an idea of earthshaking importance: the authority behind his rule comes from below, from the warrior host. He is surrounded by an aristocracy of warriors, who form an advisory assembly as found in the *Iliad*, a memory of the distant past when the warrior-hunters selected the man who was to lead them. In most places there is probably a small group of individuals – the heads of certain families, elders or whatever – particularly close to the king, who form a sort of proto-council. The remainder of the population, the tillers of the soil and the craftsmen, are outside important society and are politically nonexistent.

Given the fluid nature of society during these chaotic years and the rudimentary development of the state, kinship relations are far more important than those based on the state or territory. The family is the strongest unit of society, and it is to the family or the clan, rather than to the state (which barely exists) that allegiance is owed. Consequently, such things as justice are essentially in the hands of the family. The justice dispensed by the king is really limited to arbitration, and criminal offenses, such as homicide and theft, are left to the family to deal with. There is no law as we and the classical Greeks know it, but only custom, as in the Homeric world. (See Chapter IV for more on the development of justice.)

Because of the unsettled conditions and especially because of the values of the warrior society, land is temporarily out of the picture as the primary form of wealth. As in the epics, true wealth is measured in herds and flocks and movable goods, and despite the need for pasturage and arable land motivation for serious territorial aggrandizement is lacking. The means are also lacking, since these primitive communities are not at all equipped for wars of conquest. The warrior aristocracy is just that: a bunch of warriors, who are primarily interested in individual success and whose greatest tactical achievement was likely all getting into battle at approximately the same time. War is perhaps too grand a term for what they do; raiding and cattle rustling is more accurate. Like the Greeks at Troy they take their booty and go. Also like the Greeks at Troy they are spared the burden of a church, that is, an institutionalized religion with an ideology defended by a priest class.

The king serves only as chief religious functionary in matters concerning the community, and priests are simply specialists in matters pertaining to the gods. The absence of a church is of extreme importance, because it will allow for greater progress in all areas and ultimately allow the emergence of rationalism. (See Chapter IV for the evolution of Greek religion.)

Such is a capsule impression of Greek society at the beginning of the Dark Age. Who would have guessed that out of these grubby little villages would emerge the glory of Greece and the foundation of western civilization? How could these Greeks possibly match the achievements and magnificence of Egypt and Babylon? But they would. The grand societies of Egypt and Asia were heading nowhere, while these flyspecks in the Balkan Peninsula were about to explode with political and intellectual development and contribute more to the progress of the human race than any other single civilization. Unfortunately, we know almost nothing about the first stages of this process, how the rude agricultural community just described evolved into the aristocratic, republican polis (plural: poleis; a more accurate term than city-state) of the mid-eighth century. But the process must have been generally something like the following.

As life in Greece began gradually to calm down in the generations following the Catastrophe, more settled conditions brought on the first momentous step in the political development of the polis and the emergence of constitutionalism – the elimination of the kingship. With the arrival of more peaceful conditions (relatively speaking) and the first stirrings of re-urbanization land reemerged as the primary form of wealth, as it must in any agricultural society, and those getting in on the ground floor in real estate constituted a new force in these little communities. It is one of those "laws" of history that in any but the most primitive society economic power is political power, and economic change will consequently drive political change, as new economically powerful groups naturally seek access to the political apparatus. In the early Dark Age a new land-owning aristocracy emerged to challenge and supplant the warrior aristocracy, whose position was being eroded by more stable conditions and the developing economy. The primitive warrior host was in a way co-opted by the new nobility, which inherited their heroic value system and became the fighting force in the community. But the defining element and power base of the new aristocracy was ownership of land; warrior status was simply incidental. Further, though the land-owning aristocracy was initially open and probably drew heavily from the warrior group, as time went on and the big landowners developed a sense of their power and superiority it became a closed circle, limited to certain families. The power base is still control of the land, but the defining element is now birth. Access to power based on simple strength, the warrior aristocracy, gives way to access to political power based on birth, the land-owning blood aristocracy, which would dominate Greece until the seventh century.

In the narrow environment of the proto-polis the new nobility quickly developed a consciousness of their own power, and the monarchs began to disappear. The need for a pure warrior leader declined, and the community sought more sophisticated leadership, leaving these Indo-European kinglets in an awkward position. Their kingship was not protected by the gods or any powerful religious establishment, as in the Near Eastern monarchies, and there was no strong institution or long tradition to back them up. And if the community was considered, however vaguely, the source of the ruler's authority, then so much easier was it for the community, or at least a part of it, to remove that authority. The process by which the kings were eliminated was apparently peaceful, since there is virtually no word of violence in the Greek traditions about the disappearance of monarchy, as there is in the Roman. The monarchy might simply be abolished by the new aristocracy upon the death of a king, particularly a lackluster one, but more likely the process was gradual, the king's power being slowly chipped away until the office was severely limited or completely powerless. Something like this happened in Athens, which in the days of the democracy still had a "king," a yearly, essentially ceremonial office filled by lot. Actual hereditary monarchy survived at Sparta, but the official power of these kings was limited to commanding the army in the field.

By whatever process, kingship had generally disappeared from Greece by the end of the Dark Age, surviving intact only in backwaters like Macedon. This is already a tremendous achievement. Since the birth of civilization in Sumer some two thousand years earlier monarchy had been the rule in human society, and generally, the more sophisticated the society, the more developed the monarchy. Now, in the Balkan Peninsula in the eighth century we find hundreds of little republics, controlled by landed aristocracies of birth, either a family or more often a combination of families. These states have the basic machinery of constitutional government: elected, limited term magistrates and a citizen assembly that was the source of political authority and actually passed the laws. Of course, this political apparatus was tightly controlled by the aristocrats, but the fact is, it was there. And what is more, embedded in the very fabric of the polis are some pretty radical ideas. More or less dormant now, they will soon emerge as distinctive features of the matured classical polis and may be regarded as the essentials of constitutionalism.

Most important is the concept of the individual in society as "citizen" rather than "subject," that is, the notion that the authority exercised by the state comes from below, from the people, rather than from above, from heaven. It cannot be emphasized enough that this idea is the absolute foundation of constitutionalism, and without it your society will never progress beyond some form of absolutism. An aspect of this concept is the universality of law, the idea that all members of the community, including the rulers, are equally subject to the law, because the community is the authority behind the law, regardless of who actually makes it. Another obvious derivative is the basic democratic idea: those in authority – the government – are in some manner responsive to the will of the citizen body, because it is from the citizen body that they derive their authority. And being incubated within the idea of man as "citizen" rather than "subject" and awaiting further stimulus to develop is the notion of man the individual.

Once again, all these eighth century poleis were tightly and oppressively controlled by their aristocrats, and it probably brought that dispossessed farmer scant comfort to know that he was theoretically the source of authority behind the laws that were making his life so miserable. But the important thing is that these vital concepts were there, ready to bloom with the proper stimulus into full-blown constitutional government. And these concepts, so utterly essential to the constitutionalism that virtually all modern states possess or claim to possess, first appeared in the tiny poleis of Greece.

Why? What is it about this people at this time in this place that these republican states appeared, survived and produced the first constitutional governments in history? This is clearly not an easy question to answer with any precision and certainty, but some general reasons may be suggested.

First of all, the emergence and survival of the tiny polis as an autonomous political entity is in itself a bit strange. The general trend in political organization since the birth of civilization had – with occasional setbacks – clearly been towards larger and larger units. Yet in the Greek world, despite a common language and culture, fragmentation remained the rule, and the fragile polis survived and flourished. The rugged terrain of the Balkan Peninsula surely played a role, since the difficult communications would have created a degree of economic isolation for the average polis. Greece after all had no grand aquatic interstate like the Nile River to pull the region together politically. But the importance of geography must not be exaggerated; there were areas, such as Boeotia in central Greece, where there were independent poleis not separated by natural barriers. Far more important is the fact that the social structure of the polis was built around kinship ties, both real and imagined. The members of the community felt that they were all in some sense part of an extended family, different from the extended family that was the community just down the road. This helped the individual polis develop more quickly a corporate and unique identity that set it apart from others despite the common culture.

Most important of all, though, and the basic key to understanding their society and history is the Greek character. The days of the warrior society were gone, but the spirit of competition and struggle, the spirit of *agōn*, remained alive. *Agōn*, the need to compete, this is the single most important aspect of the Greek character and has in fact survived to the present, nurtured by centuries of competition for scarce resources in the Balkan Peninsula. As a sense of community developed in the emerging polis, the need for competition and enhancement of the self that was so vital to the individual warrior in the shame culture was transferred in part to the group, and from the warriors the community inherited narcissism and the compulsion to demonstrate superiority. This competitive urge provided a strong brake against the greater unity prompted by a shared language and culture, which in fact provided a common stage upon which the competing poleis could strut their stuff. Within the relatively limited horizons of the Dark Age ones identity as an Athenian or a Corinthian quickly became far more important than the commonality of being a Hellene. *Agōn* was present in its purest form in the man-to-man violence of the warrior society; it would now manifest itself in virtually every aspect of the polis society and ultimately be responsible for much of what was good and evil in the Greek experience. It would stimulate the explosion of cultural creativity, prompting the Greeks to compete for excellence in everything – the arts, athletics, feats of engineering, you name it. But it would also goad them into the constant inter-city warfare and civil strife that would be the downfall of the polis.

So the narcissistic little polis was born, prevented from growing into anything larger by the innate competitiveness of the Greeks. It was nurtured by the power vacuum that existed in the Aegean world since the Catastrophe, the same power vacuum, incidentally, that allowed another flyweight state, Israel, to make its brief appearance. There was no one to disturb the experiment, no strong power in the eastern Mediterranean to spur the Greeks towards unity or impose it upon them. And by the time a new powerful neighbor, the Lydian kingdom in Asia Minor, appeared in the seventh century the polis was firmly established as the political unit of the Greek world.

As for the constitutional elements of the polis, they were the result of a complex of interrelated factors, but certainly extremely important was the Indo-European background. There is no reason to believe that without the distinctive Indo-European kingship and warrior assembly the Greeks would ever have developed political systems any different from the absolute autocracies of the Near East. The concept of authority derived from the community that was inherent in the nature of the northern kingship is absolutely necessary for the gestation of constitutionalism. Of course, while such institutions were necessary, they were not alone sufficient, and most of the Indo-European peoples never even came close to producing constitutional states. Extremely important for the Greeks was the fact that the Catastrophe had so completely swept away Mycenaean society, creating a kind of blank slate in the Balkan Peninsula. As a result the Greeks had the opportunity to develop their strange new political forms free of corrupting influences.

The size of the polis was very probably a factor. Keep in mind that these were tiny places with small populations; the Balkan Peninsula, Aegean islands and Anatolian coast supported some 750 independent poleis! Excepting Sparta, whose situation was bizarre to say the least (see Chapter III), Athens, with about a thousand square miles, was easily the largest polis in the peninsula. Few others reached even half that, and the average was considerably smaller, less than forty square miles. Population figures are pretty much guesswork, but Athens at her height in the fifth century may have had as many as 50,000 plus citizens and a total population of more than a quarter million. Most poleis, however, would have had citizen bodies of fewer than a thousand, and all would have been considerably smaller during the Dark Age. This small size helped keep alive the Indo-European political concepts even after the warrior king and his host had headed for the scrap heap of history. And together with the tradition of a common family background, the size also hastened the development of a group awareness among the people as a whole, the feeling that they were all Corinthians or Thebans or whatever, regardless of their economic position in the society. Such would naturally create a more tightly knit society, one more resistant to the inevitable pressures pushing the economic levels apart and creating a subject-ruler situation.

The abolition of the monarchs must have aided immensely in the development of the constitutional forms. For one thing, the aristocrats had to divvy up the king's power among themselves, which led to the establishment of limited term magistracies, which themselves were something quite new. State officials of course existed in the Near Eastern governments, but they were simply extensions of the king and were frequently of an *ad hoc* nature. The new Greek magistrate, typically called an archon, held a regular office with a fixed term and was chosen by the community, another momentous innovation. The origins of the idea of election are completely obscured, but it must certainly have something to do with the nature of the abolished kingship, which had depended heavily on the support of a warrior host that could reject an unacceptable chief. It would be a short series of steps from the group giving the king his authority to the group giving the magistrate his authority to the group actually choosing the magistrate. The old kingship had not been, strictly speaking, elective, but the idea was inherent in the relationship between the king and the warrior group. The election of state officials (from a narrow field of aristocratic candidates) simply brought that idea into the open and into regular practice.

Further, in creating new political machinery to replace the deposed king the aristocrats had to formulate new, more precise rules about how that machinery worked, who had access to it, etc. The result: actual law begins to replace custom. Law, like custom, is simply a body of rules, but unlike custom these rules are consciously decided upon by a group of men, are more precisely defined and most important, have the authority of the state behind them. Further, in the absence of a king the notion of the rule of law emerges, as the aristocratic elites realize they have no choice but to subordinate themselves to the rules they were formulating, thus establishing the idea – at least in theory – that all were subject to the law. The idea that the group is the authority behind the law, regardless of who actually makes it, is another natural evolution of the basic idea of authority from below, particularly in connection with the emergence of the citizen assembly. The warrior tradition of gathering to advise and hear the king survived the disappearance of the kingship and warrior society and increasingly became a meeting of ordinary citizens. As the concept of law developed, the advice took on the form of actual legislation, and the legislative assembly was born. It would be a long time before any Greek citizen assembly was free enough actually to govern, but by the eighth century this curious new institution existed, if under the tight control of the aristocrats.

Finally, the Greeks were graced with a churchless religion. The invariable pattern in the Near East had been for the religious and secular authorities to fuse or at least support one another in defense of the status quo, thus shutting down possibilities for social and especially intellectual progress. It is simply a lot harder for the existing order to change or be challenged when it has the mandate of heaven, which is to say, the support of the religious establishment. The Greeks were fortunate in that their inherited religion was ideologically very diffuse and lacked any institution and priest class that could establish and defend religious dogma and emerge as a center of political power in the state. Religion would be very important in the civic life of the Greeks (see Chapter IV), but it would not be an impediment to progress. The polis maintained the all-important separation of church and state for the simple reason that there was no church.

Such are the reasons for the birth of the polis, a phenomenally new kind of society on the face of the planet. City-states had existed before – in ancient Sumer and in Syria-Palestine – but this was something more than a city-state. Essential to the definition of the polis was its constitutional underpinning; a city-state that did not have some form of constitutional government simply could not be a polis. A polis in which power did not, at least in theory, derive from the people was an impossibility. The people were in fact understood to be the polis, rather than the place it occupied, and the Greeks inevitably spoke of the Athenians doing this or the Spartans doing that, rather than referring to Athens or Sparta. When considering the state, the Greeks were far less inclined to think in terms of territory than we are, and when during the Persian invasion of 480-479 the Athenians threatened to move their polis to Italy, it was no empty bluff. In many ways the polis was as much a state of mind as a geographical entity.

# # # # # # # # # # # # # # # # # # # #

SUGGESTED READING

M.I. Finley, *The World of Odysseus*² (1977) is the book to read on Homer and the Dark Ages, and the first part of this chapter is copiously cribbed from this excellent work. Outside of Homer all the information on the Dark Age is archaeological, so most books on this period tend toward the tedious, but do try A.R. Burn, *The World of Hesiod. A Study of the Greek Middle Ages c. 900-700 BC* (1997) or A.M. Snodgrass, *The Dark Age of Greece* (1971); C.G. Thomas & Craig Conant, *Citadel to City-State. The Transformation of Greece 1200-700 BCE* (1999) is also readable and traces the period site by site. I have already recommended the Lattimore *Iliad*; Robert Fitzgerald has produced a good *Odyssey*. Rather than reading these epics, for greater authenticity you might try getting someone to read them to you, especially in a crowded, noisy place. Charles Beye, *The Iliad, the Odyssey and the Epic Tradition* (1966) is a readable introduction to the epics, and M. Edwards, *Homer. Poet of the Iliad* (1987) is more accessible than most such works.

#################

III. MONEY TALKS, ARISTOCRACY WALKS

THE AGE OF TYRANTS

My trusty shield adorns some Thracian foe; I left it in a bush –not as I
would!
But I have saved my life; so let it go. Soon I will get another just as good.

- Archilochus 6[3]

Emerging from the gloom of the Dark Age, the young polis had shed the
kingship and acquired the basic apparatus of constitutional government,
and by the end of the eighth century many, perhaps most, poleis possessed a
citizen assembly, which was theoretically the law-making body in the state.
Things had certainly come a long way from the wretched, warrior-dominated
villages of the tenth century, and for the first time in history the people were
the ultimate source of authority in the community, at least in theory. And
there was the rub: it was all political theory, which could bring very little
comfort to those suffering under aristocratic oppression.

The aristocratic families had control of the polis firmly in their grasp. The
magistracies may have been elective, but they were only open to aristocrats, as
was the council invariably found in control of the agenda and the preparation
of legislation for the citizen assembly in each polis. Lacking the power of
initiation, the Greek assembly could only deal with business put before it
by this council, and these eighth century assemblies were consequently little
more than rubber stamps for their aristocratic governments. All the important
religious functions of the community were in the hands of the aristocrats,
and they had an entrenched position in the social structure, an important
source of power in a society where the family and kinship ties were still of

primary importance. They owned the best land and directly controlled the bulk of the wealth, and as the only ones who could afford the weapons and horses, they constituted the military power.

So life in the polis was great – if you happened to be born into the right family. For most of the inhabitants times were tough and getting tougher. The growing wealth and power of the land-owning aristocracy was continually depressing the position of the peasant farmers, who constituted the bulk of the population, and this process was being accelerated by a rapidly increasing population. In the late eighth and seventh centuries the free Greek farmer was under tremendous pressure, continually forced to walk an economic tightrope. A bad year could easily mean the loss of the farm and the prospect of farming some aristocrat's land as a tenant or sharecropper, obliged to hand over a portion of the yield in return for use of the land. Further bad luck and the failure to meet the obligations owed the landlord led to a final abject state – debt-slavery. The last bit of collateral the poor farmer could offer to cover a loan was his own freedom, and if he defaulted on that loan, he became the slave of the lender.

A few words on slavery. The Greeks lived in a world in which slavery was automatically accepted as part of the natural order of things, an aspect of civilization present from its very birth in Sumer all those millennia ago. The primary sources of slaves were war, piracy and slave births, which meant that many of the slaves in Greek society were in fact Greeks. The extent of chattel slavery in any period of Greek history is completely unclear, though it is generally accepted that by far the largest category was domestic slaves, which would include slave assistants in small workshops. There were certainly a small number of state-owned slaves in classical Athens, used in policing, street cleaning, temple repair and so forth, and mines were typically worked by gangs of slaves leased from private contractors. How extensive agricultural slavery was is hotly debated, but the relatively small farm units (averaging about ten acres) and seasonal nature of the work suggests the numbers of slaves were not overwhelming, as they would be in Italy in the late Roman Republic. Overall population figures for slaves are pretty much guesses, and the numbers varied according to the wealth of the society, classical Athens probably possessing more slaves per capita than any other polis (understanding the helots in Laconia to be serfs rather than chattels – see below).

The circumstances of slaves varied, especially by occupation, and life as a slave in the Laurion silver mines was certainly far more brutal and short than that of a slave nanny in a wealthy household. But in general the treatment of slaves was better than what was found in late Republican Rome or pre-Civil War America, as the complete absence of slave revolts (helots aside again) suggests. Domestic slavery always has a kinder face, since the slaves are not just nameless agricultural work units, but personalities who interact with the family. Further, not only were slaves not a distinct ethnic group, like Blacks in America, but a great many of them were Greeks, which surely eased their treatment, since it is difficult to consider one's own people sub-human. The Greeks could be incredibly haughty about their culture, but they were spared the intense ethnicity-based racism that plagues modern America.

Not until the fourth century would Greek thinkers bother with attempting to justify the institution of slavery, so much was it an accepted part of civilized society in the Mediterranean world. And even then the attempts were half-hearted, suggesting, as Aristotle does, that some people – a few Greeks and most barbarians - were by nature better off as slaves. Certainly it was a rare Greek who advocated abolishing slavery; even the Hellenistic philosophical schools that postulated an essential equality among all men (see Chapter XVI) never seriously spoke against slavery. In fact, mass chattel slavery would only disappear with the collapse of the Roman Empire and the end of antiquity, not because of some abolitionist movement, but because the institution made little sense in the economic and political circumstances of early medieval Europe.

Discontent was rising rapidly in Archaic Age Greece, and lacking the mechanisms of social control supplied by modern technology, Greek society had no alternative to serious change. The aristocratic governments of the poleis were rolling towards a crisis of some sort, but the pressure was temporarily bled off a bit through the great colonization movement, a veritable explosion of Greece that from the late eighth to the sixth centuries showered poleis across the Mediterranean. The movement followed the trade routes and planted Greek cities around the Black Sea, all over southern Italy and Sicily (which became known at Magna Graecia – "Great Greece") and as far west as the coast of Spain. These settlements, ultimately numbering some 300, were not colonies as we understand them, but completely independent states, which did not always maintain good relations with the mother-city. The driving forces behind the adventure were political discontent and hunger for land, and for these reasons the movement was probably encouraged by the ruling aristocrats. It was an easy way to bleed off excess population and get rid of potential troublemakers, who would be the most likely to sign up for a chance at a new life in foreign lands.

But the colonization movement could only delay the day of reckoning for the aristocracies. The root problem, aristocratic political and economic oppression, remained, and the cry that was the hallmark of every Greek revolution grew louder: "Cancel the debts and redistribute the land." By the middle of the seventh century the conflict had reached the crisis stage, and the first tyrants began appearing. Two factors in particular contributed to bringing matters to a head at this time.

The first was a tremendous increase in trade and manufacture, stimulated in part by the colonization movement, which served to plant Greeks at both ends of many of the trade routes and give them a bigger piece of the Mediterranean commercial pie. This expanding economy caused new wealth to flow into the polis, wealth that primarily went not into the coffers of the land-owning aristocrats, but into the hands of the merchants and manufacturers who were creating it. The result was the creation of a new class of citizens in the polis, a class that was neither poor peasants nor wealthy nobility, but rather commoners whose means ran from moderate to great. This growing group did not develop any class consciousness and was not a true bourgeoisie, but among them were individuals increasingly impatient with the aristocratic monopoly of political power, especially those getting rich off the new economy. Many of these commoners were now as wealthy or more so than the old nobility, and they saw no difference between themselves and the aristocrats except the accident of birth, which to many seemed to make no difference. Wealth, especially wealth in land, had formed the basis of power for the old nobility, and now the new money wanted into the charmed circle of the old. Economic power is ultimately political power, and the same economic forces that undermined the old warrior aristocracy and allowed the rise of the land-owning nobility now threatened it in turn. There was a new economic power in the polis, and it demanded access to the political apparatus.

This economic development was accelerated in the second half of the seventh century by the introduction of coinage into Greece from its origins in Lydia in Asia Minor. The first stage of economic transaction was simple barter, a very cumbersome mechanism, since each has to have something the other wants and there is constant haggling over relative value. The next step was to employ some commonly accepted medium of exchange, which has usually been gold, silver and copper, but which could be pretty much anything that is relatively scarce and that society agrees upon – salt, cowrie shells, cigarettes or whatever. The medium itself is typically of little inherent value, but it can serve as a convenient stand-in for real goods of any kind in a transaction. This is a big step forward in efficiency, but there is still the question of the weight and purity of the precious metal in each exchange. The third stage is for some authority – at first the merchant, but very quickly the state – to stamp a piece of metal as a guarantee that it is of a certain weight and purity. This is coinage, and it makes the conduct of business much more efficient. The next step, which the ancient world never took, is token money, the system in which the government supports a totally worthless medium, such as printed slips of paper, and the industrialized societies appear now to be heading towards perhaps the ultimate stage, which is no money at all, just the movement of data.

The second factor was a change in Greek warfare, the development of the hoplite phalanx. Battle in the Bronze Age had generally shunned massed close combat, involving instead chariotry and lighter infantry and concentrating on missile fire in a sort of skirmishing on a grand scale. The Dorians had introduced new weaponry into the Balkan Peninsula and brought down the chariot based states of the Mycenaean world, but as Homer and archaeology suggest, apart from the absence of chariots warfare in the Dark Age was similar to what had come before. Lacking the Mycenaean urban power bases, it was naturally on a much smaller scale and was likely primarily an aristocratic affair, inasmuch as they were the ones who could afford the equipment. They may have ridden to the battle, but seem to have generally fought on foot, equipped as light and medium infantry with swords, throwing and thrusting spears and lighter shields. Poorer folk presumably supplied even more lightly equipped skirmishers and archers and slingers. Tactics were non-existent, and the front was very fluid, as individuals and small groups moved in and out of missile range and limited close combat. The whole affair was highly individualistic, and the participants, at least the aristocrats, were more warriors, concerned with personal honor, than soldiers, concerned with group objectives. As Greece developed economically in the Archaic Age better arms became available to the more substantial small farmers, and the advantages of massed formations of infantry and close combat became more apparent. Weaponry consequently evolved to match the changing conditions of battle, driving in turn the further evolution of heavy infantry and shock tactics, and by the middle of the seventh century the hoplite phalanx had certainly emerged, if not in its completely finished form.

The new hoplite (from *hopla*, arms, armor) was a soldier, a heavily armed infantryman who fought in a phalanx or line formation. His equipment was formidable, both in terms of protection and of encumbrance. He wore a full bronze helmet, which protected his head and face but obstructed his hearing and vision, a two piece bronze corselet and snap-on metal greaves on his shins. On his left arm he carried the distinctive and novel shield, the *hoplon*, a round concave shield with both a central armgrip and a handgrip, which allowed the weight to be born by the entire arm rather than just the wrist. The shield was made of wood, typically with a thin facing of mostly decorative bronze, and measured about a yard in diameter. It weighed in at about fifteen pounds, but the revolutionary concavity of the shield with its inward bending rim allowed the shield to be hung on the hoplite's left shoulder to relieve the strain on his arm. The sources in fact talk about the "hollow" shield, and almost certainly it was this bowl design that made such a heavy shield at all practical. His primary armament was a six to eight foot long thrusting spear, though there is some evidence that a throwing spear was also carried in the Archaic period. He might also be equipped with a short sword, but this would be a weapon of desperation, to be used when the spear was lost or broken, as it apparently often was when the opposing front lines crashed into one another.

Carrying all this equipment around (some seventy pounds of it), the hoplite was not exactly quick on his feet, and caught alone by light infantry or missile men or cavalry he was in a very awkward situation. To the front, his defenses were formidable, but taken from behind he was extremely vulnerable. Arrange your hoplites shoulder to shoulder in a line several ranks deep (the phalanx), however, and you get a formation that is irresistible. A disciplined hoplite phalanx in proper circumstances could successfully face any other kind of military formation (short of firearms), including a charge of heavy cavalry, and because of this superiority, this style of fighting becomes the norm for the rest of antiquity. The Macedonian armies and the Roman legions are simply variations and improvements on the hoplite theme, which is recapitulated a millennium later in the pike armies of the fourteenth and fifteenth centuries. Cavalry goes into an eclipse, and the infantryman begins a thousand year dominance of the military scene. Cavalry regains supremacy after the collapse of the Roman Empire only because the political and economic structure of early medieval Europe would not accommodate trained infantry armies.

The advent of the hoplite phalanx represented a quite new idea about warfare. It has in fact been argued that the circumstances of hoplite warfare demonstrate a distinctive approach to war that was to become characteristic of the west: the inclination to settle a conflict with a single, brutal, decisive engagement of heavy forces. It is very likely that Greek society so enthusiastically indulged in war partly because hoplite combat made it palatable by generally limiting the destruction to one brief battle, which because of the defensive equipment rarely produced excessive casualties. The more traditional eastern Mediterranean warfare of extended campaigns, devastation and occupation of territory and cities and destruction of enemy forces would have quickly drained the resources of the polis and led to the utter ruin of Greece. There were of course serious limitations inherent in fighting with heavy infantry in rigid formations: hoplite armies were not very mobile and the phalanx, essentially unable to fight on rough or broken terrain, required a flat, open battlefield. The circumstances of warfare in Archaic Age Greece minimized these deficiencies, however. Fought primarily by farmers, hoplite warfare was intimately connected with agriculture, and the threat of crop devastation by an invading enemy is what typically brought on a battle. Consequently, so long as it was a case of Greeks fighting Greeks in border disputes involving arable land, the army did not have to travel far and always found suitable ground for battle.

The inherent limitations of hoplite warfare were gradually augmented by generally agreed upon conventions, such as no surprise attacks, limited pursuit and no slaughter of captives, many of which conventions derived naturally from the nature of the tactics and equipment. These conventions and the very nature of hoplite combat served to turn war into a sustainable and culturally important game, a violent expression of *agōn* that was within the restricted means of the polis. The poleis could indulge in continuous warfare without bankrupting themselves and devastating their territories and populations. Further, since a hoplite battle was essentially a tug-of-war in reverse, in which two forces first literally crashed into each other and then engaged in a shoving and poking match, the hoplite needed little or nothing in the way of special skills, only the strength and endurance to carry half his body weight in armaments into the fray. Hoplite combat was thus the ultimate in amateur warfare, allowing the society to field effective military forces without the expense of extensive training or the need for skilled generals. Never has war been so frequent yet so constrained.

These were also people's armies, the first citizen militias in history. Unlike all previous forces, which were simply an instrument of the king and heaven, the hoplite phalanx was a manifestation of the entire community, something unthinkable before the advent of the constitutional polis with its idea of citizen as opposed to subject. In the phalanx young, middle-aged and even old men found their place, bound together as members of the polis community through a shared, intense and ongoing experience. More accurately, those citizens of moderate means were bound together, since the very wealthy supplied the now marginalized cavalry and the poor could not afford the hoplite equipment. The lower income citizens fielded the light troops – archers, slingers, javelin men, etc. – that the Greeks would hold in contempt during the generations when the hoplite heavy infantry dominated the battlefield. So complete was that domination that during the Archaic Age hoplite status came to be virtually synonymous with citizenship, generating a political ideology that would be severely strained by the rise of Greek naval power during the fifth century (see Chapter VI). The fifth century, beginning with the Persian wars (490-479), would also see changes in the circumstances of land combat that challenged hoplite supremacy. Classic hoplite warfare depended upon the belligerents having a common understanding of war and how to fight it: a set infantry battle at a particular time and place. Not being Greeks, the Persians of course did not have that understanding, and while Greek infantry was in general vastly superior to the Persian, the invasions began to reveal some of the limitations and weaknesses of traditional hoplite warfare. These deficiencies became more apparent through the remainder of the fifth century, as the Greek world moved away from afternoon wars between individual poleis to long struggles between coalitions of states. By the end of the century the hoplite, whose own armor had already become much lighter, was increasingly compelled to share the battlefield with lighter, more specialized troops, including mercenaries. And Greek warfare rapidly became a much more bloody and destructive affair.

That is all in the future, however, and in the seventh century the hoplite phalanx swept the Greek world. For the political order this meant three things. First, the nature of phalanx warfare, with its utter dependence on your fighting neighbor, strengthened the sense of community in the polis. Hoplite warfare was a team sport, with little room for individual glory, and the man who charged out ahead of the army only endangered his comrades by breaking the line. The glory went to the group, to the polis, which process aided in developing the importance of the community and undermining the authority of the family and kinship ties, which were at the heart of the old aristocratic structure. Second, middling income commoners were now fighting and dying for the state, and this could only sharpen their interest in the governance of that state, in some realization of the political authority that was theirs in theory. Some two and a half millennia later, similar thoughts would occur to voteless eighteen year old Americans in Vietnam. Finally, the most obvious: military power was no longer an aristocratic monopoly.

The result of these interrelated factors was a wave of revolutions that generally eliminated the aristocracies of birth from Greece. In their place came the tyrants. Sometimes a commoner, but more frequently a member of the old aristocracy, the tyrant was a man who capitalized on the social discontent and generally used the new military forces to depose the aristocrats and establish himself in power. He was simply an "unconstitutional ruler," a man who had seized power illegally, and the label "tyrant" did not at first have the pejorative meaning that it does for us. First generation tyrants were typically effective rulers and enjoyed the support of the commons, certainly the solid middle income types who carried out or at least passively supported these revolutions. The lowest strata of society, the poor peasantry and what we might (somewhat inaccurately) call the proletariat, invariably took no active part, and their plight was in fact not always alleviated. The exact form and results of these revolutions varied and some poleis never experienced one, but enough tyrants appear in the seventh and sixth centuries that the period may justly be called the Age of Tyrants.

The tyrants would transform Greek society, serving in most poleis as the mechanism for a change that was in any case inevitable: the switch from access to political power based on birth to access to political power based on wealth. As the economy of a society develops, this change from aristocracy of birth to oligarchy of wealth (or plutocracy) can hardly be resisted, since wealth is power. The young Roman Republic would make this same transition in the fifth and fourth centuries, and in the later Middle Ages the revival of commerce and manufacture would create wealth outside the feudal nobility and Church and thus contribute to the collapse of feudalism. Wealth as the basis of political power of course hardly creates a perfect society, as Americans are increasingly aware, but it is nevertheless a great leap forward from rule based on birth.

The tyrants also accelerated, both consciously and unconsciously, the weakening of the role of the family in the overall affairs of the community, though kinship ties would always remain very important. As the state became more sophisticated it naturally began to challenge the family and the local noble clan as the primary object of loyalty for the citizen, and the tyrants encouraged this development: they after all *were* the state. This growing importance of the state was accompanied by a greater emphasis on the individual, both being the result of the declining role of the family. Greek society now begins to develop yet another aspect of the tension that is so characteristic of the classical polis, that resulting from the conflict of a strong sense of individuality and an equally strong sense of community.

The Age of Tyrants did not last all that long, a century or so, and the period is ended with the expulsion of the tyrant Hippias from Athens in 510, although the Persians would continue to use local tyrants as their mechanism for controlling the Ionian cities until they revolted in the 490s. The tyrants generally outlived their usefulness as instruments of social change after the first generation, and the second generation, often sons or nephews, tended to become more overtly despotic and oppressive as a reaction to their growing unpopularity and were booted out. But as brief as it was in the great scheme of things, the Age of Tyrants was of extreme importance in the development of the polis; it contributed to the breaking down of the old order and the establishment of the new.

The nature and forces behind the Age of Tyrants is well illustrated by an examination of the political development during this period of what would be the two most important states in the classical Greek world: Athens and Sparta. The first is a variation on the tyranny theme, while the second is revealing as an example of a state that avoided tyranny.

ATHENS

The situation in Athens at the end of the seventh century is a perfect example of what was happening in Greece at that time. All the political and social power was in the hands of an aristocracy of birth, the Eupatridai ("those of good fathers"), but their control of economic and military power was being rapidly eroded by a growing class of commoners, whose means ran from moderate to filthy rich. For the poor peasants times were rough, and many, if not most, had been reduced to virtual, if not literal, slavery. Many Athenian farmers were known as *hektemoroi*, "sixth-parters," because in return for use of the land or some other aid they contracted to hand over a sixth of the crop, a stiff obligation for a small-time farmer.

Athens was ripe for an explosion, and it came in c. 632 when an Athenian named Cylon attempted to seize power with military support from neighboring Megara. His coup failed because of lack of any substantial support among the Athenians, but it did force a response from the Eupatridai. In 621 the aristocrat Dracon published Athens' first law code. These laws were very harsh (indeed, draconian) and came down hard on the poor, especially in matters of debt, but at least they were written down. Knowledge and interpretation of the law was no longer murky and a complete monopoly of the aristocrats. Publication of the law would also be one of the first demands made by the Roman plebians of their aristocrats during their own transition from birth to wealth. This was certainly not enough, however, and by the beginning of the sixth century the Eupatridai were perceptive enough to realize that something must be done to stave off a revolution. The unarmed poor hardly represented a threat, but if they were joined by the middle income and wealthy commoners, that is to say, the hoplite army, the Eupatridai could begin packing their bags. Unlike most entrenched aristocrats, those in Athens saw the need to act before they were acted upon, and one of their number, Solon (d. c. 560), was appointed in 594/3 to an extra-constitutional position in order that he might reform the state.

Solon immediately undertook a number of economic measures intended to help relieve the plight of the poor. He responded to one of the two traditional revolutionary demands and canceled all the debts, an event henceforth celebrated as the *seisachtheia*, "the shaking off of burdens." He also freed all the Athenian debt-slaves he could locate and forbade the use of freedom as collateral for any loan in the future. A measure prohibiting the export of any agricultural products except the olive immediately aided the poor consumer and more important, ultimately directed Athens towards becoming a commercial, grain-importing state.

There were other such economic and social reforms, but more critical were Solon's constitutional arrangements. He divided the citizen body into four classes according to wealth and distributed political power on the basis of these new classes. The measurement employed for these groupings was income in kind, how many bushels of grain a year a man's land could produce or his income buy. The wealthy were represented by the *pentakosiomedimnoi* ("500 big-bushel men"), whose income was equivalent to 500 or more *medimnoi* (roughly a bushel and a half) a year, and the *hippeis* ("knights"), who fell into the 300-500 *medimnoi* bracket. At the 200-300 level were the *zeugitai* ("yoke men" or "teamsters"), who were small farmers and businessmen, the solid middle income types who made up the hoplite army. The vast majority of the population, whose income fell below the 200 *medimnoi* mark, was placed in the bottom category, the *thetes* ("laborers").

These classes defined access to the state offices. The highest positions, the nine annually elected archonships, were open only to the *pentakosiomedimnoi* and possibly also the *hippeis*, who were in any case eligible for the lesser magistracies. The *zeugitai* could hold only very minor posts and the *thetes* none at all. Unlike before, however, the *thetes* could now vote in the assembly and sit as jurors in the Heliaia, the system of popular courts established by Solon as a guard against abuse of power by the magistrates. Solon also created the Council of Four Hundred, an annually elected body made up of one hundred citizens from each of the four traditional Athenian tribes. This new council took over from the old, aristocratic Council of the Areopagos (made up of ex-archons, who held the job for life) the all-important probouleutic power, that is, the right of preparing the agenda for the assembly, which itself lacked the power of legislative initiative.

Solon's constitutional reforms were of extreme importance in the development of the Athenian democracy. The switch from birth to wealth as the basis of political power broke the aristocratic monopoly and brought the constitution into line with the new economic realities. It was a still a long haul to real democratic government, but the admission of the *thetes* to the assembly and the juries was a giant step in that direction, bringing the people nearer the realization of their role as the ultimate decision-making body in the state.

Unfortunately for Athens, the one thing the reforms did not provide was stability. Solon's economic measures, important as they were, attacked only symptoms, and the poorer farmers remained at the mercy of the rich landholders and moneylenders. The wealthy commoners were of course satisfied with the constitutional arrangements and joined the old aristocracy to form a new nobility of wealth. But the great mass of citizens was still denied access to the important offices, and that included the middling class, who were the military backbone of the state and thus a great potential threat. Further, Solon's new council and voting system were still based on the traditional four tribes, thus maintaining in the constitution all the old family loyalties and feuds.

Why had Solon not gone further? As an aristocrat himself, he was probably opposed to such a revolutionary tactic as redistributing the land, but it was undoubtedly political realities rather than personal inclinations that stayed his hand. The new money wanted a piece of the political pie, and he gave the richest among them a full share. To have further diluted the power of the aristocrats, however, would in all probability have lost him their support and brought on the revolution he was trying to avoid. It was a game of compromise, and as is often the case with compromise, no one was satisfied. Political feuding among the new ruling circles broke out very soon after Solon stepped down from power and continued until 546, when after two earlier failures an Athenian named Peisistratus (d. 527) established a tyranny. Peisistratus seized power with the aid of a thousand Argive mercenaries and maintained a bodyguard throughout his rule, all of which makes him hardly seem the social revolutionary. But so far as can be seen he was broadly supported by the lower classes, who were tired of the bickering and incompetence of the existing government and hoped that any change would be for the better. More important, Peisistratus apparently received at least the passive support of the middle income groups, who felt gypped by the Solonian constitution. He could after all hardly have taken Athens with only a thousand troops if the potential hoplite strength of the city had been arrayed against him.

Peisistratus maintained the constitution, creating what has been called a "constitutional tyranny," but he took care to insure that his men held the important offices. He successfully faced the problem confronting the victorious revolutionary: reconciling the opposition to the new order without alienating your original supporters. In return for their support members of the noble families were offered careers in his government; the alternative was mute opposition or exile. Most of the nobility apparently decided that second fiddle under the tyrant was better than no fiddle at all. At the same time Peisistratus embarked upon a program to help the common people and strengthen the sense of national unity. For example, he provided low interest loans to farmers and sent circuit judges out into the countryside. He encouraged manufacture and trade and especially pushed the development of national cults and institutions, such as the Panathenaic festival and Theseus as the national hero. The intention behind these measures was the breaking down of the particularism and localism that supported the power of the old nobility. Peisistratus wanted the farmer in Marathon, the fisherman in

Sunium and the shopkeeper in Eleusis to look to the central government in Athens for help, rather than to their local noble families. Such not only undermined the strength of the tyrant's opposition, but also increased the power of the Athenian national government, which was of course himself.

Peisistratus was an eminently successful ruler, and his opposition seems to have been confined to disgruntled nobles. Significantly, the people never rose against Peisistratid rule, and when the old tyrant died in 527, he was succeeded by his son Hippias (c. 570-490) who continued the peaceful and prosperous administration. After his brother was murdered in a lovers' quarrel in 514 Hippias' rule became more oppressive, but in 510 it was not the Athenian people, but a Spartan army that finally threw him out.

SPARTA

Sparta is a strange anomaly among the Greek poleis, in fact, among all human societies. The Spartans found a solution to the problems leading other states to tyrannies, but that solution arrested all political, social and economic development and turned the society into a huge quasi-socialist military camp. This bizarre turn of events was traditionally attributed to a single lawgiver, Lycurgus, who supposedly reformed the entire structure of the Spartan state and society in one revolutionary stroke. Like the role assigned to Theseus in early Athenian history, however, this story is most improbable. All the ancient sources place Lycurgus in the ninth century, and the basic reforms were enacted in the seventh, by which time Lycurgus was probably only a name to the Spartans. He was likely associated with the reforms, as Theseus was with the unification of Attica, because of the Greek habit of seeing individuals as the cause of great events and changes.

Sparta's early political development, insofar as it can be seen, paralleled that of other poleis, which is hardly surprising, since she began with the same institutions and existed in the same environment. Sparta was already different, however, in that she had not one, but two kings, representing two distinct royal houses. No one really knows how this oddity developed – perhaps two communities fusing into one in the early Dark Age - but true to the general pattern, by the eighth century the aristocrats had limited the power of these monarchs by creating five annually elected magistrates, the ephors. The kings were left only with command of the army and whatever indirect political influence they could muster, but the fact is, unlike any other polis Sparta retained a hereditary kingship into classical times.

Sparta was also different in that there were virtually no chattel slaves, but rather much, if not most, of the population of Laconia (the territory controlled by Sparta) was composed of helots, state-owned serfs created, it appears, from the conquered pre-Dorian population. Laconia also included a number of non-Spartan communities, the *perioikoi* ("dwellers-around"), which were nominally free and locally autonomous, but ultimately subordinate to the Spartan state, in which they had no political rights. The *perioikoi* contributed hoplite contingents to the Spartan army, and the Greek world grouped them with the Spartans under the collective name Lacedaemonians, the label most commonly attached to the Spartans.

By the eighth century Sparta was feeling the population pressures common in the Greek world at that time, but instead of colonization she turned to conquest for an outlet. Two primary factors appear to have prompted this almost unique recourse to direct territorial aggrandizement on the part of a polis. For one thing the Spartans were already accustomed to ruling over a subject population in the form of the helots. Second, immediately to the west of Laconia were the rich agricultural lands of Messenia, beckoning the Spartans to extend their helot system. Thus, with no naval tradition and little inclination to take to the seas, the Spartans instead crushed the Messenians and took over. In the seventh century Sparta, like everyone else, adopted the hoplite phalanx, and towards the middle of the century she found herself involved in a complex of local wars with her neighbors to the north, Argos, Arcadia and Elis. Sparta emerged victorious, but these were tough little conflicts, and hard on their heels came a major revolt of the Messenians, which took the Spartans as long as twenty years to suppress. It appears that the hardships connected with these wars, especially the Messenian revolt, led to political agitation in Sparta, and together with the power of the hoplite army these troubles made the polis ripe for tyranny.

But the ruling circles saw the handwriting on the wall and took action. In the *Great Rhetra*, an oracular response from Delphi, the numbers, composition and powers of the Spartan council and assembly were fixed. The council, called the Gerousia, was composed of thirty individuals: the two kings and twenty-eight men over the age of sixty, all elected for life. The assembly was made up of all Spartan citizens (that is, adult males), who numbered several thousand and were called Spartiates or *homoioi* ("equals"). Together with the kings and the five ephors these institutions comprised the new government of Sparta. The problem of economic inequality, which plagued Athens and helped undermine Solon's efforts, was dealt with simply: it was eliminated by making all Spartan citizens completely equal. Henceforth, every male citizen in Sparta was of hoplite status, though the two kings would continue to enjoy a privileged position. All the land was redistributed, and every citizen was given an equal and supposedly inalienable plot, which came with a team of helots that would work the land while the master spent his time training for war. The formal qualification for citizenship was in fact your ability to contribute to the communal mess – thus, no land, no citizenship.

Either at this time or closer to the end of the seventh century a number of distinctive Dorian institutions were tightened up and directed solely towards military training. Children were inspected at birth by a state board to determine their fitness, and those babies that did not make the cut were exposed – left out to die. While Sparta was unique in making this a state decision, exposure was a common practice throughout Greece, a sort of postpartum birth control mechanism. There was in fact frequently a specific location outside the city where the infants were left, thus providing an informal adoption agency for childless couples. The Spartans apparently judged only on the basis of fitness, but the other Greeks were more concerned about gender, and females were apparently more often exposed than males, since they represented an economic liability. This practice, which still lurks in hidden corners of the modern world, is a reminder that civilized societies can differ dramatically in their moral attitudes.

At the age of seven the youth entered the *agogē*, the Spartan system of military training. This institution seems to have combined, it has been said, the worst aspects of the English boarding school and the Hitler Youth, but it was nevertheless Greece's first and for centuries only educational system. For the next thirteen years of his life the young Spartan lived in age groups under the absolute control of slightly older boys and endured nightmarish conditions of deprivation and brutality, all aimed at producing tough, uncomplaining soldiers. At twenty he entered the military and could marry, but he was still forced to live in barracks with his comrades and was encouraged to develop his stealth skills by sneaking out to visit his wife. At thirty he became a full citizen and could live with his spouse in his own place, but he still dined with his mess mates. Women followed a parallel course of rigorous physical training, designed in their case to produce healthy mothers for the next generation of Spartans. Spartan women were indeed as tough as their men, and it was commonly believed that Spartan men, so terrifying on the battlefield, were henpecked at home.

In order to maintain economic equality and avoid distractions from the business of producing soldiers, various austerity laws were also promulgated. The most serious of these was the prohibition of silver coinage, which left the Spartans with an obsolete and cumbersome currency of iron spits. The effect of this on the development of Spartan commerce can be easily imagined – it stopped it cold. It is hardly a coincidence that the archaeological remains show that around 600 imports into Sparta cease and Spartan arts, hitherto developing normally, rapidly decline into oblivion. Little in fact remains today to reveal that Sparta was one of the dominant powers in Archaic and Classical Greece.

So Sparta gained the first "hoplite constitution" in Greek history and was clearly way ahead of her time. That constitution provided her with great stability and the only semi-professional army in an age of amateur militias, an edge that allowed her to dominate her neighbors. That domination took the form of a system of military alliances, accurately called "the Lacedaemonians and their allies" by the Greeks and inaccurately the Peloponnesian League (it was neither strictly Peloponnesian nor a league) by modern historians. Sparta abandoned the direct seizure of territory after Messenia and instead began binding defeated foes and voluntary allies with treaties that required them to contribute troops whenever Sparta called. A lot of scholarly energy has been expended trying to determine the precise constitutional structure of the League, when in fact its real nature is quite clear: Sparta did what suited her and what she could get away with. When she was strong, she called the shots and might even interfere in the domestic affairs of a member state. When she was weak or momentarily distracted or facing a major undertaking, such as war against the Athenian Empire, she treated the allies with deference, calling meetings of representatives and attempting persuasion rather than simple command.

By the end of the sixth century the League included all the states of the Peloponnesus except some of the Achaean cities and Sparta's age-old enemy, Argos. In the course of the following century Sparta would also gain allies in central Greece, most importantly Thebes, but her inclination to go beyond the bounds of the Peloponnesus was severely limited. For all her powerful war machine, until the end of the fifth century Sparta's foreign policy was extremely conservative and insular, concerned almost exclusively with the security of the Peloponnesus, and that only as a mechanism for the defense of Laconia itself. With a potentially explosive helot population that may have outnumbered them by a factor of ten, with an eternally hostile Argos right next door and with surrounding allies not always enthusiastic about their leadership, the Spartans were definitely loathe to send their military off to some distant spot, which generally meant anywhere outside the Peloponnesus. Sparta was that odd militarized society that was not inclined to employ its military offensively, but when necessary, she could gather a force of more than thirty thousand hoplites, at the core of which would be her own Spartiates, Greece's toughest troops.

There were serious defects in the Spartan system, however. A society keyed to producing obedient cogs for a military machine does not readily produce great leaders, and the Spartans were in fact suspicious of the few clever and imaginative men who emerged despite the system. Further, creating tough soldiers insensitive to their own suffering unfortunately also creates soldiers insensitive to the suffering of others, and the brutality inherent in Spartan society was often imposed upon others. The primitive living standards and rigid social rules also produced citizens who were notoriously corruptible and greedy when confronted with the outside world. The greatest weakness lay in the fact that over the long run the system could not maintain the economic and social equality that was at its heart. There were too many loopholes and too much mobility for a closed system, and over the years land concentrated in the hands of fewer and fewer families, particularly under the inheritance laws. The result was that more and more Spartans were economically marginalized and fell into a disenfranchised group called *hypomeiones* ("inferiors"), and as a consequence the citizen body shrunk from 8000 Spartiates in 480 to only 1500 in 371, diminishing the quality of the Lacedaemonian army.

Sparta's internal harmony and the virtues of her citizens were greatly admired in a world of political and social instability and continual warfare, but nobody in his right mind wanted to live in Sparta. Her citizen equality and fantastic military machine were purchased at the expense of virtually everything else and her stability was rooted in an absence of change, and what was progressive in the seventh century seemed archaic in the fifth. And once they had this constitution, the Spartans could not abandon it even had they wished to. Such would have meant the loss of their military superiority and dominion over the Peloponnesus and the probable end of Sparta as a meaningful power.

################

SUGGESTED READING

The primary and just about the only sources for this period are the historian Herodotus and the biographer Plutarch (lives of Solon and Lycurgus), both of whom flesh out the political developments with a host of amusing stories. Far and away the most entertaining survey of the Archaic Age is A. R. Burn, *The Lyric Age of Greece* (1960); Anthony Snodgrass, *Archaic Greece* (1980) and O. Murray, *Early Greece²* (1993) are also good. A. Andrewes, *The Greek Tyrants* (1963) is a nifty survey of tyrants, and W.G. Forrest, *A History of Sparta 950-192 B.C.* (1980) is a zippy little history of this bizarre place. If you want to get a little less serious, try Larry Gonick, *The Cartoon History of the Universe. Vol. 5: Brains and Bronze* (1980) and *Vol. 6: Who Are These Athenians?* (1981). And for you cut and slash types, easily the best introductions to the Greek military are F.E. Adcock, *The Greek and Macedonian Art of War* (1957) and Victor Hanson, *The Western Way of War* (1989); Hanson's book directly addresses the question of what it was actually like in a hoplite battle and is in my opinion the best book ever written on hoplite warfare. Far less exciting, but still readable and very informative is his *Warfare and Agriculture in Classical Greece²* (1998), which deals with the intimate connection between hoplite warfare and agriculture (destroying vineyards, olive trees and grain in the field is not anywhere near as easy as you might expect!). John Warry, *Warfare in the Ancient World* (1980) is noteworthy for its lavish and detailed illustrations. A good introduction to slavery is N.R.E. Fisher, *Slavery in Classical Greece* (1993); M.I. Finley, *Economy and Society in Ancient Greece* (1982) is a collection of essays, half of which deal with slavery. You might also try M.I. Finley, *Ancient Slavery and Modern Ideology* (1980), a fascinating and broad examination of Greek and Roman slavery, particularly in the light of modern concepts of servitude.

# # # # # # # # # # # # # # # # # # # #

IV. FINALLY, THE DISCOVERY OF MAN

THE DEVELOPMENT OF GREEK THOUGHT

...Thales, when he was looking up to study the stars and tumbled down a well.

-Plato *Theaetetus* 174A[4]

And to think I always used to believe the rain was just Zeus pissing though a sieve.

-Aristophanes *Clouds* 375[5]

During the Archaic Age, that period from the mid-eighth to the beginning of the fifth century, the Greeks made tremendous progress in ordering their society and developing constitutional government. Even more spectacular progress was made in the realm of ideas, as Greek concepts of justice and religion evolved, leading ultimately to the birth of the rationalism and humanism so vital to western society.

It is necessary to drop back into Homer to pick up the threads. The justice found in the epic world is completely characteristic of the highly individualistic heroic society: the defense of right is essentially a private affair. When Menelaus charges Antilochus with committing an illegal act in the chariot race in Book XXIII of the *Iliad*, the dispute is settled by Menelaus challenging Antilochus to take an oath in the name of the god Poseidon that he did not cheat. Antilochus refuses to perjure himself before the god and admits his guilt. If Antilochus had sworn the oath, the matter would also have been settled, since it is assumed that the offended deity would punish the perjurer. Two other recourses were available to the men. They could appeal to a higher authority, such as Agamemnon, for arbitration or they could fight it out, hoping that victory would crown the man in the right. Justice, incidentally, was a matter for equals, and Menelaus would no more call for an oath from a non-hero like Thersites than an English aristocrat would challenge a coal miner to a duel.

If a crime was committed against a man, it was up to him or his kinsmen to deal with the injustice. The justice dispensed by the king, who was as close as the heroic world came to a state, was limited to arbitration, and consequently such things as homicide and theft were strictly a family affair. Society would not punish the wrongdoer, so unless you were willing to leave the matter in the somewhat questionable hands of the gods, it was up to you and your family to bring the criminal to justice. And since justice normally meant retribution, there was a distinct tendency towards blood feuds.

This is the picture presented in the Homeric epics, and it likely approximates the realities of the actual Dark Age community, though in a far more stylized manner than was actually the case. In the real world, where fights are rarely fair and the ideals of behavior never consistently observed, the accuser was probably more inclined to punish the perjurer himself if divine attention seemed too long in coming. By the beginning of the Archaic Age this picture has already changed, and justice has essentially made the move from being primarily the concern of the individual and family to being the concern of the state. This is the natural result of the individualistic warrior society giving way to the settled community of the polis with its social consciousness and sense of group responsibility and obligation. Order and harmony became prized goals of society, and the development of a true government provided a mechanism to help achieve those goals. As the representative of the community, the state would deal with those who violated the community by committing crimes against its members. In Greek society justice would never be completely out of private hands (indeed, the Greeks, unlike the Romans, would never develop a coherent vision of the law or a juridical system that was autonomous and detached from the political-social structure), but nevertheless the fundamental idea that the community is the seat of justice has emerged by the end of the eighth century.

This change in the concept of justice can be seen in a vocabulary shift. In Homer what is right or just is indicated by the word *themis*, which means "the correct way" (i.e., custom), and to a lesser extent by the word *dikē*, which has the same concrete meaning. *Themis*, however, is backed by divine authority, while *dikē*, which will become the classical Greek word for "justice," derives its authority from the community. In Homer *themis* is far more important and is personified as a goddess, while *dikē* is simply a word. But as the polis developed and emphasis moved from the family to the community, *dikē* grew in importance while *themis* declined, especially after the disappearance of the monarchy, with which it was closely associated. In the works of the farmer-poet Hesiod (fl. c. 700) *dikē* has in fact become a divinity, Dikē, the daughter of Themis and Zeus and sister of Eirēnē ("peace") and Eunomia ("good laws"). Very cleverly put by Hesiod: from the union of tradition (Themis) and legitimate authority (Zeus) spring justice, peace and good laws, the three attributes of the well-ordered community.

According to Hesiod, "whenever anyone hurts Dikē with lying slander, she sits beside her father, Zeus, the son of Kronos, and tells him of men's wicked heart, until the people pay for the mad folly of their princes who, evilly minded, pervert judgment and give sentence crookedly." (*Works and Days* 258-62)[6] Key here is the fact that the bad guys no longer personally offend Zeus or some other particular deity, but rather they injure Dikē, who for all her recent elevation to godhood is essentially an abstract concept, justice. Further, a violation of Dikē, justice, now brings retribution upon the entire community, not just the individual criminal, and consequently the community must concern itself with lawbreaking. What might appear to be a lot of mythological nonsense in Hesiod is in fact a revealing statement about the understanding of justice in the early seventh century: it is an abstraction defended by the community. The historian works with whatever he can.

Though first presented in 458, several hundred years after the period being considered, the *Eumenides* of Aeschylus (c. 525-455) is especially illustrative of the development of the concept of justice. The *Eumenides* is the last play in the *Oresteia*, the only surviving dramatic trilogy, and deals with the final chapter in the bloody history of the house of Atreus. Atreus and Thyestes, the sons of Pelops, quarreled over the kingship of Argos and over Thyestes' seduction of his brother's wife, and Atreus, pretending reconciliation, served his brother his children for dinner in a disguised dish. When Thyestes discovered he had just eaten his own offspring, he dropped a curse on Atreus and fled with his surviving son, Aegisthus. Atreus' two sons, Agamemnon and Menelaus, inherited the rule of Argos and Sparta, and it was the abduction of Menelaus' wife, Helen, that led the brothers into the Trojan War. In order to get favorable winds for the expedition Agamemnon sacrificed his daughter Iphigeneia, which certainly annoyed his wife, Clytemnestra, who in her husband's ten year absence took up with another man - Aegisthus. The *Oresteia* picks up the story here, and the first play, *Agamemnon*, deals with the king's return from Troy and his murder at the hands of his wife and her lover, who has usurped the throne of Argos. The second, *The Libation Bearers*, details the murder of Clytemnestra and Aegisthus by Orestes, the son of Agamemnon, while in the *Eumenides* Orestes, pursued by the avenging Furies (the Erinyes), is brought to trial in Athens.

This last drama centers on Orestes, but he himself is of no great concern to us. Like Dred Scott or Ernesto Miranda or Norma McCorvey (Jane Roe), Orestes represents an issue, and it is the issue that is important. And the issue is the old versus the new concept of justice and all the ramifications of that struggle. Orestes' murder of his mother is only the most recent episode in the bloody soap opera of his family. The original crime of Atreus placed a pollution, a blood guilt, upon his family, and this guilt was passed through the generations, crime invoking counter-crime. This is the old retributive justice, the clumsy justice of Zeus, in which sin is countered with further sin in an inherited pollution. Orestes is only the last link in a bloody chain, but his crime is especially horrible, since he has killed his mother. As a matricide he has the Furies hounding him, bent on the extraction of vengeance.

The Furies or Erinyes are one side of the dichotomy in the play. They are dark divinities of the earth, numbered among the "anonymous gods," who are so terrifying that their names are rarely spoken, lest their attention be attracted. Instead they are commonly referred to by the ironic name Eumenides ("well-intentioned ones"), which they most definitely are not. They are primitive and female, a sign of their antiquity, and they deal with the most primitive and instinctually horrible crime – the killing of immediate kin. And they deal with it in the most primitive way – unreasoning vengeance. Concerned only with the fact of Orestes' crime, the Furies are blind to the ideas behind it and the circumstances surrounding it. They only see a mother's blood on a son's hands and demand his death as atonement. They are representatives of a pre-Hellenic past, barbaric and cruel and single-mindedly driving for the punishment of the wrongdoer.

Opposed to the Furies and arguing for the defense is the god Apollo, perhaps the highest expression of the new Olympians. Young, male and the epitome of careful reason, he represents that which is new, that which is of the light, in short, that which is Hellenic. He is concerned not with Orestes' murder of his mother, but with her murder of her husband. For Apollo Clytemnestra's act was a double crime, the murder of Agamemnon the male, the head of the family, and more important, the murder of Agamemnon the king, the head of the community. By killing the head of state Clytemnestra struck a blow at order and authority in society, and for that reason Apollo gave Orestes his blessing and encouragement. Apollo stands for the male principle over the more primitive female, for reason over unreason, for the community over the family. He is every bit as ruthless as the Furies, but there is reason behind his ruthlessness. His way is not the simple blind vengeance of the Erinyes.

To settle the dispute the goddess Athena establishes for all time a jury of mortal men to try this and succeeding cases. And this is the crux – the dispensation of justice is taken from the hands of individuals and gods and given to the community of men. As it happens, however, the community of men are unable to make up their minds on this one, and Athena must cast a deciding vote in favor of acquittal in order to break the tie. The deadlocked jury is intended, I believe, to remind us of a basic fact: primitive though it may be, what the Furies represent is still extremely important. Law and order cannot be allowed to trample on the sacred instincts; reason and the needs of the community cannot obscure the fact that crimes such as matricide move us to instinctive horror. We may respond to Apollo intellectually, but we still connect to the Erinyes at a more visceral level. Nevertheless, the new justice of Apollo must prevail, and so Athena casts her vote, giving the final verdict and all its ramifications the approval not merely of heaven, but of wisdom itself. For Athena is more than just another deity; she is wisdom incarnate, sprung full grown from the mind of Zeus, untouched and unspoiled. Female in form, but with male attributes, she, the reconciler, is herself something of a reconciliation.

Thus, though the victory goes to Apollo insofar as Orestes is acquitted of the crime, the Furies, who after all are part of Apollo's own past, are not simply turned away. Rather, they are fitted into the new order of things and given a position in the polis. Henceforth, they will concern themselves not only with strife among kin, but also with strife among brothers in the greater family that is the community. Fear, after all, is a component of justice: "What man who fears nothing at all is ever righteous?" (*Eumenides* 678-79)[7] says Athena. This is the final synthesis. The primitive, individualistic Erinyes are incorporated into the Hellenic order and transformed into defenders of the community, which is now the seat of justice for men. And so they pray: "Civil war/ fattening on men's ruin shall/ not thunder in our city. Let/ not the dry dust that drinks/ the black blood of citizens/ through passion for revenge/ and bloodshed for bloodshed/ be given out state to prey upon." (*Eumenides* 976-83)

In the area of religion vital changes were also taking place from the Dark Age through the Archaic, and it is necessary to return again to Homer and Hesiod. It simply cannot be overemphasized how fundamental these two poets are to the nature of post-Mycenaean Greek religion; they virtually single-handedly defined the religion of their entire society. As sources of information about the divine, Homer's *Iliad* and *Odyssey* and Hesiod's *Theogony* possessed an authority that was completely unparalleled in the Greek world, yet they were not sacred texts or the word of god, like the Bible, but poetry composed by men. As we shall see, this circumstance almost certainly played a role in the emergence of humanism.

The Homeric gods, whom Hesiod organized into a coherent hierarchy, might be characterized as a near perfect reflection of the heroic society over which they hold sway, which is hardly surprising, since every religion mirrors the society that creates it. Zeus and the other gods are similar to the earthly king and his retainers, to Agamemnon and his often rebellious chieftains. Zeus ascended to power by deposing Kronos, the previous ruler (and his father), just as a Homeric warrior might gain the kingship by the violent overthrow of a weak king. The Olympic gods are completely anthropomorphic: they possess tremendous power and cannot die, but otherwise they are perfectly human, as full of weaknesses and as inclined to poor behavior as any mortal. In fact, the Olympians were for the Greeks a constant source of both awe and laughter, surely an oddity among all the human approaches to divinity. It is a rare society indeed that laughs at its gods.

The Homeric deities may also be described as essentially non-ethical, at least in the sense to which we are accustomed with our Judeo-Christian-Islamic god. Unlike their colleague Yahweh in Israel, the Greek gods were quite definitely not role models. Not only does Zeus frequently engage in behavior considered socially unacceptable by the Greeks themselves, but he is also basically unconcerned with any equitable dispensation of justice. The favor of the gods is instead capricious, depending for the most part on the whim of the individual deity rather than any well established notion of right and wrong. There is consequently no real concept of sin, as we understand it, and the offenses a man might commit against heaven are identical to those he might commit against his mortal lord: treason, perjury, failure to perform obligations, etc. There is also as yet no sense of *phthonos*, divine retribution for immoderate human pride. The Greeks were most certainly not given to humility, even before their gods, and pride is an essential part of a hero's character; Achilles can even dare to struggle with the river god Skamander without fear of being struck down for pretentious behavior. The gods of course meddle in human affairs, but the Homeric heroes are nevertheless fiercely independent, ready to take their chances in a capricious world.

These are the gods of the Greek Dark Age, and as the polis developed and emerged from the gloom, these deities developed along with it, becoming intimately connected with the city. Religion has three primary functions: dealing with the psychological and emotional needs of the individual, explaining the world and cosmos and helping to secure the social order. It is the last of these that looms largest in Greek religion of the Archaic and Classical periods, when Greek beliefs and sacral practices were primarily civic in character, tied to the polis community and overwhelmingly communal in their nature. The Greeks did not have a church, that is, a centrally organized religion with a more or less fixed ideology defended by a professional priest class, like the Catholic Church or the Temple of Amon-Ra, and Greek priests were simply specialists, who typically belonged to no hierarchy beyond the local cult or polis. But Greek religion was "established," in the sense that cultic practices were part and parcel of the polis and their observance necessary to the health of the political and social order. Citizens were free privately to believe what they would, but the civic religion demanded public observance, lest the well-being of the community be threatened.

This is all very different from what little we know of Mycenaean religion, which reflected the hierarchical society surrounding the Bronze Age kingship and in its practice granted special honor and privilege to kings and priests. In the religion of the polis the citizen-as-priest performed the rituals, but the entire community took part, sharing the experience and the meat from the animal sacrifice that was at the core of Greek religion. It was not the king and his priests securing the right relationship with heaven, but the community, and the communal religious experience, with its shared emotions of awe, fear, hope and joy, helped strengthen the social bonds. As to be expected, ritual practices attended every significant passage in the life of the individual, from birth to death, but the primary thrust of these practices was civic in nature: to reestablish order and harmony or reintegrate the individual into the group after any significant event. Of prime importance was the animal sacrifice, whose origins are obscure, but whose point was clearly to confront and deal with the all-important issue of life and death in a communal setting. Some of the elements in the civic religion, like the animal sacrifice, are very old, but the religion as a whole seems coeval with the polis. At the heart of the polis was an incredibly strong sense of community, one that even overshadowed the distinctions of class and wealth, and the civic religion of the polis developed as a reflection of this, its practice inseparable from the community it served. This of course could be a problem should the polis disappear.

The civic religion of the polis, built around the Olympic gods of Homer and Hesiod, would persist for centuries and remain the most obvious manifestation of Greek religion, vitally important to the political community and vividly prominent in the art and literature of the society. But already early on in the Archaic Age societal developments were producing changes in the Greek concepts of divinity, as men responded to the increasing difficulties of the period. The seventh and sixth centuries were disturbing times for the average Greek, who was constantly at or over the edge due to the economic oppression of the aristocrats (see Chapter III). His life was filled with insecurity and anxiety, and matters only got worse when the advent of the tyrants added political uncertainty and confusion to the economic woes. This personal insecurity and social upheaval could hardly fail to affect religious beliefs.

Men increasingly experienced a lack of justice on earth, but turning to heaven, a natural human tendency, ran up against the fact that a concept of justice was not a strong feature of the inherited religion. The Archaic Age community thus attempted (quite unconsciously of course) to moralize the Olympians to some degree, but the result appears to have been a supernatural world increasingly filled with threats, as the fears and anxieties of the community were projected into heaven. The offspring of insecurity and fear, something apparently new played upon the psyche of the Greeks – guilt, and this notion of guilt was most obvious in the evolving idea of *miasma* or ritual pollution.

The idea of a pollution, a spiritual defilement (from sexual intercourse or killing or whatever) that required a purification or cleansing, is in fact found in Homer, but it is a simple concept of limited importance. In the later Archaic Age the fear of *miasma* begins to loom very large, and the definition of a pollution comes to include the terrifying notion that it is hereditary and infectious. It was clear that if the wheels of heavenly justice turned at all, they must have done so very slowly, often slower than a man's days could measure. But the punishment had to come, the guilt had to be expiated, the pollution expunged, and it had to happen in this world, since the Greek vision of the afterlife was shadowy and lacked any system of judgment, reward and punishment. So, if the punishment did not come in the wrongdoer's lifetime, the guilt must be passed on to the next generation, an idea supported by the tight family bonds of the period. The son was the continuation of the father and inherited not just his goods but also his guilt. The curse in the *Eumenides* is a perfect example of an inherited pollution.

Guilt and pollution thus came clothed in uncertainty. You were never sure whether some ancestor had committed a crime and incurred a pollution that was now upon you and about to be attended to by the gods. You were never even sure whether you yourself had unwittingly picked up a pollution, since the guilt could be the automatic consequence of an external act, such as accidentally violating a grove sacred to Artemis. This is externalized sin, quite independent of your actual intentions, and whether or not you intended the act or are even aware that you did it is irrelevant; the crime is committed and the pollution incurred. This is part of the horror of it all – you just never knew, and it was upon this uncertainty that the anxiety and guilt already in your mind played.

Grim times can produce grim visions of the nature of things, but men require some hope, and as the years rolled by, the needs and desires that had attempted to moralize the Olympians stirred the development of an alternative religious form, the mystery cult. Elements of these cults appear to go back to prehistory, but it was the pressures of the Archaic Age and the discovery of the individual that fostered their growth. The cults varied in their content, but they shared certain characteristics and all of them provided the worshipper an intense and personal emotional experience generally missing from the civic religion. They focused on a single or small group of gods, offering a more intimate involvement, and the participant would undergo some sort of initiation (*telein* or *myein*, hence "mystery"), which would ultimately lead him to the central mysteries of the cult, in theory unknown to outsiders. As the continued popularity of fraternal organizations and secret societies demonstrates, initiation and secrecy, which create special bonds and a sense of elevated status for the group, are always a good draw.

The cults also revolved around sex and most importantly the issue of death, the fear of which the cult hoped to dispel with its rites. The cult of Dionysus (or Bacchus) offered temporary release from pain and suffering through ecstatic possession (see Chapter XI), but the other important Greek mysteries, the Eleusinian, Orphic and the later Hellenistic cult of Isis and Serapis, possessed as central figures gods who died and were resurrected, either literally or metaphorically, thus confronting the initiate with the terror of death and the hope of rebirth, either in this life or the next. If this seems hauntingly familiar, it is because Christianity, while something more than just another mystery religion, was certainly influenced by the ideas of the mystery cults, which were far and away the most popular religious form in the Roman Empire into which Christianity was born. The idea of the dying and resurrected god, so critical to Christianity, played no important role in the Near Eastern religious traditions, and while the new faith may have developed a fresh understanding of death and rebirth, the notion of the suffering god appears to come straight out of the Greek experience.

While these developments were taking place in the sphere of religion, a much more exciting and portentous intellectual adventure was being born in the poleis of sixth century Ionia. There, circumstances gave rise to a purely scientific inquiry into the nature of man and the universe, and humanism and rationalism were born. Why this should be the moment for these towering discoveries is to a great degree a matter of the right combination of things coming together in the right place at the right time.

One of those right things, and probably the most important, was the nature of the inherited Olympic religion, which many of the Ionian scientists ultimately spurned. A key fact here was the absence of any church. The tenets of Greek religion were fairly fluid and permitted a broad amount of intellectual freedom. There were no stultifying dogma, no holy books and no prophets speaking the absolute word of god; the works of Homer and Hesiod may have defined Greek religion, but they were not sacred writ and their authors, while inspired, were completely human. There was no powerful organization to enforce beliefs and threaten the thinker with the stake, and "amateurs" were consequently free to speculate on questions, such as the origins of the universe, that were normally reserved for the "professionals" of the priesthood. Whatever you might think of the role of faith, it is clear that organized religions, especially the monotheisms, have invariably been a brake on intellectual progress. God requires belief without doubt, and doubt is vital to the discovery of truth.

Another important aspect of the traditional religion was that in contrast to the belief systems of the Near East the Greeks held that the ruling gods, the Olympians, did not create the universe and that men and the current gods were both subordinate to the fact of its existence. This permitted – perhaps encouraged – speculation about its origins in terms other than divinities and personalities, which constitute the causative coin of myth. In the Near Eastern mythopoeic ("myth-making") universe there could be no natural causation, because every natural phenomenon was the manifestation of a will, a personality, in a universe filled with life. The Greeks, with their belief that the universe preceded the gods, that it preceded all definable personalities, had a leg up in the process of breaking free of the restraining bonds of mythopoeic thought. And non-mythic propositions about the nature of the universe invite further examination and questions because they are not protected by the sacred inviolability that is associated with myth. Further, god and man were much, much closer than in the pre-classical religions, and the Olympians, unlike their Babylonian and Egyptian counterparts, constantly involved themselves in human affairs and frequently looked silly for it, all of which undermined their status as cosmic forces and made them easier to dispense with. Finally, the blatant immorality of their gods forced the Greeks to look more to themselves in considering their moral and social values, which focus on human society surely contributed to the birth of humanism.

A second factor is the simple existence of the poleis in Ionia. All Greece was in commercial contact with the older civilizations of the east, but the Ionian cities were especially so, forming a kind of east-west interface with the non-Greek communities in the Anatolian interior. This interface not only brought access to the accumulated scientific and technical data of the eastern societies, but more important it also provided obvious and unavoidable cultural contrasts. One did not have to walk many miles inland from, say, Miletus before coming upon communities that were definitely not Greek and that had far different customs, values and social organization. Unfortunately, most humans react to such differences by automatically assuming that the other guy is wrong, but some, however, face such a challenge by questioning the absolute validity of their own institutions, by wondering if perhaps such things are all relative after all. Perhaps what is good for Greeks in Miletus is not so good for Carians in Mylasa? Indeed, perhaps Milesians could in fact be doing things differently themselves? And thus the first stages of skepticism and relativistic thought, which are absolutely fundamental to scientific inquiry, are reached. If there is no doubt, if there is only contentment, there is no spur to intellectual progress. Old and Middle Kingdom Egypt, secure in the material bounty of the Nile valley and in its entirely positive view of the cosmos, passed fifteen hundred years with virtually no progress.

Most Greeks, like most people everywhere, of course assumed that their ways were the best, and the tremendous explosion of Greek culture in the Archaic and Classical periods was accompanied by a growing conviction that Greek culture was simply better than anything the rest of the world, which was composed entirely of barbarians, had to offer. But one vitally important component of this culture was the Ionian tradition of skepticism and examination, which made the Greeks, and subsequent western civilization, generally more receptive to outside ideas and less xenophobic than others.

Also because of the east-west interface, which put them on the cutting edge of the Archaic Age economic boom, the Ionian poleis achieved a high level of material prosperity very early on. This prosperity allowed more men the leisure time to devote themselves entirely to intellectual pursuits, just as thousands of years earlier the development of agricultural technique had freed some men from the burden of the food supply and led to the emergence of the basic arts and crafts and urban civilization. The existence of a leisure class is of course not a sufficient condition for the birth of rationalism; every civilization since Sumer had possessed a leisure class of some size, but none had produced rationalism. It is, however, a necessary condition, since men who do not have the free time just to think will rarely think new thoughts.

A final and extremely important factor was the material progress being achieved all over the Greek world throughout the seventh and sixth centuries. Archaic Age Greece was one of those very rare moments before the modern world when real change was apparent in a man's lifetime, as the Greeks began to make great advances in the arts and engineering and in their general mastery over the environment. Lyric poetry and secular drama were born, artists were learning new techniques for decorating pottery and sculptors moved heavily into marble. The trireme, the classic Greek oared warship, was perfected and led to greater control of the sea lanes. Coinage and standardization of weights were introduced and spread quickly across Greece. Especially important in these developments were the new political powerhouses, the tyrants, who could provide for more efficient government than the aristocrats ever could and who were everywhere inclined towards feats of engineering. Polycrates of

Samos (fl. c. 530), for example, built a temple over three hundred feet long and brought water to his capital by piercing a ridge with a thousand yard tunnel, the diggers meeting in the middle with an error of only six feet. This may not seem like much compared to the pyramids or the temple complex at Karnak, but those monuments were the achievements of an entire, very populous civilization, while these were the work of one tiny polis.

Because of such achievements, because of the inescapable fact that life and society were not just discernibly changing, but also generally improving, the Greeks were becoming infected with a new spirit, a totally new idea – that of progress. For the first time in history men were looking forward, rather than back to some golden heroic age. Every other society in the ancient Mediterranean had believed that if things were changing at all, they were only getting worse. The Egyptians did not even have a real concept of non-periodic change and the passage of time; as their universe was created, so it would always be. And while it is true that the Hebrews looked forward, it was only to the arrival of a messiah; they had no concept of progress. Actually, the Greeks too had a vision of an earlier golden age, but that was now giving way to the astounding notion that things were getting better. The realization that the human race was progressing had arrived.

And these deeds that stirred the notion of progress were the accomplishments of men, not gods. Men were at last becoming fully aware of their capabilities and realizing that things could be made better, even without the help of heaven, especially, perhaps, a heaven populated by often foolish looking deities. They were taking pride in human achievement and discovering that man, not god, was the most proper object of human attention, that human society and the individual human being had their own intrinsic dignity and worth. The Greeks were flexing their intellectual and spiritual muscles, and humanism was being born. The Ionian scientist Xenophanes of Colophon (c. 570-c. 478) summed it all up in a single statement: "The gods have not revealed all things from the beginning to mortals; but, by seeking, men find out, in time, what is better."[8] Such a thought would have been utterly impossible in any of the dozens of societies that preceded the Greeks.

The result of all these factors was the birth of Greek rationalism and real genesis of science and philosophy in sixth century Ionia. The Ionian philosopher-scientists asked "why" concerning the world and its phenomena and sought to make consistent and logical generalizations about nature. And unlike any before them they did not do so from religious or purely practical motives, but from simple curiosity, from the plain desire to understand and order the world about them. This is the crux of rationalism. The Near Eastern societies had developed a considerable body of scientific knowledge, but they had done so in the service of religion or practical needs and in a context of mythopoeic thought. The impressive engineering skills of the Egyptians, for example, followed upon the desire to build more elaborate temples and tombs for their god-kings, and the sophisticated astronomical data of the Babylonians was collected in order better to read the will of the gods revealed in the movements of the heavenly bodies. And whatever the motives, the mythopoeic outlook of the pre-classical societies, a world view that rejected logic, consistency, generalization and natural causation, prevented them from turning their accumulation of data into true science and philosophy. Now in Greece for the first time in any significant numbers men were studying the world around them simply to understand it and were realizing that through such understanding the human condition could be improved.

The skepticism of the Ionian thinkers was especially strong regarding the inherited religious traditions, understandably, since reason naturally tends to devalue ideas based only on faith and custom. The Ionian scientists were breaking the mythopoeic bonds and spurning the divine in their explanations of things; the traditional *mythos* was being challenged by the newly discovered *logos*. It was a rare Greek thinker who did away with divinity altogether and almost all accepted the notion of some divine first principle, but in their examination of the cosmos they focused their attention on impersonal forces and natural causation. "For many and ridiculous," says Hecateaus of Miletus (fl. c. 500) at the end of the sixth century about the inherited traditions, "so they seem to me, are the tales of the Greeks."[9] Far more astounding is the declaration of his contemporary Xenophanes: "And if oxen and horses and lions had hands, and could draw with their hands and could do what man can do, horses would draw the gods in the shape of horses, and oxen in the shape of oxen, each giving the gods bodies similar to their own."[10] In other words, the gods are mere inflations of the mortal image, which is an incredibly penetrating perception about the nature of religion, one that has not occurred to most people even today.

Thales of Miletus (fl. c. 600), earliest known of the Ionian thinkers, saw the material world as being formed of or evolved from a single substance – water. This is of course not quite right, but the systematic generalization and rational speculation involved in reaching such a conclusion was a great achievement. Thales expressed (or at least implied) for the first time the essential scientific-philosophical concept of form, that is, the idea that substance and form are separate qualities. This might seem a completely obvious conclusion, but it certainly was not to people before Thales. Mythic thought views every object as completely unique and makes no distinction between form and substance.

Anaximander of Miletus (fl. 1st half 6th cent.), a younger contemporary of Thales, elaborated on his colleague's ideas, and in his view of the development of the material world he came up with a fantastic notion. He suggested that the first generations of men were nurtured inside of fish-like creatures, which had themselves arisen spontaneously in the primeval seas. His belief that land animals, including humans, came originally from the sea is hardly a statement of Darwinian evolution, but it is nevertheless a brilliant breakthrough. Every previous conception of the origins of man had made him a special creation of the gods, either spit out or ejaculated or fashioned out of dirt or some other handy material. And here is Anaximander laying a firm foundation for an understanding of the evolution of life on the planet by dethroning man and placing him squarely in the animal kingdom.

This kind of thought is a triumph of human reason, proceeding to inquire into first principles from a basis of general physical observation. It would take the Greeks (that is, the educated elites) a while to emancipate themselves completely from the concrete imagery of mythopoeic thought, but the basic break with myth had taken place, virtually overnight. The headlong plunge into rationalism was in fact overbold: so drunk were these new rationalists on the novel notions of logic and consistency, both foreign to mythic thought, that they followed them wherever they led, even if that meant contradicting the observed world. This resulted in many mistaken ideas about the nature of things, but it nevertheless demonstrated an intellectual courage impressive in any age, as the Ionians accepted without hesitation logical conclusions that were at odds with what they saw about them.

The mythopoeic mode of thought of the pre-Greek cultures certainly worked; the longevity and achievements of these societies attest to that. But it was simply an incorrect view of the universe and placed a very low ceiling on intellectual progress. In the belief systems of these societies, including the Hebrews, man was fashioned essentially to serve the gods. True, the Egyptians provided him with some measure of dignity by understanding him to be an integral part of creation, akin to the animals and the gods, but it was a static conception that left the human potential untapped. The Greeks now dared suggest that man was not a special creation of the gods, but at the same time they boldly asserted that he did indeed occupy a special place, not because of any particular relationship with god, but because of his mind. The birth of humanism and rationalism was the discovery of the mind, the realization that unlike the other inhabitants of creation humans could examine and refashion their world and even themselves. For a moment at least, the obsession with the established order, prevalent in Greece as it had been in the Near Eastern societies, was shattered, and invention and change were in the air. Unfortunately, that moment would pass, and by the second half of the fifth century Greeks would once again fear innovation, especially in the economic and social spheres, as a challenge to the status quo and thus a path to social upheaval and ruin. But while it lasted the moment was electrifying, and in any case the humanism and rationalism would remain, woven into the fabric of urban Greek society and the cause of a spectacular cultural outburst. After two and a half millennia of human civilization the Greeks had finally discovered man.

# # # # # # # # # # # # # # # # # # #

SUGGESTED READING

Easily the best introduction to Greek religion is Walter Burkert, *Greek Religion* (1985), and if you are interested in myths, try Robert Graves, *The Greek Myths* (1964); his discussions and interpretations are even better than the myths. On mythopoeic thought and the Greek liberation from the same see Henri Frankfort, et al., *Before Philosophy: The Intellectual Adventure of Ancient Man* (1946), an excellent book that will also provide a fascinating brief look at the cultures of Egypt and Sumer-Babylonia. Werner Jaeger, *Paideia: The Ideals of Greek Culture* (1970) is the classic work on the subject, but this is serious reading. On justice Donald Kagan, *The Great Dialogue: History of Greek Political Thought from Homer to Polybius* (1965), an eminently readable book, from which I have shamelessly cribbed a lot of material. Eric Havelock, *The Greek Concept of Justice* (1978) is an interesting book that concentrates on justice in the Homeric and Archaic worlds. On the events in Ionia G.L. Huxley, *The Early Ionians* (1972) is excellent; he concentrates on the intellectual and political developments and keeps the archaeological trivia to a minimum. John M. Robinson, *An Introduction to Early Greek Philosophy* (1968) is a clear and readable, if something less than exciting, presentation of the pre-Socratic philosophers. On a related note, the first chapter of John Casti, *Paradigms Lost* (1989) is the best account I have ever seen of exactly what science is and is not.

# # # # # # # # # # # # # # # # # #

V. MORALITY FOR SALE OR RENT

THE SOPHISTIC MOVEMENT

But remember: I want his tongue
honed down like a razor. Sharpen him on the left side
for piddling private suits, but grind him on the right
for Grand Occasions and Affairs of State.

-Aristophanes *Clouds* 1107-10[11]

We hold these truths to be self-evident...

-American Declaration of Independence

A new spirit of rational inquiry was born in sixth century Ionia with the scientific endeavors of men like Thales and Anaximander. The basic concern of these men, who were primarily physical scientists, was the nature of the world about them, but a concern for the nature of things leads naturally to a more essential question: the nature of reality itself. Indeed, the subatomic physicist and cosmologist must today face this question, as they investigate the very fringes of the knowable. But the nature of reality, particularly for those who lack particle accelerators and radio telescopes, will tend to be more a metaphysical than physical problem, and thus from the fertile ground of Ionian science there quickly grew the other major branch of rationalism – philosophy.

In some sense the skepticism that had stimulated the break with the religious tradition and the rise of rationalism now began to undermine the basis of scientific inquiry. Near the beginning of the fifth century

Heraclitus of Ephesus (fl. c. 500) asserted a doctrine of flux, maintaining that all existence is change, that nothing *is*, but rather all is *becoming*. In a sense Heraclitus had stumbled upon an understanding of physical reality that has been confirmed by the most recent discoveries of particle physics, which indicate that the seemingly stable fundamental building blocks of matter like protons and neutrons are in fact made up of ever changing clouds of even smaller particles. Heraclitus of course was not thinking in such terms and had come to his conclusion through logic, and in the fifth century his ideas tended to subvert the physical sciences by undermining the permanence and reality of the material world.

More critical was the skepticism of Parmenides of Elea (b. c. 515), who is active in the first half of the fifth century. Parmenides stops just short of saying explicitly what Heraclitus only implies, that we cannot trust the information provided by our senses. Specifically, Parmenides claims that logic demonstrates the non-existence of change, which of course appears to be all around us, so our senses must be deceiving us. He explicitly states that when confronted with such a conflict, reason must take precedence over experience, thus virtually denying the validity of sensory information. Such was the power of the newly discovered rationalism: thinkers were willing to accept the conclusions of logic even when they were seemingly contradicted by the observed world. A brave new world indeed, but this distrust of the senses is clearly fatal to science, which is firmly rooted in the information our senses provide us of the physical world. This distrust, together with the consequent notion that true reality is not to be found in the perceived world around us but somewhere beyond our senses, would become a major theme in Greek philosophical thought and reach its fullest statement with Plato (see Chapter XIII).

Thus far the Greek enlightenment had been essentially an Ionian affair, but around the beginning of the fifth century the focus of intellectual activity switched to Athens, where men like Anaxagoras (c. 500-428), Empedocles (c. 492-432) and Democritus (b. c. 460) carried on the Ionian tradition of rational examination of the universe. The fifth century, however, also produced a new group of rationalists, who though concerned with a variety of subjects were united by their particular interest in rhetoric and the nature of man and society. These men, who might be considered the first sociologists or political scientists, are called the sophists (from *sophia*, "wisdom").

The term sophist as used by the Greeks referred to the teachers who began appearing in the first half of the fifth century. These were men who for a fee would teach you whatever there was to know, but most especially rhetoric, the art of persuasive speaking. The appearance and multiplication of these teachers is hardly surprising; they served a vital function in a society that had no public education or institutions of learning whatsoever. If you wanted to know something beyond what your parents taught you, you went to a sophist. The subject of rhetoric was particularly in demand, since in an age blessed with the absence of the professional attorney the ability to speak persuasively was utterly important to your ability to defend or prosecute a case in the courts. And if you lived in a democracy like Athens, rhetorical skills were an important tool for exerting influence in the assembly.

So for the Greeks the sophist was a kind of traveling tutor. For the modern historian, however, the sophists are of considerable interest chiefly because of their examination of man and society. These thinkers inherited the skepticism of the Ionian rationalists and applied it to human affairs, ultimately producing disastrous social consequences. The whole structure of law and morality in the polis would be undermined and traditional sources of authority called into question. By the last quarter of the fifth century sophists were openly attacking the polis, and sophistic ideas were providing justification for the Athenian Empire and contributing to the breakdown of Athenian society. This was serious business.

Central to sophistic thought is the distinction made between *nomos* and *physis*, literally the Greek words for "law" and "nature." For the sophist *nomos* is man-made law, that is, all the rules made by society, whatever form they take: unwritten customs, decrees of a king, legislated statutes, whatever. It is obviously mutable, changing from place to place and from one time to another. *Physis*, on the other hand, is understood to be completely unchanging and to consist of universal absolutes imposed by the nature of things, including the nature of human beings, and it is thus contrasted with man-made *nomos*. Most commonly *physis* referred to a body of natural law that served as a basis for behavior and morality, a basis rooted in nature rather than a particular human society and thus universally valid and compelling. It is a manifestation, it seems, of the instinctive feeling on the part of all normal humans that there are some things that are always right, like protecting a child, and some that are always wrong, like sleeping with your sister or taking a life without good reason. Today natural law is generally understood to be a body of moral absolutes and is frequently connected to a deity (e.g., "Thou shall not kill."), but a god is not necessary. Whether you call it natural law or god's law or the law of the gods or higher law or conscience, it is all the same – *physis*.

An immediate question arises: What if *nomos* and *physis* are in conflict? What do you do if your vision of natural law is contradicted by some man-made law of your society? Antigone faces this problem in Sophocles' (c. 496-406) play *Antigone*. King Creon of Thebes has decreed that Antigone's brother Polyneices may not be given the burial rites the Greeks considered the absolute right of every Greek corpse. Antigone violates this order, which is *nomos*, and defends her action by appealing to *physis*: "For me it was not Zeus who made that order./ Nor did that Justice who lives with the gods below/ mark out such laws to hold among mankind./ Nor did I think your orders were so strong/ that you, a mortal man, could over-run/ the gods' unwritten and unfailing laws./ Not now, nor yesterday's, they always live,/ and no one knows their origin in time." (*Antigone* 450-57)[12] She justifies her violation of man-made law with an appeal to natural law, just as twenty-five hundred years later those who because of the war in Vietnam burned draft files, obstructed the government or in some way broke the law justified their actions with the same appeal. Antigone calls it "the gods' unwritten and unfailing laws" and Jerry Rubin and Daniel Elsberg called it "conscience" or "higher law," but they all refer to the same thing – *physis*.

There are a number of different ways to categorize the sophists, but grouping them according to their views on the nature of the polis and the relationship between law and morality is particularly convenient for examining the evolution of sophistic thought. The Greeks traditionally believed that the polis had a positive moral purpose, that is, the state, through the mechanism of its laws, should produce virtuous citizens. We have some limited experience of this with our laws against prostitution, gambling and other "immoral" activities, but essentially this idea is alien to our concept of the state, which views the law as being morally neutral. We hope our laws coincide with our notions of morality, but they are not the source of those notions; religion is. For the Greeks, however, the state and its laws had a positive moral role, and they consequently accepted a close relationship in society between law and morality.

The first category of sophists accepted this traditional view, despite their general skepticism. Men like Protagoras of Abdera (c. 490-420) and Hippias of Elis (fl. 2nd half 5th cent.) recognized the existence of natural law, but felt that it was compatible with the changeable, man-made laws of society. Skeptics that they were, they no longer accepted that the polis had a divine origin, but because they believed *nomos* and *physis* to be complementary, they did view the state as natural, a product of *physis*. They thus accepted the traditional notion that the state had a moral function and that its laws should create virtue.

Others were not so sure, and the second group of sophists asserted that the polis and its laws had no positive moral purpose. Law was simply a body of morally neutral, expedient measures that allowed society to function. It might by chance happen to reflect true morality, which was embodied in natural law, but essentially it was irrelevant to morality. The state was therefore not natural, but rather an artificial creation, a product of *nomos*.

This is in essence the modern western view: the law is a neutral agent, which the society hopes reflects its moral values, which are derived from religion. A representative of this category of sophists is Antiphon (c. 480-411), who felt that the laws of the polis were artificial, established by human convention and thus not as critically important to the individual as natural law was. Laws might be necessary to society and the state, but not to life, which in fact might be hindered by them. True morality was independent of *nomos* and could be found instead in *physis*. In a word, man-made law was irrelevant. Antiphon and his friends thus rejected two essential facets of the traditional concept of the polis: that it had a divine or natural basis and that its laws were positive moral agents. For these sophists the polis was an artificial construction, the result of a kind of social compact, and its laws were morally neutral.

The sophists of category two challenged the very nature of the classical polis, but they tolerated its existence. It was left to the final group, the radical sophists, to carry the thinking to the logical extreme and openly and directly attack the polis. These characters felt that the state, as it existed, interfered with and impeded true morality, that the state was in fact immoral. A spokesman for this position is Critias (c. 460-403), leader of the oligarchic Thirty Tyrants, who ruled Athens for a brief period after her defeat by Sparta in 404. According to him, the state was not based upon divine or natural sanction (Group 1 and the traditional view), nor upon a compact (Group 2 and our view), but upon fraud, and law was thus an agent causing men to act immorally. This of course was a very convenient point of view for Critias, whose terror-filled regime openly flouted the laws and traditions of the Athenian polis. Another member of this group, Thrasymachus of Chalcedon (fl. c. 430-400), spells it out exactly: "That is what I mean when I say that right (or justice) is the same thing in all states, namely the interest of the established ruling class; and this ruling class is the strongest element in each state, and so if we argue correctly we see that right (or justice) is always the same, the interest of the stronger party." (Plato, *Republic* 339A)[13] In other words, might makes right. This is the ultimate destination of sophistic skepticism: ethical nihilism.

Actually, Callicles (historicity disputed), who appears in Plato's *Gorgias*, takes the line of thinking a bit further. Thrasymachus says that the acts of certain extraordinary men who have power are beyond accepted standards of justice and are not subject to normal moral judgment; their might makes right. Callicles pulls out all the stops and proclaims that the actions of the superior man in fact constitute a superior form of justice; his might *is* right. And who are these superior men? Simply put, they are those who are clever and strong enough to seize power and hold on to it. For Callicles it is a fact of *physis*, a dictate of natural law that these individuals should rule and should enjoy complete satisfaction of all their desires, completely free of the restraints customarily imposed by *nomos*. This kind of thinking is a moral justification for even the most brutal sort of rule and can lead to disastrous social results, as for example in Germany in the 1930s.

Clearly, ideas like these were not going to sit that well with everyone in society, especially a society made up of Greeks. Men like Thrasymachus and Callicles were social extremists, who threatened the orthodoxy of Athenian democracy and every other form of government the Greeks considered legitimate. They could hardly fail to excite a negative reaction from the mainstream of Greek society, but even the more moderate sophists like Antiphon contributed to earning sophism a bad reputation among the more conservative elements of the population. The rhetorical skill and increasing moral relativism of the sophists combined to create a public image of amoral tricksters, who "made the weaker argument the stronger" through their clever use of words. They were accused of undermining the values that were traditionally believed to hold Greek society together, and they were especially indicted for corrupting the youth.

This negative image, particularly the charge of corrupting the young, is reflected in Sophocles' play *Philoctetes*, which appeared in 409. It is the last year of the war at Troy, and the gods have decreed that Troy will be taken only if Philoctetes and his magic bow of Heracles are present. The problem for our heroes is that Philoctetes is not at Troy, but on the island of Lemnos, where he had been abandoned ten years earlier by those same Greeks who now needed him. He had unwittingly stumbled into a sacred grove and been bitten by a sacred snake, which produced an unhealing wound, the sight and smell of which had disgusted his companions to the point that they had abandoned him. (This is, incidentally, a perfect example of a ritual pollution.) Now they need him, and they send a rescue team headed up by Odysseus and Neoptolemus, son of the now dead Achilles.

Odysseus may in this instance be seen as the sophistic figure. Already in Homer he had a reputation for cleverness, especially rhetorical cleverness. While all the other heroes carry stock epithets such as "shining" or "fleet-footed," Odysseus is always "wily," seemingly the only hero ever to use his brain. In the *Odyssey* he is constantly fabricating stories, even before the goddess Athena, who tells him: "Two of a kind, we are, contrivers, both./ Of all men now alive you are the best/ in plots and story telling." (*Odyssey* 13.296-98)[14] This inclination to easy deceit, shared by his wife, Penelope, is part of the fallout from *agōn*, information or truth being an asset in the continual competition that marked every aspect of Greek society. Deception and secrecy were inherited by the classical polis along with the constitutionalism, and they are in fact a facet of the Mediterranean community today. Odysseus' ability to lie at a moment's notice is in his value system a positive attribute, and among all the Homeric musclemen he is something of an appealing character.

In later ages, however, Odysseus is not so appealing, as the more negative aspects of his cleverness and deceit were emphasized, and such is the case in Sophocles' play. Philoctetes is not about to go to Troy voluntarily, and the team dare not use force, because the bow of Heracles fired a kind of Homeric heat-seeking missile, which hit whatever it was aimed at. Odysseus in particular could expect a magic arrow if he showed his face, since he was in fact the one who had actually marooned Philoctetes. So it is basically a negative thing that Odysseus must do, and in doing it he must corrupt Neoptolemus and his heroic ideals, since it will be necessary to obtain the bow by trickery. Odysseus himself has become non-heroic. For him individual responsibility has disappeared, and he passes the moral buck on to Zeus and other men: "It is Zeus, I would have you know, Zeus this land's ruler,/ who has determined. I am only his servant." (*Philoctetes* 989-90)[15] And with regard to his original marooning of Philoctetes he says: "I tell you I had orders for what I did:/ my masters, the princes, bade me do it." (*Philoctetes* 6) Honor is gone; pride is gone; only success matters for Odysseus: "What I seek in everything is to win." (*Philoctetes* 1052)

Reflecting such ideas, Odysseus already suggests the more radical sophists and their emphasis on expediency and success. This identification is clinched by Odysseus' use of rhetorical methods. Just as the sophists were reputed to win by making the weaker argument the stronger, so also will Odysseus succeed through verbal trickery. "Ensnare/ the soul of Philoctetes with your words," (*Philoctetes* 54-55) he tells Neoptolemus. He has abandoned the traditional heroic way of force or persuasion for other methods: "I was young, too, once, and then I had a tongue/ very inactive and a doing hand./ Now as I go forth to the test, I see/ that everywhere among the race of men/ it is the tongue that wins and not the deed." (*Philoctetes* 96-99) These are not the words of a hero, but of a sophistic cynic.

In direct opposition to Odysseus is Neoptolemus, who as the son of Achilles represents the epitome of heroic ideals, and to Odysseus' sophist he plays the young aristocrat. He is the heir to the old tradition, but is young and naïve enough to be corrupted away from that tradition. As an heroic character Neoptolemus is naturally repulsed by Odysseus' plan to trick Philoctetes: "I have a natural antipathy/ to get my ends by tricks and stratagems,/ so, too, they say, my father was." (*Philoctetes* 88-89) For the hero the means were absolutely vital, far more important than the ends. Neoptolemus recognizes the importance of the ends in this case, the sacking of Troy and the common interest of the Greeks, but they must be superseded by his own heroic conscience and he must say: "Still, my lord, I would prefer even to fail with honor/ than win by cheating." (*Philoctetes* 94-95) Now, this is a hero talking. For him the rhetorical way of Odysseus is cheating, and he prefers the open physical struggle. This is the honorable way, though Sophocles momentarily suggests that it might be a brutal kind of honor, when he has Neoptolemus say: "Surely a one-legged man/ cannot prevail against so many of us!" (*Philoctetes* 91-92) The heroic value system involves a standard of honor that naturally resists the deceit of Odysseus, but blithely accepts assaulting a cripple.

This is the team that is out to get the bow. The heroic force desired by Neoptolemus is impossible, and Odysseus' plan is to have Neoptolemus promise Philoctetes that he will take him home to Greece and thus trick him into surrendering the bow. "For you must sharpen your wits, to become a thief/ of the arms no man has conquered," (*Philoctetes* 77-78) he tells Neoptolemus, already using his cleverness on the young man by tempting him with the prize of conquering the as yet unconquered. Neoptolemus will have none of this, however, and Odysseus turns the full force of sophistic argument against him and overwhelms the lad with his logic. Philoctetes' weapons are destined to take Troy, and Neoptolemus is destined to be known as the conqueror of Troy. Thus, Neoptolemus must aid in capturing Philoctetes and his bow or give up Troy. And to the young hero the loss of Troy is virtually unthinkable, for the capture of Priam's city represents for him the epitome of the heroic ideal, the opportunity for the highest expression of his heroic nature. The logic is of course correct, and Neoptolemus chooses not to surrender the heroic goal of sacking Troy. But in deciding to play along with Odysseus and obtain the bow by deceit rather than by force or persuasion, Neoptolemus commits a crucially non-heroic act. The end here is glorious and heroic, but the means is not, and Neoptolemus has now sided with Odysseus in agreeing that the end justifies the means. He has ceased to be the son of Achilles and has become instead the child of Odysseus, who in fact now refers to him as *teknon*, "my child." The sophist has corrupted the noble youth. As Philoctetes later says to Neoptolemus, "You are not bad yourself; by bad men's teaching/ you came to practice your foul lesson." (*Philoctetes* 971-72)

The story does not end with Neoptolemus' fall from heroic stature. He is at heart disgusted by what he has done, and so he returns the bow, much to the annoyance of Odysseus, who chides him: "In your own case/ neither the words nor the acts are clever." Neoptolemus' reply reveals his regained heroic status: "Still/ if they are just, they are better than clever." (*Philoctetes* 1245-46) He has surrendered Troy to his honor. And there is more. He also agrees to honor his promise to take Philoctetes home and thereby forsakes something more than golden opportunities. By agreeing to go to Greece and not to the Greek army at Troy Neoptolemus is cutting himself off from his heroic peers and the society that gives his life meaning. In the shame culture of the heroic world it was what the other heroes thought about you that mattered, and if they are not around, then there is no definition of your heroic honor. Neoptolemus has clearly moved up the moral ladder and achieved a kind of honor that is perhaps nobler than that typical of the hero. But fortunately for Neoptolemus and the others the god Heracles, a literal *deus ex machina*, drops out of the sky and sets everything right by telling Philoctetes that he must find his destiny at Troy.

What Sophocles is surely reflecting in the confrontation between Odysseus and Neoptolemus is the popular notion that the Athenian youth were being corrupted by sophistic teachings. This idea is expressed more blatantly by the comic playwright Aristophanes (c. 455-386) in his comedy the *Clouds*, which was first presented in 423. Here all the ideas of the sophists and their Ionian predecessors are exaggerated, distorted and lumped together in the guise of Socrates and his Thinkery, a school that will teach you the "New Logic," i.e., sophistic rhetoric. The farmer Strepsiades sends his playboy son, Pheidippides, to the Thinkery in order that he might learn rhetoric and bail out his debt-ridden father in court. Pheidippides comes out filled instead with radical ideas and proceeds to demonstrate how it is correct for children to beat their parents rather than the reverse.

In one real sense this idea of corruption was true. Sophistic teachers did not, in general, consciously aim at corrupting the young or turning them against their parents, but the radical skepticism and moral relativism of later sophism indirectly achieved something like this. Sophistic ideas certainly undermined the traditional foundation values of family and community, and the impact of this was felt most strongly among the younger generation, especially the upper class youth. It was the young aristocratic types who had the means and the leisure time to learn sophistic ideas and practice what they might imply. And so too is the young aristocrat Neoptolemus corrupted – though much more directly – by the sophistic Odysseus and the young Pheidippides by a sophistic Socrates.

And what about Socrates (469-399)? Was he a sophist? That in fact depends upon exactly how you define sophism. Certainly Socrates shared with the sophists a strong reluctance to accept traditional beliefs without examination, and everyone is familiar with his habit of hanging around the agora (the market place, where all the action took place in the polis) and questioning everything under the sun. "Hello, Socrates. Nice day, isn't it?" "What is a nice day?" Now, this kind of thing can be extremely annoying, especially when it is directed at those important convictions that are so often accepted and held without examination. "Why is democracy the best form of government?" or "Why do you believe in the Christian god?" Since most people simply inherit basic social and moral values without ever examining them, such questions are difficult to answer and usually provoke anger. The Athenians were no exception, and their general annoyance made it easier to identify Socrates with the generally annoying sophists. Gadflies are rarely popular. Socrates was also obviously critical of the Athenian democracy, which he considered amateur government, and this too colored him sophist in the public's eye and hardly won him friends among the majority of Athenians.

But despite his identification with the radical sophists in the eyes of the public, Socrates lacked the common denominator of all sophists: he refused to accept a fee. Further, he was certainly a traditionalist in his view of the polis, with which view only the sophists of the first category could possibly agree. He believed the polis to be a natural entity and its laws to have the positive moral function of creating virtuous citizens. And he believed absolutely in the rule of law, which, I think, is why he sipped the hemlock in the end. The major sources for Socrates' trial are conflicting and unclear regarding the precise details of the prosecution and Socrates' defense, and there is no way to know to what extent the Socrates of Plato and the Socrates of Xenophon represent the real character rather than these authors' image of him. Nevertheless, I believe the following account to be a generally valid understanding of the philosopher's end.

The charges brought against him in 399 were impiety and corruption of the youth, both valid under Athenian law, but the real reasons behind his indictment were political. Athens' defeat by Sparta in 404 led to a year and a half of despotic oligarchic rule, the Thirty Tyrants, and in the nervous climate of the restored democracy Socrates suffered from his negative public image and earlier association with such notorious anti-democrats as Critias and Alcibiades. A general amnesty prevented Socrates' enemies from leveling overt political charges, and instead they sought to drive him into exile by raising these other accusations, taking advantage of a growing popular irritation with criticism of traditional religious ideas. Already in the sixth century the new rationalists had begun assaulting the traditional religion, which because of its extreme anthropomorphism was an easy target; the all too human gods plainly did silly things, and many of the rituals of the civic religion were absurd when viewed objectively. The sophists continued the attack, asserting that the traditional gods were simply the product of *nomos*, even, as Critias suggested, consciously formulated lies, and by the second half of the fifth century they had discovered atheism, though it is nowhere directly expressed. It was difficult, if not impossible, to refute these criticisms, especially with regard to the anthropomorphism, and the frustration of the traditionalists led to growing aggravation and public trials for *asebeia*, impiety. Traditionally, *asebeia* had involved overt acts of sacrilege, such as violating sanctuaries or profaning the mysteries, but in fifth century Athens the definition expanded to include less demonstrable offences, such as introducing new gods and not believing in the gods of the city, the charges leveled against Socrates. These accusations do not appear to be true, but Socrates was in many ways a very annoying person, and many were more than ready to accept these distortions of his real beliefs.

To the apparent surprise of his enemies, Socrates did not flee, but stood trial and was convicted by a only a narrow margin of votes, demonstrating that in this instance at least the Athenians were not given to a lynch mob mentality. The Athenian court did not have judges, and in a broad category of cases the prosecution, which consisted of the citizens who brought the charges, was entitled to propose a penalty, to which the defense would reply with a counter-penalty, leaving it to the jury to choose in a sort of post-conviction plea bargaining. The prosecution asked for death, expecting the defense to propose a stiff fine, which the jury would select as the punishment. But ever the wiseass, Socrates proposed that he pay a ridiculously small fine and receive free board from the state for the rest of his life in order that he could continue enlightening his fellow Athenians. The jury was not amused and chose death (still by a close margin), but every opportunity was given Socrates to escape into exile, since death was clearly an inappropriately drastic punishment for the crimes for which he was convicted. He insisted, however, that the execution be carried out and drank the poison.

Why? Because unfair though the condemnation might be, Socrates had been tried and convicted justly, that is, according to the laws of Athens, and such was his commitment to the law that he refused to violate it even under such extreme circumstances. Socrates was making, about as dramatically as one can, a point about the nature of justice, that it is rooted in the law, not in any vague notions of what is right. Everyone might feel that Socrates' execution was not fair or right, but it was nevertheless just. We hope that our laws embody our ideas about fairness, but the bottom line is that what is just is not necessarily also what is fair. Socrates might be generally accused of a certain intellectual dishonesty in that he used his considerable powers of argument to demonstrate only conclusions compatible with his view of things, but his death is surely one of the noblest examples in history of dying for ones principles.

Thus, we have seen how the skepticism born in Ionia and applied by the sophists to the subject of man and society led rapidly to the definition and examination of perhaps the most basic social question – the relationship between law and morality. Is morality rooted in man-made law, *nomos*, as the Greeks traditionally believed? Or are our moral standards to be found in natural law, *physis*? And if this is so, who is to define *physis*? Suppose there is conflict between *nomos* and *physis*? How should society deal with those individuals whose vision of *physis* and resulting morality is radically at odds with that of the majority?

The Athenians had to deal with these questions, and so must we. Since the collapse of the classical world the west has derived its morality from a particular understanding of *physis*, hanging its basic system of moral values from the metaphysical peg of the Judeo-Christian god and attempting to varying degrees to bring *nomos* into line with these values. This has not always been very successful, since human desires and expediency are in constant conflict with out notions of morality. Further, the moral standards required of individuals seem always to be incompatible with those applied to nations, and human beings are easily led to do as a group things they absolutely shun as individuals. The problem associated with attaching an ethical system to a particular view of natural law of course is getting everyone in the society to accept that view. If an individual does not accept the existence of the Christian god, the moral precepts of that deity can hardly be of any great weight. And even if by some totalitarian miracle the entire community accepts the metaphysical standard, the inherently relative nature of all value judgments will quickly reveal itself. Take what is probably the most basic moral absolute: thou shall not kill. Inasmuch as most human beings will grant that there are circumstances, such as self-defense, that may require one to kill, the prohibition is more accurately stated as thou shall not kill without good reason. But what exactly constitutes a good reason? Killing someone whom you believe is about to attack you? Assassinating a tyrant? The moral absolutes are never so absolute.

And those "self-evident truths" (*physis*) are never really self-evident to everyone, which leads to the most fundamental problem arising from a consideration of *nomos* and *physis* – what if they conflict? What if the morality of the community, as expressed in its laws, and the morality of the individual, which springs from his own mind, do not match? Of course the society must protect its members from physical harm, so that the man whose definition of *physis* involves god telling him to shoot certain people must be forced to follow the *nomos* of the community. But what about the most obvious manifestation of the potential *nomos-physis* conflict, civil disobedience? This is a tough one. Civil disobedience has clearly resulted in great social progress in American society, especially in the area of civil rights, but it must be remembered that a very dangerous principle is being entertained here.

Civil disobedience is the open and nonviolent violation of *nomos* justified by an appeal to *physis* and the intention of bettering society. It is at heart a political-social expression of the notion that the end justifies the means, and this is always a dangerous proposition, especially in the absence of any precise definition of valid ends and acceptable means. Since the justifying goal here depends upon the individual's vision of *physis* there can be no definition of valid ends, and the door to chaos is open. An illegal demonstration by Blacks in favor of integration and one by the Klan in favor of segregation are in essence the same, since each group will justify its breaking of human law with its particular definition of natural law. (And ironically both groups would see *physis* embodied in the same Christian god.) Therein lies the problem: *physis* is defined by the individual, whether he dreams it up himself or takes it ready-made through an inherited religion. Critias and Thrasymachus felt that justice or right was what was in the interest of the strong, whereas singer Joan Baez violated the tax laws because her view of *physis* indicated that for the strong to dominate the weak was wrong and unjust. Neither vision of natural law is more or less valid than the other. Both are quite correct or quite incorrect, depending upon your point of view. For society to allow any group, no matter how apparently noble its cause, to selectively violate the laws is thus to court disaster.

What then do you do if according to your values a law or policy is immoral and legal means to change it fail? Only you can decide that, but when you consider that decision remember that you are standing in a line that stretches back to fifth century Athens and men like Critias.

###################

SUGGESTED READING

Once again I recommend Kagan, *The Great Dialogue*, whose three category approach to the sophists I have blatantly appropriated. For the full story on the sophists try W.K.C. Guthrie, *The Sophists* (1971) or G.B. Kerferd, *The Sophistic Movement* (1981); J. de Romilly, *The Great Sophists in Periclean Athens* (1992) is also an excellent book. On the original Annoying Man go to G. Vlastos, *Socrates. Ironist and Moral Philosopher* (1991); I.F. Stone, *The Trial of Socrates* (1988) is an interesting account by a non-specialist. T.C. Brickhouse & N.D. Smith, eds., *The Trial and Execution of Socrates* (2002) includes all the sources pertaining to the trial and a number of articles interpreting those sources, but beware: this is scholarly stuff. If you want to go to the main sources on the sophists and Socrates, read the Socratic dialogues of Plato and Xenophon. Translations of Aristophanes vary tremendously; I heartily suggest William Arrowsmith's *Clouds*, which pulls no punches on the obscenities, which of course were not obscene to the Greeks, just funny.

################

VI. ONE MALE, ONE VOTE

THE ATHENIAN DEMOCRACY

...among the people there is a maximum of ignorance, disorder, and wickedness...

-Old Oligarch, *Constitution of Athens* 1.5[16]

Consideration of the sophists carried us to the end of the fifth century, and it is necessary to step back to the end of the sixth to pick up the political thread. We left Athens in the hands of the tyrant Hippias, but his days were numbered. The people do not appear to have been dissatisfied with his rule, but there were many disgruntled aristocratic types floating about, dreaming of the good old days before the tyranny. Especially active, though in exile, were the Alcmaeonids, probably the most politically important family in Athenian history. With the help of the Delphic oracle, whose new temple had been built with Alcmaeonid money, they managed to convince the Spartans, who were traditionally anti-tyrant and also interested in establishing some influence over Athens, to help them throw Hippias out. Accordingly, in 510 a small army under king Cleomenes I (c. 520-490) of Sparta came north and forced the tyrant into exile.

And it was right back to the aristocratic political feuding that had led to the tyranny in the first place. The contest was primarily between the Alcmaeonids under their leader Cleisthenes (c. 570-c. 500?) and the majority of the old noble families under Isagoras, and because of his widespread aristocratic support Isagoras was able to gain the edge in this traditional political game and win the head archonship in 508/7. Cleisthenes responded by changing the rules of the game, and according to Aristotle, "he won the support of the common people by promising to give the state into their hands." (*Constitution of Athens* 20.1)[17] Especially responsive to Cleisthenes' bid for support were middle income types, who particularly dreaded a return to the pre-tyranny instability, and many new citizens, who had already lost or feared they would soon lose their citizenship under the restored aristocratic government. With the political tide turning a desperate Isagoras called back Cleomenes, who was naturally inclined to support the aristocrats. With Spartan help Isagoras exiled Cleisthenes and his people and tried to dissolve the Solonian constitution and replace it with an oligarchy, but quite spontaneously and apparently without any aristocratic leadership the Athenian people rose up and besieged Cleomenes and his small band of soldiers on the Acropolis. Unprepared for a siege, the Spartans were forced to leave Athens after two days, taking Isagoras with them, and Cleisthenes returned and got to work.

You will recall that the essential machinery of democratic government was already established in Athens: universal suffrage among the citizen body, a sovereign assembly open to all citizens, and a council and limited term magistracies unrestricted by birth. Cleisthenes' task was to solve the problems, especially the localism and strife among the aristocratic clans, that prevented this machinery from functioning smoothly. The tyrants had made substantial progress along these lines, helping to break down the particularism that supported the power of the old nobility, but much of the old social structure was still entrenched in the Solonian constitution. What Cleisthenes had to do was get down and reorganize Athenian society from the ground up.

All of Attica (the territory of the Athenian polis) was already divided into about 170 little districts called demes. Cleisthenes' first step was to divide these units into three geographical groups: the demes of the city of Athens and its immediate surroundings, the demes of the coastal regions and the demes of the inland area. He then divided the demes of each region into ten equal subgroups, named *trittyes* ("thirds"), selecting for the most part noncontiguous demes for each *trittys*. He then chose, by lot, a *trittys* from each of the three regional groups and combined them to form a tribe, thus producing ten new tribes, each formed of roughly equal numbers of citizens from the three main geographic areas of the Athenian state. And this was the point of all the gerrymandering: to mix up the population insofar as the political structure was concerned. Each tribe was made up of a mixture of people from varying backgrounds and loyalties, and this helped undermine the social and political divisions upon which traditional aristocratic factional politics had rested. It also helped Cleisthenes politically, since his support was apparently particularly strong in the city, which meant he now had adherents distributed through all ten tribes.

The ten new tribes formed the basis of the military and political structure of the state. Each contributed a regiment of hoplites and elected a general to command them, creating an annual board of ten generals or *strategoi*, which would later become the most important group of officials in the state. The old Solonian Council of Four Hundred was thrown out and replaced with the Council of Five Hundred, composed annually of fifty members from each tribe. At first councilors were chosen by lot from a group elected by each tribe, but the election was later done away with and selection to the Council became completely a matter of chance. The Council of Five Hundred became the supreme administrative body of the state, acting as a ministry of foreign affairs, finance, public works – you name it. It also had some judicial functions, serving as an impeachment court, but most important it had the probouleutic power: it prepared the agenda for the sovereign assembly, though frequently the agenda items were simply calls for discussion and proposals on an issue. The Council was thus a sort of standing committee of the assembly, dealing with routine affairs and undertaking the preliminaries for important issues that required deliberation by the full assembly.

Sweeping though his reforms might be, Cleisthenes did maintain some conservative elements of the Solonian constitution. With its power of scrutinizing magistrates and reviewing the "constitutionality" of laws passed by the assembly, the Council of the Areopagus remained a key ingredient in the constitution, and being made up of ex-archons, who sat on the Areopagus for life, it definitely had a conservative flavor. Moreover, the elections for the archonships were held outside the new tribal system, thus allowing the traditional political forces more leeway, and democratic voters continued to return to the high offices members of the noble clans, thereby preserving the Areopagus as an aristocratic bastion.

Cleisthenes also maintained the Solonian property qualifications for officeholders, thus retaining a constitutional bias towards wealth, but two observations must be made with regard to this. In the first place, Athenian society had on the whole grown far more wealthy since the days of Solon, and this had the effect of expanding the Solonian classes downward. Second and more important, the *thetes*, the people of the lowest classification, were apparently not that concerned about holding the archonships. They had neither the time nor the money to hold unpaid positions and were satisfied with having the power of election and legislation. For a long time to come they would continue to elect for the most part men from the old noble families, which is hardly surprising, since these characters were the ones with the political ability and the reputations.

Cleisthenes' reforms centered around substituting a purely political arrangement (the ten new tribes) for an originally social one (the four old tribes) that had been adapted to political needs. Helping secure the permanence of this complex and artificial structure was the fact that the basic units, the demes, were

Richard M. Berthold

The Structure of the Athenian Democracy

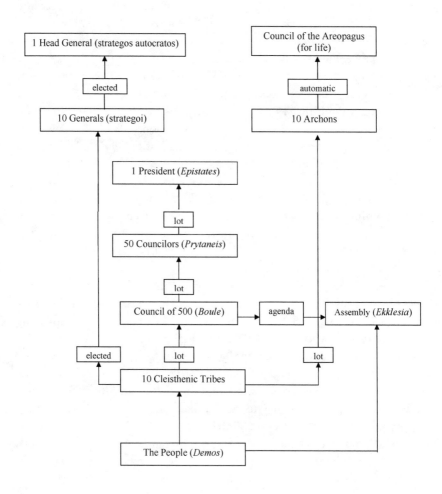

not artificial, but already existing divisions of the countryside. Further, Cleisthenes was sensible enough not to mess with the old tribes once they had been removed from the political structure, and they were left with their traditional role in social and cult affairs.

There is a final institution of Cleisthenes, one of little importance to the democratic structure, but of interest as a curious political mechanism – ostracism. Once a year the assembly voted whether or not to hold an ostracism, and if the decision was yes, a date was set. On that day any Athenian citizen could come to the agora and cast a ballot by simply writing someone's name on a potsherd (*ostrakon*; this is the scrap paper of the Greek world) and tossing it onto the pile. If 6000 such votes were cast, it was a valid ostracism, and the lucky person receiving the most votes was required to leave Athens for ten years. He did not lose his property, and he resumed his citizenship without disability when he returned. A clever device, ostensibly designed to guard against tyrants, but in fact created by Cleisthenes as a weapon to hold over the heads of his opponents. Opposition aristocrats and supporters of the exiled tyrant apparently got the message, and the first ostracism did not take place until twenty years later, when this dangerous weapon was turned against the Alcmaeonids themselves.

Though Cleisthenes has traditionally been called Athens' first democratic leader, the government he created was hardly a democracy. Athens at the end of the sixth century was far from being a modern political entity and was in fact still considerably short of even the kind of civic state familiar to Aristotle. As it had been for centuries, the state was still essentially in the hands of a network of aristocratic families, for whose members political activity was virtually an end in itself, a sort of timocratic game in which they competed for temporary advantages in power and prestige. With the majority of Athenian citizens still barred from holding the important offices and thus excluded from the political leadership, the Athens of Cleisthenes was far more like that of Solon than Pericles.

What was now different and made Athens more "democratic" was as much a result of the process of Cleisthenes' reforms as it was of the reforms themselves. When Cleisthenes stepped out of the traditional aristocratic political clubs and appealed to the people in order to defeat Isagoras, he established the *demos*, the Athenian people, as a new political faction, one with which every future politician, whatever his stripe, would have to contend. As yet it was still a rather passive faction, but the people themselves would quickly come to understand the new rules and demand more and more for their support, steadily propelling the state down a democratic path.

Cleisthenes did not so much create the Athenian democracy as he enabled it.

The new government continued to develop for the next half century after Cleisthenes, becoming increasingly liberal, until under Pericles (c. 495-429) and his less competent successors Athens became the most complete and radical democracy the world has seen. A number of forces fostered this growth, including the socio-political thought of the sophists, who initially supported the egalitarian notions basic to the democratic idea. They were saying that tradition was not a valid justification for holding power and that one man's opinion was as good as another's, and this sort of talk could hardly fail to keep things stirred up. Probably most important in the political development, however, was the emergence of Athenian naval power and the empire that would be built upon it. Partly because of poor soil and partly because of old contacts with Ionia, Athens had early turned to the sea and commerce. Solon's reforms and Peisistratid policy had pushed her further in this direction, but at the end of the sixth century the Athenian navy was still insignificant and it was the hoplite army that really counted. Athens seriously turned to a naval policy only after the Persian invasion of 490 (see Chapter VII), and that change in policy was the work of one man – Themistocles (c. 524-459).

Pericles gets all the credit today and it is a rare person who has even heard of Themistocles, but more than any other individual it was Themistocles who made Athens great. In the 480s he built the Athenian navy, and it was that navy that was the salvation of Greece and foundation of the Athenian Empire. Themistocles' naval policies undoubtedly reflected his convictions about where Athens' future would be found, but they also fit nicely with his domestic political situation. From a minor noble family, he was outside the Alcmaeonid coalition that had dominated the government since Cleisthenes, and rather than join them as a junior partner he took a page from Cleisthenes' handbook and appealed to the people. Unlike Cleisthenes, however, his pitch was not directed towards the middle income farmers and merchants of the hoplite class, but rather at the great mass of lower class citizens, the *thetes*, who could only benefit from the development of a war fleet.

Contrary to what you may think, rowing a galley was a skilled occupation, and Ben Hur notwithstanding, the rowers in Greek and Roman navies were typically free men, serving for pay. The standard warship of the classical period, the trireme, required as many as 170 rowers, who were usually recruited from the poorer folk, who could not afford to serve in the hoplite ranks. Expansion of the fleet thus provided jobs for these people and in a sense gave them increasing power at the expense of the middle class types who made up the army. Her huge hoplite army of course remained important to

Athens, but the navy would rapidly become the real backbone and instrument of Athenian power, and the navy was the *thetes*. Such could only tend to radicalize the democracy. Like Cleisthenes, Themistocles set in motion forces that would carry Athenian politics into unanticipated arenas, and while he himself could hardly be described as a radical democrat, he was in many ways the political ancestor of those who would be a half century later.

In the decade between the two Persian invasions Themistocles used his support among the *thetes* to develop his naval policies and to eliminate through ostracism all his political opposition. He led Athens and Greece through the crisis years of 480-479, but during the 470s he fell victim to a conservative resurgence in Athens and was himself ostracized. But the democracy with its staggering naval power was out of sympathy with conservative leaders like Cimon (c. 510-c. 451), son of Miltiades, and the ever-boring Aristides the Just (d. c. 467), and in the 460s the opposition forces struck back under the leadership of Ephialtes (d. c. 461) and the young Pericles. They launched their attack at the most conservative element in the constitution, the Council of the Areopagus, which had been badly weakened by a law of 487/6 that switched the selection of archons from election to sortition. This reform meant the political decline of the archonship and the simultaneous rise of the generalship, since the ten *strategoi* were now the only important elected officials. Chosen by chance, the archons were now mostly political nonentities, and since the Areopagus was formed of ex-archons, the quality and influence of that body was also in decline, rendering it more vulnerable to attack. In 462 Ephialtes pushed through reforms that stripped the Areopagus of its important political powers and distributed them to the assembly, the Council of Five Hundred and the popular court. Henceforth the Council of the Areopagus would concern itself only with homicide cases and care of the sacred olive trees of Athena on the acropolis. Ephialtes' reforms were something of a watershed in the history of the democracy: Athens as a "radical" democracy is typically dated from 462 until the installation of the Thirty Tyrants in 404.

A year later Ephialtes was murdered by persons unknown, and the young Pericles was suddenly catapulted to leadership of the liberal forces. From then until his death in 429 Pericles was almost never out of office, and for the last fifteen years of his life he was elected *strategos* every year and was clearly the director of Athenian affairs. Under his leadership the final steps in the completion of the democracy were taken in the 450s. Not that it mattered much, but the archonship was opened up to the middle class *zeugitai* and perhaps later unofficially to the *thetes* as well. Much more crucial was the introduction of pay for jurors and members of the Council of Five Hundred and the dramatic expansion of the courts. The provision of pay, minimum wage though it was, gave the poorest citizens access to state offices, and while this may not have had much effect on the composition of the Council, it has an overwhelming impact on the judicial system. Because of the tremendous increase in jurisdiction and cases, the Heliaia was supplemented by the creation of several other popular courts, all of them filled by lot from an annual juror pool of 6000 citizens of at least thirty years of age (the Athenians wanted greater wisdom on their juries). Pay meant that most of these jurors were *thetes*, and given the Athenian penchant for large juries (501 or more) and the fact that in the absence of attorneys and judges the jury *was* the court, this meant in turn that the *thetes* pretty much controlled the judicial system. And because the jurisdiction of the popular courts was so sweeping – they were in effect almost as important a part of the political structure as the assembly - the poor thus had a powerful political base, second only to the assembly, which by virtue of their numbers they could also dominate.

As is probably clear, amateurism and voluntarism were keynotes of the Athenian democracy. Athenians believed politics was something you could engage in during your spare time, and there was consequently a hostility towards and fear of professionalism in government. The widespread use of the lot to fill all but a handful of the 700 or so public offices and the prohibition (in most cases) against holding an office twice prevented the emergence of a professional bureaucracy that might challenge the power exercised by the assembly and courts. By the same token, the huge juries, the absence of judges and the prohibition of pay for advocates kept the legal system on an amateur basis, one of the reasons Greek law, unlike Roman, would have virtually no impact outside Greece. All of this of course required a truly astonishing degree of citizen participation, though for the vast majority that participation was essentially passive: listening to arguments and voting. (It also required a great deal of political "publicity" in order that those citizens be constantly informed, not an easy thing in a pre-paper age.) The extensive use of the lot and of boards of officials was also designed to limit the potential power of any single magistrate, the Athenians believing, perhaps more realistically than we, that corruption lurked somewhere in the heart of every man. There were consequently also a myriad of mechanisms for calling officials to account and hitting them with serious penalties, including death. This was a citizen government in a way no other ever has been or again could be.

By the middle of the century, then, Athenian society had completed its final constitutional transition. Solon had transferred political power from the blood aristocracy to the merely wealthy, Peisistratus and Cleisthenes passed it on to the hoplite class, and Themistocles and Pericles insured the final supremacy of the proletariat. The Athenian democracy had reached its highest point of development, at least structurally, and the people directly controlled just about everything of importance in the state. And by the middle of the century that everything included a powerful naval empire that controlled half the Greek world.

There is a tendency among Americans to assume that democracy, and especially our brand of democracy, is the only sensible form of government for any civilized society, which is of course wrong. It would be equally mistaken to assume that the Greeks viewed the essentials of democracy in precisely the same way as we. True, like us the Greek democrat regarded freedom and equality as the particular requirements and virtues of a democracy, but he saw these essentials in a slightly different light, defining them in purely political terms. The result was a government that was much more genuinely democratic than our own, but at the same time far less caring about the nonpolitical life of its citizens.

To the Athenian freedom essentially meant three things: freedom to participate in the government, freedom to live your life as you pleased and freedom of speech, which was considered crucial to the other two. The introduction of pay made freedom of participation theoretically economically feasible to all, but when it came to living your own life, it was sink or swim. Greek society of course had private support structures, usually kinship based, but the freedom to fail or even starve was inherent in the nature of the Greek state. On the other hand, the Athenian would find unpalatable the limitations placed by the government in the name of security and social welfare on the personal freedom of his American counterpart. He would also find our general lack of participation in government hard to reconcile with his notion of democracy, which, remember, was nurtured in a relatively tiny societal unit with a very strong sense of community. Being a good citizen meant more than obeying the laws and occasionally voting; in the words of Pericles: "We do not say that a man who takes no interest in politics is a man who minds his own business; we say that he has no business here at all." (Thucydides 2.40.2)[18]

Now, this might seem a bit foreign to us, since we tend to consider politics, especially at the national level, a game for full-time professionals, which is hardly surprising given the size and complexity of modern American government. What must be kept in mind when considering the Greeks is the small scale of their politics. It is estimated that only three poleis, Athens and the Sicilian cities of Syracuse and Acragas, had citizen bodies greater than 20,000, and most were far smaller, fewer than 1000. To our reckoning these were pocket states, with no complex bureaucracies and no developed public services. The day-to-day running of the government was fairly simple, and foreign affairs, while just as devious and violent as ours, were far less complicated and did not require lightning reaction times. And on the more critical issues there was in Athens the guiding hand of the board of *strategoi*, who, in theory at least, reflected serious political talent. The polis was a small and highly politicized place. Even in the oligarchic states the average urban citizen knew the issues and their ramifications, and in a democracy like Athens he was expected actually to take part in the government, which would simply not have functioned were it not for the incredible number of citizens – literally thousands – willing to serve in the courts and assembly on a regular basis. All of this fostered a greater political awareness, if not wisdom. Much more than in our abstract way the Athenian felt he was the government, and in fact he was.

Equality, that foundation stone of democracy, meant to the Greek democrat theoretical equality of political opportunity and equality before the law, and he rarely confused this with economic and social equality. The most radical Athenian democrats never once proposed directly upsetting the traditional social structure or redistributing land or wealth; that would be revolution and unwarranted meddling in the private lives of citizens. But when it came to political equality, the Athenians meant business, as can be seen in the widespread use of the lot. Sortition is your ultimate democratic mechanism. We see free elections as a pillar of democratic government and certainly have a mania for urging them on various third world countries, but they were ironically one of the *least* democratic elements in the Athenian constitution.

The equality issue has traditionally been the favorite line of attack by the opponents of democracy. The oligarchic types in history have said: "Take a look around. It's clearly absurd to maintain that men are equal in anything, including the ability to deal with political affairs." The radical sophists took this position, and Socrates' favorite *shtik* against democracy followed this line: we do not expect shipwrights to sculpt or sculptors to make shoes or cobblers to build ships, so why expect any of them to practice the craft of politics? Well, the democrat would reply that he agreed that men were not equal in their ability to govern and would claim that the system in fact rewarded those with the political talent. In Athens the important officials, at first the archons, later the ten *strategoi*, were always elected, and all those officials selected by lot performed functions that were routine or unimportant and they most often served on boards that made group decisions. Further, the system, unlike our own, included several automatic checks that threatened the seriously incompetent with stiff fines, and this probably scared off the real airheads.

The sensible democrat would agree with Socrates that politics is indeed a craft, but he would also maintain that it is hardly on a par with brain surgery, nuclear physics or writing history and could in fact be practiced casually by any citizen. His underlying assumption is that every man has some share of political wisdom, no matter how small that share might be, and this makes the collective opinion of the people of value in governing the society. The sophists of course would be quick to point out that this assumption is not demonstrable and thus suspect. It is one of those "self-evident truths," which are so important to our own political system. Whether or not the assumption is true may be judged, I suppose, by considering the success of democratic governments throughout history. Unfortunately, there have been very, very few democracies (or even constitutional states), and most of them are found in the modern world, where the existence of representation insulates the average citizen from any severe testing of his political wisdom. As we shall see, the Athenian democracy certainly developed some serious problems.

While discoursing on freedom and equality, the Greek democrat would not fail to mention the importance of law. The rule of law is of course an essential of any constitutional government, but it was regarded as particularly important in a democracy, which allows for so much freedom for the individual. It should be noted right off that the Greek conception of law differed from ours in one very major way: the law was not "autonomous," that is, it was not a self-contained entity, sporting its own technical language and possessing mechanisms theoretically isolated from considerations outside itself. Like everything else in Greek society the law and its practice were highly politicized, and economic and social factors were allowed to intrude, blurring the boundary between official legal procedures and other mechanisms for judgment within the society. There is, perhaps in consequence, a sense of informality, even hesitancy, in the Greek practice of law, and the precision and exact definition characteristic of any modern legal system is missing. This is why there were no real attorneys, only professional speechwriters, and courtroom argument – at least in Athens – mostly ignored scrutiny of statutes and precedents and provision of formal proofs in favor of simply convincing the jurors through persuasion. Arguing the guilt or innocence of a defendant consequently differed little from arguing for or against a bill before the citizen assembly and typically involved blatant appeals to emotion and other extra-legal considerations.

Exactly what the Athenians considered law changed as the democracy developed to its fullness and various checks on the power of the assembly were removed by the reforms of Ephialtes and Pericles. By the middle of the century law was defined simply as an act of the assembly, and the assembly was limited in its action only by the laws that had established the democracy. Beyond this, the assembly - which any citizen off the street could attend – was the absolute and final political authority in the state. What the sovereign assembly said, went. Period. This is total radical democracy. The fourth century democracy, reacting to the conduct of the radical democracy during the Peloponnesian War (see Chapter X), would become more moderate, differentiating between "laws" and "decrees" of the assembly and attempting to put the law above the people (see Chapter XII).

There is of course a potential problem here: what about the rights of the political minority? Essential to the concept of democracy and the rule of law is the element of persuasion, and the democratic legislative process may be seen as the majority being persuaded – by reason, emotion or whatever; so long as force is not involved – to a particular action. But what about the unpersuaded minority? They were not convinced that the new law was a good thing, yet they are compelled to obey it, implicitly threatened by the force with which the state backs up its laws. The rule of the majority over the unpersuaded minority might thus be considered the rule not of law, but of force, and in fact critics of the radical democracy in Athens accused it of exercising a "tyranny of the majority." Well, the democrat can only reply that the majority may be assumed to be acting in the best interests of the community and for the minority that is life in the big city. True enough, but suppose that political minority may be identified with a group defined as a minority for some other reason, such as religious views or skin color or sexual inclinations. Suppose the majority enacts a law that prohibits a religious minority from worshipping their gods or an ethnic minority from holding certain jobs. These by definition are democratic acts, but they hardly seem fair.

What is a good democrat to do, then? There is no final solution, only three alternatives. You can make unanimity the basis of law in your society, which means of course that if your society has more than three people in it, you will never pass any laws. Or you can establish a body of laws and mechanisms that safeguard the basic rights of all your citizens, laws that even the will of the people cannot change, at least not without extreme difficulty. This is essentially the path we have chosen with our Constitution and Bill of Rights. This is well and good, but bear in mind that by doing so you are robbing the people of some of their power, that you are making the democracy a little less complete. The final course is to follow the Athenian way and make the people absolutely sovereign in all matters. This is complete and true democracy and requires the greatest trust in the collective wisdom of the people, a trust that is not likely to be well founded in the mass democracies of the twenty-first century.

There is one final area in which Greek democracy was subjected to attack by its oligarchic critics. As we saw in the discussion of sophism, the polis was traditionally expected to fulfill a positive role of producing virtuous citizens, and according to the critics, in this regard democracy utterly missed the mark, failing to mold its citizens in any way whatsoever. Conservative nonsense, says the democrat. Rather than force its citizens to conformity, he would argue, democracy, with its liberty and total political participation, allows each to find his own particular excellence. Pericles put it more elegantly in the funeral oration he delivered to the Athenians after the first year of the great war with Sparta:

> …we place our dependence, not so much upon prearranged devices to deceive, as upon the courage which springs from our own souls when called to action… For we are lovers of beauty with no extravagance and lovers of wisdom yet without weakness… For in truth we have this point also of superiority over other men, to be most daring in action and yet at the same time most given to reflection upon the ventures we mean to undertake; with other men, on the contrary, boldness means ignorance and reflection brings hesitation… In a word, then, I say that our city as a whole is the school of Hellas, and that, as it seems to me, each individual amongst us could in his own person, with the utmost grace and versatility, prove himself self-sufficient in the most varied forms of activity. (Thucydides 2.39.1, 40.1, 40.3, 41.1)[19]

Idealistic to be sure, but I suspect the Athenians came much closer to this ideal than any other people in history.

This then was Athens in the fifth century, the most radical democracy the world has seen. Yet there were already those in antiquity who claimed that the Athenian democracy was perhaps not so democratic. Thucydides, the Athenian historian, who certainly had an intimate knowledge of Athens, points to Pericles' extremely long tenure of power and says: "So, in what was nominally a democracy, power was really in the hands of the first citizen." (Thucydides 2.65.9) Is this true? Was Pericles a kind of Greek Joseph Stalin? Of course not. Thucydides' judgment is a transparent one, made because he is not at all sympathetic towards the post-Periclean radical democracy, and he is thus forced to conclude that what Athens had under Pericles was not really democracy. Long tenure of power does not necessarily invalidate democratic government, though it easily can. Pericles had to be reelected *every* year, and he could fail and possibly did in 444. He could at any time be ejected from office by the people, which in fact happened in 430. Throughout his career the democracy continued to function, and though old "Squill Head," as he was affectionately known because of his curiously elongated head (which is why his statues always show him wearing a helmet), might lead the people this way or that, he had to retain their confidence to retain his job. That seems far more like democracy than some of the modern varieties, in which removing an individual from national office is almost impossible and in which the power of incumbency virtually guarantees unlimited tenure in office.

There is a valid criticism that may be leveled, however. Athens was a near perfect democracy, but only if one looks at the active citizen body. That group – adult males born of citizen parents – comprised probably less than a fifth of the total population of the state. Excluded were slaves, *metics* (resident aliens) and an extremely large group, women. These people lived in Athens, they worked for Athens and in the case of the *metics* they even fought for Athens. The women and *metics* shared to a degree in equality before the law, but they could not participate politically. In this wider sense the Athenian democracy, represented by the citizen body, was a kind of oligarchy ruling over a far greater number of nonparticipants. It has in fact been argued that the democracy was possible at all only because of the empire and slavery.

The empire argument is easily disposed of: in the fourth century, when Athens had no imperial revenues, the democracy flourished, even though it apparently cost more than it did in the fifth century, approximately 100 talents a year (by way of comparison, it cost about a talent to maintain an operational trireme for a month). As for slaves, it is certainly an exaggeration to say the democracy depended on slavery. All but the poorest Athenians apparently did own at least one slave, but most Athenians also had to work, suggesting that slaves did not create huge amounts of free time for their masters. Further, the political participation of most Athenians was very limited and in the most common venues, the juries and the Council, paid for. Actually, a better argument might be made that the democracy rested on the backs of women, who with the exception of plowing seem to have performed most of the routine tasks of daily life.

And was the citizen body a kind of oligarchy over the rest of the population? Of course, but this is to judge the Athenians by our more universal modern standards. Slavery was an institution that few Greeks stopped to question, and no one would ever consider giving a chattel political rights. In the case of the *metics* it certainly seems unfair, since they not only lived in Athens – some for generations – but also paid taxes and fought for her. But one must keep in mind the intimate connection between citizenship and ancestry that existed among the Greeks; even the reforms of Cleisthenes and the radicalization of the democracy could not eradicate this notion. No polis ever had a process for naturalization, and only on rare occasions would a foreigner be voted the citizenship. As for women, suffice it to say that even two and half millennia after the Athenian democracy their liberation is far from complete.

# # # # # # # # # # # # # # # # # # # #

SUGGESTED READING

Far and away the best book on the structure and functioning of the democracy in the fifth and fourth centuries is M.H. Hansen, *The Athenian Democracy in the Age of Demosthenes* (1991); it is intimidatingly large and detailed, but actually eminently readable. More anecdotal and focusing more on development, A.R. Burn, *Pericles and Athens* (1966) and Donald Kagan, *Pericles of Athens and the Birth of Democracy* (1991) are also excellent, and Kagan, *Great Dialogue* discusses democratic theory. Carl Richard, *The Founders and the Classics* (1994) examines the impact of Greek and Roman political ideas and models on the American founding fathers and Constitution and is a wonderful example of why the study of history is so important; by way of contrast, Victor Hanson and John Heath, *Who Killed Homer?* (2001) offer a clear account of the perils of abandoning the study of the Greeks, as they track the decline of classical studies in the last generation. For the horse's mouths read Herodotus, Aristotle's *Athenian Constitution* and Plutarch's lives of Themistocles, Aristides, Cimon and Pericles; the Plutarch is filled with amusing anecdotes about these characters. For the anti-democratic view see the Old Oligarch (or Pseudo-Xenophon), *Constitution of Athens*, which is usually found among the works of Xenophon, to whom it was falsely attributed.

# # # # # # # # # # # # # # # # # # #

VII. THE EMPIRE STRIKES BACK

HERODOTUS AND THE PERSIAN WARS

The storm lasted three days, after which the Magi brought it to an end
by sacrificial offerings, and by putting spells on the wind,
and by further offerings to Thetis and the sea-nymphs – or, of course,
it may be that the wind just dropped naturally.

-Herodotus 7.191.2[20]

While the Athenians were busy honing their democracy during the first half
of the fifth century, life outside Athens did not of course come to a halt. In
fact, these were pretty lively times for the Greeks, who found themselves the
priority target of the giant Persian Empire to the east. Detailing the events
of the Persian wars is hardly necessary for understanding the development of
Greek society, but the wars do illustrate some of the strengths and weaknesses
of the Greeks and provide an occasion to talk about the historian Herodotus.
Besides, the battles of the Persian wars are among the most celebrated in the
history of the west and consequently deserve some attention in any Greek
history. And it can be exciting stuff; it certainly was for the Greeks who had
to live through it.

The historian of the wars is Herodotus (c. 480-c. 425), the "Father of
History," who was born in Halicarnassus in Asia Minor and lived for some time
in Periclean Athens. He traveled widely in the Near East and consequently his
work is a mine of geographical, cultural and historical information about the
Persian Empire, for which he is the primary source. His book is essentially a
narrative examination of Greek-Persian relations down to the defeat Xerxes,
but it is also an ethnological study of the peoples of the Great King's empire.

This sort of *National Geographic* material is characteristic of early Greek historical writing and was very popular with Greek audiences, especially a more cosmopolitan one like the Athenians.

Herodotus actually represents the second generation of Greek historians, but he is the first for whom we have more than just a few fragments surviving. In many ways he stands between two worlds, looking back to the epic tradition of Homer and looking forward to the truly modern history of Thucydides (c. 460-c. 400?). At the beginning of his history he states as part of his goal "to preserve the memory of the past by putting on record the astonishing achievements both of our own and other peoples" (Herodotus 1.0.0), an aim that hearkens back to the bards who sang the deeds of great men that they might be preserved for future generations. And like Homer he makes his characters speak his observations on the events he describes, and he engages in the long digressions typical of the epic. But he also has a second goal, which constitutes the major theme of his work: an examination of the struggle between two different types of civilizations, Greek and Persian. In this sense, analyzing the conflict between oriental autocracy and slavery and Greek constitutionalism and freedom, he is a historian of a more modern cut, attempting to provide some understanding of the great deeds he preserves. By doing this, he creates a kind of universal history, which expounds ideas that are valid even beyond the confines of the particular struggle between Greek and Persian.

Herodotus' sources were primarily oral, his information gained through his extensive travels and in the case of the wars through interviews with old men who had actually participated in the campaigns. A product of the Ionian enlightenment, he is inclined towards natural causation and skeptical of the mythic tradition, except when he is dealing with events in the distant past. Generally he is noncommittal when it comes to fabulous stories: "My business is to record what people say, but I am by no means bound to believe it." (Herodotus 7.152.3) But you nevertheless get the impression that he does believe a lot of the outlandish things he was told about distant lands. Reading his material on Egypt, for example, one has an image of the Egyptian priests, his primary informants, nudging one another and saying: "Get ready. Here comes that gullible Greek again."

A certain gullibility about far off places is excusable, but Herodotus displays a few more serious shortcomings. Though an Ionian by birth, he has a pronounced anti-Ionian bias, which naturally colors his entire account of the Ionian revolt. He is also pro-Athenian, but his admiration is kept within bounds and on occasion he is willing to criticize the democracy. He favors the Alcmaeonids and is definitely anti-Themistocles, which is awkward since Themistocles is at the heart of the defense against Persia. Herodotus cannot deny Themistocles' role, but he attempts to downplay it and consistently assigns him the worst possible motives and character, anticipating in this practice many a modern historian. Finally, Herodotus is typically Greek (or perhaps just human) in that he is inclined to explain events in terms of individuals and personal relationships, missing the deeper social and economic causes, and he really does not seem to understand grand military affairs, a serious weakness in a book focusing on a great war. Despite all these problems, however, he is undeniably good, especially contrasted with the average historian in antiquity. He is certainly a better read than most of his modern scholarly counterparts, and though you should reach for the saltshaker when he explains *why* something happened, you can generally accept *what* he says happened.

In a sense, the chain of events leading to Xerxes' mammoth invasion of Greece begins back with the conquest of western Anatolia in the 540s by Cyrus II the Great (559-530), the founder of the Persian Empire, but more immediately it was the Ionian revolt that started the ball rolling. Now, Herodotus explains the origins of the revolt with a complex story about the intrigues of Aristagoras (d. 496), tyrant of Miletus, but while the tale may be basically true, it says nothing of the underlying causes – economic and political oppression. The Persian Empire was actually a light touch compared to most, but Greeks did not take kindly to having their autonomy limited by anybody, even (or perhaps especially) other Greeks. The Persian mechanism of control of the Ionian poleis was the local tyrant, but by the end of the sixth century the Age of Tyrants was past and these leaders were resented perhaps more than another type of puppet government might have been. Also resented was the burden of tribute that the Great King demanded from his wealthy Greek cities, a burden that apparently became heavier when the empire decided to build an Aegean fleet in the years immediately preceding the revolt. Aristagoras' activities may have set off the revolt, but it was these more mundane factors that made the Ionians ripe for it.

Events kicked off in 499 and the Ionians immediately appealed for aid from their brothers across the Aegean, but only Athens and the Euboean city of Eretria responded. The Eretrians had a debt of honor with Miletus, the center of the revolt, while the Athenians, who had economic and emotional ties with Ionia, saw this as an opportunity to gain some valuable PR by supporting a popular cause, especially since Sparta, the traditional anti-Persian power in Greece, had refused to get involved. Like everyone else, the Athenians undoubtedly did not have any idea of just how immense and powerful the Persian Empire was and fell for Aristagoras' promises of easy victories and loot. They sent twenty ships and a complement of hoplites, which force could hardly tip the scales, but this was a serious move. That score of vessels represented most, if not all, of

Athens naval strength, and she was now aiding and abetting revolting subjects of the Great King, something an empire held together by the threat of force was not likely to take kindly to.

In 498 the allies managed to burn Sardes, seat of the chief Persian satrap (provincial governor) in Asia Minor, but were themselves defeated at Ephesus later that year, and the Athenians sailed home, deciding that a wait-and-see posture was best. The revolt was effectively lost when the Ionians were defeated at the naval battle of Lade in 495, and the last nails were hammered into the coffin the following year with the Persian sack of Miletus. So the Ionians remained subjects of the Great King, but the uprising did at least convince him to abandon the tyrants and rule the Greek cities through their individual constitutional governments; forming alliances with the local elites was the most efficient imperial mechanism in antiquity. Meanwhile, the Athenians could expect some serious trouble to be coming their way.

Darius I (522-486), the Great King, was not amused. Athens and Eretria, those impertinent flyspecks to the west, would have to be punished in order to show the world the Persian Empire was not to be trifled with. As

Ahuramazda's deputy on earth, it was the king's duty to expand the empire in any case, and it must also have occurred to him that so long as the Greeks to the west were independent, his grip on Ionia would never be completely secure. Accordingly, in 490 a fleet carrying some 20-25,000 troops under the command of Datis and Artaphernes put out from Asia Minor and headed directly across the Aegean. With a force this size Darius was obviously not contemplating the conquest of Greece, but he had in mind something more than just vaporizing the two cities and returning home. With the expedition was old Hippias, the ex-tyrant of Athens, and it is reasonable to conclude that Darius intended first to punish Athens, probably by burning her temples and executing her leaders, and then to install Hippias as head of a Persian puppet government, creating a convenient beachhead for a full-scale assault on the Balkan Peninsula.

As the expedition moved across the Aegean it visited the Cyclades islands and enrolled them in the empire, collecting supplies and hostages. Eretria was dealt with first, its gates betrayed for gold after a week of bloody siege, and the expedition then landed at the bay of Marathon, one of only two places on the Attic coast able to accommodate the Persian fleet (the other was Phaleron just outside Athens). Datis parked his army at the northern end of the plain and waited for the Athenians to make their move, Hippias filling his ear with promises that his supporters would seize the city in a coup. Meanwhile, back at Athens, Miltiades (c. 554-489), who had seen action during the Ionian revolt, was exhorting the Athenians to take the bold move of marching out to meet the invaders. With the fate of Eretria on their minds they agreed and sent the hoplite army, some 9000 strong, north to Marathon. Notified by a runner, the Spartans, who had promised help, were eager to mix it up with the Persians – this after all was their idea of an excellent time – but a religious festival prevented them from marching until the moon was full, a week or so hence.

The Athenian army, under Callimachus (d. 490), the war archon, camped in the southern part of the plain and was joined there by the 600 hoplites of Plataea, which owed Athens for earlier favors. Now the ball was in Datis' court. He could not support his army at Marathon forever, and he must have known that sooner or later the Spartans would show up. But he dare not attack the Greeks in their well-protected position, and since that position either flanked or straddled the main road to Athens he could not simply begin moving his army out either. What he did was to re-embark a small part of his force, including all his cavalry, it seems, and send them sailing south. The Athenians could not stand idly by and allow the defenseless (and possibly wall-less) city to be captured, so they were forced to move out into the plain to meet the bulk of the Persian army, which Datis had formed up facing the Greek camp.

So the battle would be fought on terrain favorable to the Persians: a wide open space where they could bring the superior numbers and mobility of their essentially light infantry to bear. Realizing the danger of being enveloped, Callimachus and Miltiades lengthened their line to match the Persian and strengthened their wings at the expense of the center. Moving double-time, the Geeks literally crashed into the enemy line and began chewing up the lightly armored Asiatic troops, who were at a tremendous disadvantage in nose-to-nose combat with hoplites. But there were a lot of them, and they managed to break through the Athenian center, something that usually meant doom for a phalanx. Rather than turning and attacking the Greek wings from behind, however, the undisciplined Persian troops headed straight for the Athenian camp and plunder, allowing the victorious Greek wings to wheel inwards and crush the Persians in a classic double pincer.

Datis managed to get his fleet away and head for Athens, but some 6400 of his soldiers had bought the farm at Marathon. The Athenians, who had lost only 192 killed, immediately hustled back to the city and arrived there before the Persian strike force. Not about to attempt a landing against armed resistance, Datis gathered his Eretrian prisoners and sailed back to Asia. A couple of days later the Spartans finally showed up and toured the battlefield, impressed by the Athenian achievement and disappointed they had missed all the sport. Incidentally, it is just short of twenty-six miles from Marathon to Athens by the main road, but there was no Marathon runner. Absent from Herodotus, the story was created by later writers, and the first marathoner was apparently Spyros Louis in AD 1896.

Marathon was hardly a disaster for the Great King, for whom the battle was a relatively minor engagement on the periphery of his empire, and the manpower losses could be made up in a moment. But the defeat was a tremendous loss of face, which meant that a rematch was absolutely necessary. For the Athenians and Plataeans Marathon was an unparalleled triumph. Outnumbered more than two to one, they did not just beat the Persians, they humiliated them, slapping back a force that for more than half a century had seemed invincible. And this was the importance of Marathon. The victory did not stop the Persians, who would be back ten years later with ten times as many troops, but it gave the Greeks the confidence to face that juggernaut when it came. Had there been no Marathon, there would probably have been no serious resistance to Xerxes in 480.

Darius began preparations for another assault, but Egypt revolted from the empire in 486 and Darius himself died of old age soon after, all of which upset the invasion timetable. This is not say that the Greeks used the extra time to prepare their defenses; the average polis could not see beyond its immediate neighbors, with whom it was usually in conflict. But Athens under Themistocles was not your average polis, and the delay in the east gave the Athenians time to build a navy. In 483 a big silver strike was made at the Athenian mines at Laurion, and Themistocles was able to persuade the Athenians not to divide the windfall among themselves, but to use it to lay the keels of new ships. Two years later Athens possessed a fleet of 200 warships, bigger than all the other Greek navies combined, and it was that fleet that would save Greece.

In 483 the King's engineers began preparing the expedition's route around the northern Aegean, and by 481 Darius' son and successor, Xerxes I (486-465), had collected his forces in western Anatolia. Herodotus describes an army of more than two million, which was accompanied by another three million followers, but these figures demand immediate skepticism. What Herodotus is really providing in his description of the army is a catalogue of the peoples of the empire, many of whom had little value in a military expedition. What fool would transport Stone Age Ethiopians all the way to Greece to fight hoplites? Actually, Xerxes might have been able to assemble a million man army, but there was no way he could ever feed it. Food supply put a limit on the size and movement of an ancient army, and the poor state of land transport put a serious limit on the food supply for any army away from the coast. Xerxes' forces numbered perhaps about 180,000 men, who would have required something like 270 tons of food each day, and in order to keep all those bellies filled he was compelled to keep his army in close contact with his fleet of some 600 to 800 ships. It suited him to keep this navy on a short lease anyway, since those sundry Egyptians, Phoenicians and especially Ionians who manned the ships could not be completely trusted.

Xerxes' aim was to conquer Greece, and his strong suit in this endeavor was the sheer size of his army and navy. At sea it was sufficient to remain on the defensive and guard the lines of supply and communication, while on land he had only to win one major victory and Greek morale would probably collapse. Like Datis before him, he wanted his army to fight in big open spaces, where his huge numbers and superior cavalry would have the edge and help compensate for the generally poorer quality of his infantry. His navy also required elbow room for its battles, both because of its size and because of its skill, which could be put to good advantage only when there was plenty of sea room for maneuver. The problem with all this of course was that the Balkan Peninsula does not offer that much in the way of wide open spaces and seemingly favors the defense.

Naturally, the Greeks were delighted with their terrain. Dramatically inferior in mobility and numbers, their hoplite infantry was virtually invincible when fighting in confined places, as Thermopylae would demonstrate. The rugged terrain also favored the defensive, which was obviously the posture the Greeks would have to adopt on land, at least initially. With a fleet of about 375 warships, the Greeks would also be on the defensive at sea, but here the opportunities were greater, since Xerxes' expedition would be in serious trouble should he lose control of the Aegean. The greatest problem the Greeks faced was themselves. The animosities among the poleis ran deep, and some states would join the Persians because their neighbors intended to resist. For those who were determined to fight, the political difficulties involved in creating a unified effort were tremendous. For example, to facilitate the defense an Hellenic League was formed in 481, but while Sparta was given the command on land, envious and hostile members balked at giving Athens the naval command, despite the fact that she was supplying two thirds of the fleet. Incredibly enough, the solution was to appoint a Spartan! A major problem for the alliance was Sparta's inclination to write off the north and defend only the Peloponnesus, a political fact of life that explains some of the otherwise confusing military moves of the Greeks. It cannot be emphasized enough how much trouble the Greeks had getting along with one another, even in the face of a common danger. This Hellenic League, shaky though it was, is as close as Greece ever came to voluntary unity.

The size of Xerxes' army and the geography of Greece pretty much determined the path of the Persian advance would be along the Aegean coast, and along that route there were three natural choke points: the passes around Olympus in the north, the pass at Thermopylae in central Greece, and the narrow isthmus linking the Peloponnesus to the mainland in the south. Accordingly, in the spring of 480, before the enemy had even crossed to Europe, an army of 10,000 hoplites was sent north to Tempe, on the frontier between Macedon and the plains of Thessaly. The hearts of the southern Greeks, especially the Spartans, were, however, just not into fighting so far from home, and within a few days the relatively small army, having failed to obtain the support of the Thessalian hillmen, left without seeing hide or hair of a Persian. With the evacuation of Tempe, a result of the political disunity, all of northern Greece promptly went over to the Persian side, despite threats of dire punishment from the Hellenic League. Meanwhile, the defenders fell back on Thermopylae, a pass running east-west between the cliffs of the Oite mountains and the waters of the Malian gulf. In antiquity the pass was truly narrow, less than fifty feet wide in spots (silt has subsequently moved the coastline out several miles), and like the German Wehrmacht 2400 years later, Xerxes had absolutely no choice but to come this way. The terrain to the west was simply too rugged for his huge army, and in any case his men would quickly begin to starve if they left contact with the fleet.

In late summer the Greek force arrived at Thermopylae, some 7000 hoplites under the command of king Leonidas I (490-480) of Sparta. Leonidas' army illustrates perfectly the Greek problem: only 300 full Spartans out of a potential 8000 and only 400 hoplites from Thebes, the strongest polis in central Greece. Theban hatred of Athens had her just going through the motions and ready to switch sides, while the Spartans were extremely unenthusiastic about defending so far north. Under pressure from Athens, the Spartans were willing to risk a smallish number of Peloponnesians at Thermopylae and send one of their kings to show they meant business, but they would not risk the final defense of the Isthmus of Corinth by sending all their forces. Actually, 7000 hoplites would have been sufficient to hold the pass for a long time had Leonidas played his cards right. He was aware that Thermopylae was turned by a narrow track, the Anopaea path, through the mountains, and he posted 1000 Phocian hoplites at its highest point, where they could easily fend off any attack. His failure was in not leaving a Spartan to command them.

Defending Thermopylae was pointless unless the Persian fleet was also held back, and accordingly the Greeks sent more than 250 warships, half of them Athenian, to take station at Artemesium on the northern tip of the island of Euboea. Probably to ease the fears of the Spartans, a squadron of about 100 ships was kept back in the Saronic Gulf, between Attica and the Peloponnesus. There were no full-scale battles at Artemesium, only skirmishes, in which the Greeks made a good showing, and the real damage to the Persians came in the form of two storms, one of which devastated a squadron of 200 ships that was attempting to round Euboea. The Greek fleet was still outnumbered, but the odds had been reduced, and though they abandoned the position after a week, Artemesium could be counted a victory for the Greeks. They had stopped the southward advance of the enemy fleet, and only when Thermopylae had fallen did they retreat to the Saronic Gulf.

Meanwhile, back at the pass the Spartans were having the time of their lives. Xerxes delayed his attack at first, hoping the Greeks would be scared into retreating, but instead of fleeing the Spartans spent the time combing their long hair and thinking up clever one liners for posterity. For example, when told there were so many enemy archers that their volleys blocked out the sun, the Spartan replied: "All the better, we'll fight in the shade." The Great King unleashed a frontal assault, which had little effect other than piling up Persian casualties, and even the crack guards division, the Immortals (so named because their number was never allowed to fall below 10,000 actives), could not make a dent in the hoplite line. Xerxes was getting, in spades, the message only suggested to Datis at Marathon: a disciplined hoplite phalanx on favorable terrain could withstand just about anything short of firearms.

Without much hope of forcing it, the King finally sent a detachment of Immortals up the Anopaea path, and Ahuramazda smiled on Xerxes this day. Surprised and unprepared (or bought off), the Phocian guard retreated into the heights and left the path free for the Persians. Leonidas was now in serious trouble.

But Leonidas was also a Spartan king, and once he got the bad news, he sent south everyone except his 300 Spartans and their helot attendants, some 700 Thespians, who volunteered to die, and the 400 Thebans, whom he didn't trust. There was an oracle to the effect that a Spartan king must die if the Greeks were to win the war, but more compelling, there needed to be a rearguard if the rest of the army were to escape the more mobile Persians. Leonidas and his lads were the obvious choice, and besides, what better death could any Spartan hope for? As expected, the Thebans surrendered as soon as they could, but the Spartans and Thespians fought on, actually charging the enemy on several occasions and waging a veritable Homeric struggle over the body of the fallen Leonidas. Spears lost, swords broken and fighting with hands and teeth, they made their last stand on a small hill, which today bears a marker with the famous epigram of Simonides: "O stranger, tell them in Sparta that here we lie, having obeyed their orders." The stuff of epic.

The fall of Thermopylae meant that central Greece was now open to the invaders, and most of the states in the area promptly surrendered, while the Peloponnesians began furiously building their maginot line across the isthmus. The Athenians, however, refused to give in and used their navy to ferry most of their population to the islands of Salamis and Aegina and to the Peloponnesus, an evacuation that Herodotus pictures as a last minute panic and failure of Themistocles' leadership. But Herodotus does not like Themistocles and is clearly distorting what was obviously the back-up plan in the event the Thermopylae-Artemesium line was lost. Certainly clever enough to plan for such a contingency, Themistocles was also clever enough to know that the hopes of the Greeks now rested on a naval victory, without which the isthmus wall was a complete waste of time. And he knew that the best shot at victory was to lure the Persian fleet into battle in the bay of Salamis, whose confined waters would not only offset the superior enemy numbers, but also favor the Greek style of naval combat.

The Greek trireme (and its slightly larger descendants, the quadrireme and quinquereme) was a fragile, unseaworthy affair, less a ship than a giant racing scull. Measuring 125 to 135 feet in length and about 13 feet (18 with the outrigger) amidships and drawing very little water, the trireme was equipped with a ram protruding from the prow just below the waterline and in battle was propelled by some 170 rowers. Easy to build, but expensive to maintain, the trireme sacrificed everything to speed under oar and barely had the free space to carry water for the crew, let alone provisions and other supplies. There were two ways to fight an engagement with this sort of vessel: ramming and sinking or closing and boarding. The former involved rowing like hell at the enemy ship, punching in its side with your ram, then backing off and watching your opponents founder. These tactics required a great deal of maneuvering and coordinated action and consequently were favored by those with strong naval traditions and skilled crews. Landlubber types, like the Macedonians and Romans, were attracted to the second approach, which required only the skill to get close enough to throw over the grappling hooks, draw the ships together and send over the marines. This was especially effective when your marines were a compliment of hoplites or legionaries. Now, later in the fifth century the Athenians would be highly skilled and dreaded masters of ramming, but in 480 they and the other Greeks were definitely inferior to Xerxes' sailors and thus inclined to the less demanding boarding tactics. So it behooved the Greeks to fight in crowded waters, where boarding was easier and the enemy had no room to maneuver.

Unfortunately, many of the Greek commanders failed to appreciate this fact, and Themistocles was forced to threaten to take the Athenian fleet and people off to Italy to found a new Athens if his plan was not adopted. Even the Spartans could understand that the departure of the Athenians would spell doom for the Peloponnesus, and so the fleet was stationed at Salamis, where it was a tempting target for the Great King. Xerxes must have known from his advisors that a battle in the open sea was more attractive, but here was a chance to trap the entire Greek fleet and capture Salamis and all those Athenians. So he sent his armada in, and the resulting battle went pretty much as Themistocles had expected. The Persian ships became hopelessly crowded together and confused in the narrow waters and fell easy prey to the Greek boarding tactics. In a day of hard fighting they suffered heavy losses and finally withdrew in disarray.

In the wake of Salamis Xerxes promptly packed up most of his army and returned to Asia, leaving behind some 60,000 troops under his cousin Mardonius (d. 479). Herodotus describes this retreat as a mad panic, but Xerxes in fact had good reason for his actions. At Salamis he had lost command of the sea, which meant that provisioning his huge army went from difficult to critical, while his line of communications back to Anatolia was now seriously threatened. Further, a serious defeat of Persian forces was usually the signal for someone in the empire to revolt, and the Ionians could certainly be counted on to entertain such disloyal thoughts. The Great King had little choice but to pare down his land forces and get his royal presence back to Asia.

Salamis took Greece off the critical list, but the Persians still controlled everything of interest north of the isthmus. Mardonius moved north into Thessaly for the winter, and when he came south again in the spring of 479, the Athenians, who had returned to their devastated homeland, listened in vain for the sound of marching hoplites. With the Persian navy on the run and the Peloponnesus apparently safe the Spartans saw no compelling reason to pick a fight in central Greece, and Attica was evacuated a second time. The Athenians now made it clear that unless they got immediate help they would take Mardonius' offer of alliance, and even Spartan brains could grasp that Mardonius plus the Athenian navy equaled useless fortifications at the isthmus. The Peloponnesian levy was promptly mobilized and sent north under Pausanias (d. c. 470), regent for Pleistarchus (480-459), the underage son of Leonidas. Picking up contingents from Athens and other allies, he went looking for Mardonius with an army of 35,000 hoplites, accompanied by perhaps an equal number of not too valuable light-armed.

The Persian general, meanwhile, had withdrawn from Attica and taken up a position near Plataea, just south of his ally Thebes. He had more troops than the Greeks, but apart from his Thebans and other turncoats they were all light infantry and no match for the hoplites at close quarters. His strong suits were his archers and excellent corps of 10,000 cavalry, which caused the Greeks endless hassles during the several days of maneuver that preceded the battle. In the end Mardonius was induced by an apparent Greek withdrawal to attack in circumstances less favorable to his forces, and once the infantry was engaged the superior armament of the hoplites carried the day. The Spartans were not inclined to pursuit, so a portion of the Persian force managed to withdraw in good order and make it back to Asia Minor. Greece was free.

The Persian invasions were a severe test for Greece, the first massive external challenge to the polis society. Militarily, the Greeks passed the test with high marks. Marathon, Thermopylae, and Plataea had all demonstrated the superiority of hoplite heavy infantry when used in the proper circumstances, though it must be noted that the Greek victory was due in large part to the Persian failure to employ their own military assets in the most efficient manner. On the other hand, Xerxes' assault had also revealed the great weakness of the Greeks, the one that would destroy them in the end – their disunity. Even in the face of foreign conquest the poleis found cooperation difficult or impossible. Pride, jealousy, selfishness and the reluctance to give up even the slightest bit of autonomy had brought the Greeks to the brink, to be saved in the end by the sacrifice and determination of Athens. Xerxes' failure would initiate the liberation of the Ionian Greeks, but the Persian Empire itself would totter on for another century and a half, using its immense financial resources to interfere in Greek affairs. Had they been able to achieve any measure of unity, the Greeks of the generation of the Persian wars could have begun the destruction of Cyrus' empire. Instead, they and their descendants would squander the heritage of Salamis and Plataea in a seemingly endless series of destructive local wars, until unity was finally imposed upon them by Macedon. Only then would the Greeks return Xerxes' call.

###################

SUGGESTED READING

Obviously, the best thing to read for the Persian wars is Herodotus, supplemented by the appropriate lives of Plutarch: Themistocles and Aristides. For a modern analytical account, start with A.R. Burn, *Persia and the Greeks. The Defense of the West 546-478* (1962, 1984). This is an excellent book, filled with anecdotes as well as serious analysis, and it provides background on the Persian Empire and an account of the Sicilian Greeks' struggle with the Carthaginians. Two more sober, but still readable accounts: Charles Hignett, *Xerxes' Invasion of Greece* (1963) and J.F. Lazenby, *The Defense of Greece 490-479 BC* (1993). Steven Pressfield's novel about Thermopylae, *Gates of Fire* (1998) is a good read, and of course you shouldn't miss the account in Larry Gonick, *The Cartoon History of the Universe. Vol. 6: Who Are These Athenians?* (1981). The movie *The 300* is fun and the Spartans would certainly enjoy it; going into a battle wearing only a leather speedo is certainly the height of bravado.

# # # # # # # # # # # # # # # # # # #

VIII. THE GREATER AEGEAN CO-PROSPERITY SPHERE

THE ATHENIAN EMPIRE

Not that we hate Athens – heavens, no.
And not that dear old Athens isn't grand,
that blessed land where men are free – to pay their taxes.

-Aristophanes *Birds* 36-38[21]

At the end of the Persian War it appeared that Sparta might have the Greek world at her feet. She was far and away the strongest land power and under the energetic leadership of the regent Pausanias had emerged from Plataea with enhanced prestige. (The blackmail that was needed to get her to the battle was conveniently forgotten.) But Sparta just did not have what it took to lead the Greeks to unity or impose it upon them. Spartan society was simply too conservative and insular and created neither the brains nor the initiative needed to run a Panhellenic organization of any kind. Men of ability were smothered by her system, and she had no navy, an absolute necessity for any power that would establish an hegemony over Greece. On the other hand, there was Athens – open, dynamic, commercial Athens. Her sacrifices had earned her a reputation as great as Sparta's, and she possessed the largest navy outside the Persian Empire. A society that favored talent rather than suppressing it, she had a realistic shot at Hellenic leadership.

A few days after the battle of Plataea the Greek fleet landed on the Anatolian coast at Mycale and defeated the Persian force there, and this victory touched off a second revolt of the Ionians. Sparta's reaction to their request for aid was to offer to settle them in the Balkan Peninsula, which was not quite what they had in mind. To make matters worse, when

Pausanias took over the fleet in 478, he managed to alienate all the allies with his tyrannical behavior and was recalled. So the Asiatic Greeks turned instead to the Athenians, who were definitely interested. Not only did they have growing commercial contacts with Ionia, but more and more of their food supply was coming from the Black Sea region through the vital Hellespont, where they in fact had colonists. The invitation also meant an opportunity for Athens to increase her power and influence, while at the same time making the Spartans look bad.

And so the Delian League was formed, so called because its official headquarters was on the sacred isle of Delos. It was a voluntary association of states interested in furthering the liberation of Ionia and providing collective security for the Aegean basin. Its membership came to include the poleis of Ionia, the Propontis (Sea of Mamora and the Bosporus) and the north coast of the Aegean, all but one of the cities on the big island of Euboea, most of the Aegean islands and of course Athens. The League was essentially an alliance of sea states, so the basic contract was to furnish ships and some troops for a common fleet. Many of the very small poleis, for whom the maintenance of even one or two triremes would be an unfairly heavy burden, agreed to contribute money. Policy would be decided by a representative assembly on

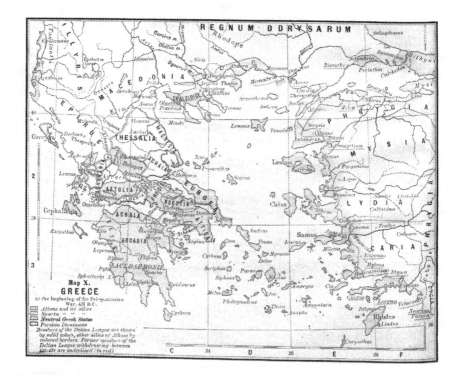

Delos, but Athens was permanent operational commander of the League forces and supplied the treasurers of the organization. The alliance was to be permanent, and the members tossed iron bars into the sea and swore to keep their treaties until the weights floated to the surface. Diplomacy used to be much more colorful.

Certainly the allies had to cut Athens a good deal to get her participation, but such a deal! The Delian League just begged to be turned into an Athenian Empire. Not only was Athens installed as permanent hegemon, but she was also in an excellent position to dominate the League assembly by using her economic strength to influence the votes of the small states that constituted most of the membership of nearly 200. (This gives an idea of just how small the average polis was: almost 200 independent states on just the islands and coasts of the Aegean.) Allied ships remained the property of the allies, but the triremes Athens built with the cash contributions became for all practical purposes part of her own fleet, thus increasing her strength at League expense. And gradually more and more members slipped into the tributary category, because it was easier to make a cash payment than maintain a squadron of warships and their crews. The allies practically asked Athens to take over, and the dynamic, aggressive Athenians could hardly refuse such an invitation. It is very hard to turn down an empire on such a silver platter.

The early operations of the League fleet were perfectly legitimate. Under the leadership of Cimon the allies cleared the Persian strongholds in Europe and northwestern Asia Minor and liberated cities in Caria and Lycia in the southwest. These last operations culminated in c. 466 in the battle of Eurymedon, a joint land and sea engagement in which the Greeks annihilated a huge Persian armada and ended for the moment the threat from the east. But meanwhile, the fleet had already conducted operations against Greeks. In 472/1 the Euboean city of Carystus was forced into the League, the allies claiming with some justification that it was reaping the benefits of the alliance without shouldering any of the burdens. In 470/69 Naxos attempted to secede and was crushed, and Thasos revolted in 465, only to capitulate two years later. Athens could correctly claim that the alliance would collapse if members were allowed to secede once the Persian heat was off, but the case of Thasos was ominous. The island was the first ally to lose her fleet, and Athenian interests in the area certainly prospered once she had been defeated. Even more ominous was the creation in the wake of these events of a new class of allies, those who were partially subject and thus open to interference in their internal affairs by the League, which increasingly meant Athens.

And so the Athenians began the process of transforming the League into an empire, tightening their control over the allies and strengthening their fleet while the allied squadrons declined. The process was gradual, and the allies helped every step of the way. Athens made no blatant moves to suppress her allies, but instead was a very picky hegemon, immediately crushing and reducing to the subject category those who did not promptly meet their League obligations. The result was that within a generation of the creation of the League there were besides Athens only three ship contributing allies left – the wealthy islands of Chios, Lesbos and Samos. The remaining allies all paid tribute and supplied troops, and of these a large number were subject and so more directly controlled. By the fifties Athens had suspended meetings of the League assembly, and in 454 the League treasury was moved from Delos to the Athenian acropolis, where Athena began receiving a rake of one sixtieth. The move was supposedly to protect the funds from the Persians (who had not been seen in the Aegean for a quarter century), but it sure seemed a sign that the Delian League was now formally the Athenian Empire.

Athens exercised control over her allies through a variety of mechanisms. The most potent of course was her awesome naval strength. The mere existence of the Athenian fleet was in normal circumstances enough to keep disaffected elements in check, and if push came to shove the coastal and island cities that made up the empire could be easily crushed. More subtle means of control were provided by Athens' economic power, especially her growing influence in the Aegean grain trade, and the requirement that all cases involving Athenians or capital punishment be tried in Athenian courts. In the case of the subject allies Athens could intervene in their internal affairs and typically did so by supporting democratic government, sometimes installing a garrison to help guarantee the security of the democratic faction. There were some loyal oligarchic regimes that survived the war years, but for the most part the internal politics of the allied states came to reflect the polarization that emerged in the wider Greek world: democrats looked to Athens while the oligarchs pinned their hopes on Sparta.

The Athenian organization was a light touch compared to the average empire, at least until the pressures of the great war with Sparta. The tribute was reassessed every four years, and the allied state could appeal if it thought the amount was too high. In return for their money the allies got the Athenian fleet, which not only protected them from the Persians and from their own neighbors, but also suppressed the normally endemic piracy, probably the most appreciated benefit of the empire. The obligation to supply troops was a burden, but perhaps better the allied hoplites should be defending and expanding the empire than fighting one another, which is what they would otherwise be doing. Because of the strong feelings the Greeks had about the autonomy of the polis, however, the empire was probably generally resented and Athenian meddling in the internal affairs of the subject allies certainly was, but it could have been worse. After all, Athenian interference was primarily concerned with maintaining democratic governments, which by definition involved the majority of the locals ruling themselves. (At least by the Greek definition, which required direct participation; representative government readily allows the creation of sham democracies.) And in fact, it would be worse: when Sparta took over the empire after Athens' defeat in 404, she ruled it through oppressive little ten man oligarchies.

Athens had her ups and downs with her allies, but it was the Peloponnesian War of 431-404 that really turned the empire sour. Initially there was little problem, since Pericles pursued a purely defensive strategy (see Chapter X), which made very small demands upon the allies, especially in terms of troops. But old Squill Head died in 429, and Athenian policy became increasingly aggressive and expansionist, putting heavier and heavier demands on the allies. For example, in 425, the seventh year of the war, Athens more than doubled the tribute demanded of the allies. At the same time growing political difficulties led to bungling and folly in the prosecution of the war, culminating in the disastrous Sicilian expedition of 415-413. The empire became an increasing burden on the allies, wasting their resources and lives in dubious operations and providing no discernible benefits in return. In 412, prompted by Athenian losses in Sicily and Spartan promises of aid, almost all the allies revolted and went over to the enemy camp. In the next few years the energetic Athenians would reconquer most of their former dependents, but a few years after that they would lose the war and with it the empire. Then the allies would get a taste of empire Spartan style.

Athens' decaying relationship with her allies in the course of the war is neatly reflected in her own changing view of the empire and foreign relations in general. In the famous Funeral Oration given at the end of the first year of the war Pericles alludes to the relatively benign imperialism practiced by Athens: "We make friends by doing good to others, not by receiving good from them…When we do kindnesses to others, we do not do them out of calculations of profit or loss: we do them without afterthought, relying on free liberality." (Thucydides 2.40.4-5) Well, the reality of the empire was of course far from this ideal, but Athenian imperialism was almost a gentle presence compared to the heavy-handed Spartan brand, which had virtually enslaved the southern part of the Peloponnesus. In any case, it is the ideal we are interested in, how Athens viewed herself and her relations with other states.

Only one year later the tone has already changed. In a speech given by Pericles at the end of the second year of the war the will to power is now clearly apparent:

> The whole world before our eyes can be divided into two parts, the land and the sea, each of which is valuable and useful to man. Of the whole of one of these parts you are in control – not only of the area at present in your power, but elsewhere too, if you want to go further. With your navy as it is today there is no power on earth –not the King of Persia nor any people under the sun – which can stop you from sailing where you wish…And do not imagine that what we are fighting for is simply the question of freedom or slavery; there is also involved the loss of our empire and the dangers arising from the hatred we have incurred while administering it…In fact you now hold your empire down by force: it may have been wrong to take it; it is certainly dangerous to let it go. (Thucydides 2.62.2, 63.1-2)

After only two years of war the friendly, mutual aid concept of empire expressed in the Funeral Oration has given way to a more realistic appraisal of the empire as a kind of tyranny. But the empire cannot be given up now, and justification of it can be found in the mere fact that it exists. Further, in his description of Athenian naval strength Pericles defines a power that has no limit and suggests that Athenian ambitions might not be contained within the confines of the present empire. Knowing what is to come, we can understand these words as an ominous forecast.

In 428 Mytilene, the chief city on the island of Lesbos, revolted from Athens and was crushed the following year. In a fit of emotion the Athenian assembly voted to put to death the entire male population and enslave the women and children, a rare and extreme form of punishment that was unfortunately becoming less rare as the war progressed. The harshness of the reaction is a vivid sign of the brutalizing effects of the war, but what happened next is also revealing of the changing Athenian attitude towards the empire. The day after the decision was made cooler heads prevailed, and an extraordinary second meeting of the assembly was called to debate the issue again. The demagogue and radical imperialist Cleon (d. 422) argued that the heavy punishment was necessary to set an example and that policy could not take a back seat to irrelevant humanitarian concerns. The opposition, led by the moderate Diodotus, countered with the argument that the slaughter would not serve as a deterrent, but rather would cause those who did revolt to fight to the death, since that would be all they could expect anyway. Moreover, Mytilene was an oligarchy and the people had been compelled to go along with the revolt, so punishing them would only disaffect the democratic factions in other states.

The penalty was repealed and the Mytilenians were saved at the last minute, but look at the arguments delivered in their defense. Nowhere does Diodotus say anything about justice or what is right or what Mytilene deserves. His arguments are based entirely on expediency, on what course of action would be best for imperial Athens, and he comes right out and says so: "But this is not a law court, where we have to consider what is fit and just; it is a political assembly, and the question is how Mytilene can be most useful to Athens." (Thucydides 3.44.4) Whatever Diodotus may have felt about the inhumanity of the punishment and the plight of the Mytilenians, he understood that the Athenian people would only be moved by a cold appeal to their imperial self-interest. As the war dragged on, Athens' concept of empire was clearly growing harsher. And Athens was not alone in the growing brutality. In 427 Plataea surrendered to the Spartans after a two year siege, and despite the city's role in the Hellenic victory of 479, it was razed to the ground. Prompted by the Thebans, the Spartans acted in a particularly nasty fashion. Each defender was asked if had done anything of service to the Spartans and their allies in the war, and when each answered no (what else?), he was executed.

The moral rock bottom came in 416, when the Athenians attacked the tiny island of Melos in the southern Aegean. The Melians had not joined the original Delian League and had managed to escape the attention of the Athenians in the following years. At the outbreak of the war the island was neutral, although her sympathies were with Sparta, since she had been colonized from there. She resisted an Athenian invitation to join the empire and because of this uncooperative stance was in 426 the object of an unsuccessful Athenian attack. Now, ten years later the Athenians extended their invitation again, and once again the Melians refused. This time, however, the Athenians captured the city and killed all the males and enslaved the women and children. Actually, this was the second occasion that such drastic measures were taken; Athens had already inflicted this same terrible fate upon her ally Scione after an unsuccessful revolt in 421. But in the case of Scione the Athenians could at least claim, rightly or wrongly, just desserts for an ingrate ally, whereas Melos quite obviously involved nothing more than naked and brutal aggression.

And indeed the Athenians made no claim that there was anything more. In their dialogue with the Melians before investing the city they boldly state their reasons for pressuring the island: "If we were on friendly terms with you, our subjects would regard that as a sign of weakness in us, whereas your hatred is evidence of our power...So that by conquering you we shall increase not only the size but the security of our empire. We rule the sea and you are islanders, and weaker islanders too than the others; it is therefore particularly important that you should not escape." (Thucydides 5.95, 97) When the Melians protest that what is happening to them is hardly just, the Athenians reply with one of the most cynical statements of foreign policy principles in history:

> You know as well as we do that, when matters are discussed by practical people, the standard of justice depends on the equality of power to compel and that in fact the strong do what they have the power to do and the weak accept what they have to accept...Our opinion of the gods and our knowledge of men lead us to conclude that it a general and necessary law of nature (*physis*) to rule wherever one can. This is not a law we made ourselves, nor were we the first to act upon it when it was made. We found it already in existence, and we shall leave it to exist for ever among those who come after us. We are merely acting in accordance with it, and we know that you or anybody else with the same power as ours would be acting in precisely the same way. (Thucydides 5.89, 105.2)

Such honesty in foreign affairs is certainly refreshing, but it cannot obscure the total moral bankruptcy of Athenian policy. It has come to this for the Athenians – might makes right. Taking a cue from the radical sophists, they have abandoned the normal standards of civilized behavior and justified their violation of accepted international *nomos* by appealing to a brutally defined *physis*, as many a great power would do in the twentieth and now the twenty-first century, precisely as Thucydides predicted.

The affair at Melos set the stage for another expression of Athens' growing will to power, one of far greater impact. In 415 the Athenians sent a great armada to Sicily to attempt the conquest of Syracuse and the rest of the island. In this and a second relief force dispatched two years later Athens and her allies sent out over 200 triremes and 10,000 hoplites, for a total force of more than 50,000 men. The ostensible goal of the expedition was to bring aid to beleaguered Athenian allies, but the real reason for the trip was blatant aggression. The Athenians were being transported by visions of unending empire, by dreams of extending their control to the western Greeks, whose resources could then be used to crush once and for all the Spartans and their allies. Then it was on to Persia, Carthage, Italy, Spain and Zeus knows where else. Alcibiades (c. 450-404/3), the flamboyant and talented proponent of the expedition, defined for the Athenians the new concept of empire: "The fact is that we have reached a stage where we are forced to plan new conquests and forced to hold on to what we have got, because there is a danger that we ourselves may fall under the power of others unless others are in our power." (Thucydides 6.18.3) Athens had come a long way from "making friends by doing good to others."

Sometimes there is justice in history and sometimes it is almost poetic. Despite having everything in its favor the Sicilian expedition was a failure and not because of the strength of the enemy, but because of the blunders of the Athenians. Again and again Syracuse was saved by the political squabbling and military incompetence of the Athenian leadership, and in the end those failings guaranteed that the expedition would not just fail to capture Syracuse, but would culminate in unqualified disaster. In 413 all the ships and almost all the men who had constituted the proud armadas that had sailed from Athens were lost, and this catastrophe led in the following years to the revolt of almost all of Athens' empire. Thucydides puts it succinctly at the end of his account of the Sicilian debacle: "Out of many, only few returned." (Thucydides 7.87.6.) The odd Melian slave could only smile.

Making a judgment call on the Athenian Empire is a difficult proposition, since it all depends upon your point of view and what you consider valuable in society. Because of our strong bias towards democracy, we are certainly inclined to look favorably on Athens and her activities, particularly in contrast to Sparta and her support for oligarchy. Encouraging democratic governments around the world seems part of America's historic mission these days, and we can hardly fail to be sympathetic to an empire that frequently ruled by imposing democracy. One might assume that inasmuch as democracy allows the masses to share in the government, a poll taken of the denizens of the Athenian Empire might have revealed substantial support for the organization, at least in the democratic cities. Not necessarily. Central to the concept of the polis was its complete autonomy and the freedom of its citizens to manage their affairs in a totally sovereign manner, which frequently meant fighting the neighboring polis or generally screwing things up. It is necessary to keep in mind that there were really two "Greeces," the better-educated and very politicized urban populations, who shaped Hellenic culture and history, and the illiterate and probably mostly apolitical rural populations (Athens is almost certainly an exception), about whom we know next to nothing. The latter probably appreciated the peace and prosperity the empire brought, at least before the war, but the urban Greeks were extremely touchy about the autonomy of the polis, be it for better or for worse, and would probably have instantly voted against the empire. And if the fact that Athens did not have much to deal with in the way of serious revolts until the war is seen as evidence of contentment in the empire, it must also be viewed as evidence of a healthy respect for the long arm of the Athenian fleet. Even non-Greek peoples (like the Iraqis) have demonstrated a typical unwillingness to have their sovereignty violated by the most caring conqueror.

From the point of view of most Athenians of course the empire was without question a good thing. It brought Athens immense power and considerable profit, part of which financed the architectural treasures found on the acropolis. (When the allies complained about wasting funds "gauding up the whore Athens," Pericles reply was to the point: "See any Persians around?") One would, I suspect, have been hard pressed to find before the Peloponnesian War more than a tiny handful of Athenians who did not support the empire. After the outbreak of the conflict there were probably still only very few who advocated surrendering power, but the increasingly aggressive approach to empire did create critics of the system. The most familiar and entertaining of these was Aristophanes, who in general in his comedies enthusiastically satirized the war and in the *Birds* specifically lampooned Athenian imperialism. In this comedy, produced in 414 in the midst of the Sicilian expedition, two Athenians seeking to escape the turmoil of wartime Athens decide to reside among the birds in the air and build a city called Cloud-cuckoo-land. Instead of finding peace, however, they end up ruling over a new empire of the birds and attempting to dominate humanity below and the immortals above. The birds can easily be seen as the Athenian allies, actually helping the Athenians to establish power over themselves, as in fact happened with the Delian League. Appropriately, at the end of the comedy the Athenians and their bird allies celebrate by feasting on birds, just as the Athenians in the real world were devouring their allies in their imperialist adventures.

In the *Birds* Aristophanes is also poking fun at that quality in their character that the Athenians called *polypragmosyne*. This was a kind of restless or nervous energy that drove the Athenians in their varied activities, both good and bad. Aristophanes suggests that the Athenians could not avoid this facet of their character even if they wanted to; the two Athenians who join the birds in their search for peace quite naturally build an empire. The Athenian Empire was a result of *polypragmosyne*; Melos and the Athenians themselves in Sicily were victims of it. This dynamism was the source of Athens' greatness and the reason she became the "school of Hellas." But this same restless energy was also her downfall, leading her to rush and thereby ruin her mission of unifying the Greek world.

# # # # # # # # # # # # # # # # # # # #

SUGGESTED READING

If you want to go to the source on the Athenian Empire, read Thucydides: Book 1.89-117 provides an account of the growth of Athenian power during the period between the Persian War and the great Peloponnesian War. For everything you wanted to know about the empire (600 pages worth), you might try Russell Meiggs, *The Athenian Empire* (1972); Simon Hornblower, *The Athenian Empire* (1988) is a collection in English of all the evidence relating to the empire. And when you have tired of this weighty stuff, take a break with Aristophanes' *Birds* for the anti-imperialist view; once again I recommend the Arrowsmith translation, which pulls no punches.

# # # # # # # # # # # # # # # # # #

IX. WHERE HAVE ALL THE FLOWERS GONE?

THUCYDIDES AND THE OUTBREAK OF WAR

> But then some tipsy, cottabus-playing youths went to Megara
> and kidnapped the whore Simaetha.
> And then the Megarians, garlic-stung by their distress,
> in retaliation stole a couple of Aspasia's whores,
> and from that the onset of war broke forth upon
> all the Greeks: from three sluts!
>
> -Aristophanes *Acharnians* 524-29[22]

As all the talk of war in the last chapter suggests, Athens and Sparta had something of a falling out after the defeat of the Persians. In fact, relations between the two states deteriorated steadily after Plataea, and while Athens was fine-tuning her democracy and building her empire, she was also trading the occasional punch with Sparta and her friends. This sparring erupted in an actual, if somewhat half-hearted war in the 450s and led finally in 431 to the outbreak of the great Peloponnesian War, the championship match that culminated in the ruin of Athens.

The historian of this war and the period leading up to it is Thucydides, the greatest and most modern historian of the ancient world. Born into a wealthy Athenian family around 460, he pursued the expected political career until 424, when he was ostracized, allegedly for failing in his responsibilities as one of the ten *strategoi* for that year. The ostracism was definitely unjust, but Athens' loss was humanity's gain, for Thucydides used his newly imposed free time to write a history of the war. And he turned out to be a far better historian than general, producing not just a lucid account of his times, but also one of the most penetrating studies of society in conflict in all of history.

Though from an aristocratic background, Thucydides was a Periclean democrat, a political inclination that causes him some problems in his analysis of the Athenian democracy. He clearly understands the vital role of democratic forces in Athens' rise to power and unlike Herodotus praises Themistocles, but he is also disenchanted with the more radically minded democracy that emerged after Pericles' death. Indeed, he makes the abandonment of Pericles' defensive strategy and the adoption of expansionist policies his central explanation for Athens' defeat. And he himself was personally affected: his exile in 424 seems the result of his being made a scapegoat for the loss at Delium by the radical imperialist Cleon. Disappointment and bitterness thus soured Thucydides on the post-Periclean democracy, but he could not deny the achievements made in the age of Pericles, when the democratic government was structurally no different. Perhaps betraying a bit of his aristocratic background, he consequently accentuates the role of Pericles over that of the democracy and claims that it was really government by a first citizen, which, as we saw, it of course was not. He would not abandon his hero Pericles, but the experience of the war years turned Thucydides more conservative, and he describes the limited democracy of 5000 citizens proposed in 411 as "not the worst" form of government, indicating that it was certainly better than the radical democracy.

Thucydides' intellectual background appears to have two main components. One is the Hippocratic medical tradition, which for all its nonsense about biles and humors nevertheless instilled in him an inductive or scientific approach to his material and allowed him to write a thoroughly objective account and analysis of the Peloponnesian War. The other is sophism, whose influence can be most easily seen in Thucydides' emphasis on the generic and his search for truths drawn from the observation of human actions. He is writing his history not just to preserve an account of the war and celebrate the deeds of those involved, but to provide something much more important: an understanding of this particular war and of human nature and behavior in all wars. "It will be enough for me, however, if these words of mine are judged useful by those who want to understand clearly the events which happened in the past and which (human nature being what it is) will, at some time or other and in much the same ways, be repeated in the future. My work is not a piece of writing designed to meet the taste of an immediate public, but was done to last for ever." (Thucydides 1.22.4) Thucydides recognizes that though he is writing about a specific war, he is dealing with eternal questions, an understanding of which ought to help one to understand other contexts, other wars in other times and places. More than his careful recording of data, it is this search for general historical truths that makes Thucydides one of the greatest of western historians.

Sophistic input is also obvious in the kinds of arguments Thucydides uses, in the mechanisms he employs to analyze events. The most general is the argument from likelihood, which is based on the assumption that the circumstances and interests of a group determine how that group is likely to act. This involves a somewhat mechanistic view of history that accepts the notion that similar groups of people in similar situations will tend to behave in similar ways, and the study of history has convinced me that this idea is basically true, if not pressed to far. This argument becomes a powerful tool in the hands of Thucydides, who for the first time applies it to classes of people, to understand both how they acted in the past and how they will act in the future. The speakers in his history are constantly predicting what will happen, and Thucydides sees this ability to foresee events as an absolute requirement for an effective leader. And so his history "was done to last for ever," to provide a basis for predicting and understanding the conduct of future wars.

Derived from the argument from likelihood are two, more specific varieties of argument, both used extensively by Thucydides. One is the argument from expediency, which states that a group will tend to act according to their self-interest, which very often means acting in conflict with accepted notions of what is right or just. This is a cynical, but unfortunately reasonable appraisal of human behavior. The second is the argument from *physis*, that is, the assertion that people will tend to act as human nature directs them. This depends of course on how you define human nature – is it all sweetness and light and spark of divinity or is it basically animal? Thucydides' definition is perfectly clear and is most expressly stated in his account of the horrors of the civil war on Corcyra: "Then, with the ordinary conventions of civilized life (*nomos*) thrown into confusion, human nature (*physis*), always ready to offend even where laws exist, showed itself proudly in its true colors, as something incapable of controlling passion, insubordinate to the idea of justice, the enemy to anything superior to itself." (Thucydides 3.84.2) Thucydides (like Euripides and Aristotle; see Chapters XI and XIII) is thus a *nomos* man, believing that the *physis* of human beings is animal and antisocial and only kept in check by the *nomos* of civilized society. And when you look at the sad history of human conflict, especially in the twentieth century, it is extremely hard to disagree with him.

For all his commitment to the general, Thucydides, who is after all a Greek, does not lose sight of the specific and would be a poor historian if he did. As he discovered, truth emerges from a union of the specific and the generic, and in his work the specific is found in the coldly objective narration of events, while the generic is generally brought out in the speeches his characters deliver at critical moments in the history. "My method has been, while keeping as closely as possible to the general sense of the words that were actually used, to make the speaker say what, in my opinion, was called for by each situation." (Thucydides 1.22.1) In other words, the speeches are filled with analysis and judgment and thus provide a balance for the purely factual reporting of the narrative (though of course this approach is very annoying to modern classical historians, who would prefer to know *exactly* what a speaker said). Incidentally, the speeches typically come in pairs, each providing the arguments and reasoning on one side of whatever issue is at hand; this contrasting of opposing arguments, or antilogy, is another sophistic device.

Finally, Thucydides is too clever an historian to allow himself to be carried off the deep end in his appreciation of the vital impersonal forces and develop, as the Marxists have, a too rigidly mechanistic approach to human affairs. He admits the important role that key individuals can play in shaping events, and for him Pericles is clearly one of those pivotal characters. He also recognizes the inexplicable in history, the fact that sometimes the course of things is determined by nothing more than chance. An example is the coincidental eclipse of the moon the night the Athenians were to retreat from Syracuse; this chance event caused the superstitious Athenian commander Nicias (c. 470-413) to delay the withdrawal and thus turn failure into disaster.

As Thucydides informs us, there was little action between Athens and Sparta during the first two decades after the Persian War. There would certainly have been more had the anti-Spartan Themistocles stayed in power, but he was only able to complete the fortification of Athens and her port, the Piraeus, before the conservative, philo-Laconian opposition engineered his ostracism in the late 470s. Led by Cimon, the conservatives then cooperated with the Spartans to chase Themistocles out of Greece altogether, and in one of the great ironies of history the man who had been instrumental in spoiling Xerxes' invasion spent his sunset years as an honored guest of the Great King. The Athenians soon came to regret their actions, however, as the conservatives fell from power and détente with Sparta began to unravel. Matters came to a head in 462, when at the invitation of the Spartans Cimon took a force of 4000 hoplites south to help them capture the mountain stronghold of Ithome, held by revolting helots. Cimon and his men no sooner arrived, though, when the Spartans, probably disturbed by the free thinking, free speaking Athenians, arrogantly informed them that their help was not needed after all. This insult completely sunk the conservatives and their policy of détente, and in the following year Cimon was ostracized and Pericles took over.

When Athens broke with Sparta in 461, she immediately formed a new alliance with Argos, Sparta's next door neighbor and traditional enemy, but this was a pointed message, not an invitation to war. War came out of another and somewhat surprising quarter. In 460 Sparta's two allies at the isthmus, Corinth and Megara, got into a typical border dispute, and the Megarians, fearing that Spartan arbitration would favor the more important Corinthians, took the unexpected step of appealing to Athens for protection. Since occupation of Megara meant complete security against a Peloponnesian invasion, the Athenians were quick to take the deal and promptly found themselves at war with Corinth, Epiduarus and Aegina, commercial competitors of Athens and all members of the Spartan alliance. But where was Sparta? At home; the Spartans were always reluctant to go to war, especially outside the Peloponnesus, and this was a particularly bad time. The helot revolt in Messenia was still not completely cleaned up, Argos was a big threat on her frontier and how could she get the army through Megara anyway? So for the moment Athens was left free to walk all over her lightweight opponents. The job was so easy in fact that the Athenians found the time to send a 200 ship expedition off to help the Egyptians in a revolt against the Great King. Athens was now involved in war on two fronts, a sign of her growing confidence and power. Give us more, said the Athenians.

They got more. The Spartans could not stand idly by forever, watching their credibility crumble as their allies were roughed up by Athens, and with the helot affair in its last stages and Argos still quiet they decided in 457 to move. Over 11,000 hoplites crossed the Corinthian Gulf into central Greece, ostensibly to help the tiny state of Doris, which had been attacked by its neighbor Phocis. The real aims of the expedition, however, were a demonstration of force and aid to Thebes, a Spartan friend and a first rate power when she was able to control the other cities in Boeotia, a situation traditionally opposed by Athens. Having propped up Thebes, the Spartans encountered and defeated the Athenian army at Tanagra, but all they won was a free passage home through Megara. Two months later an Athenian expedition seized all of Boeotia except Thebes, and soon after that the island of Aegina was captured. In that same year the Athenians also completed the long walls (almost four miles of them) linking Athens with the Piraeus, thus creating a kind of super fortress that could be supplied from the sea. Athens was now virtually immune to attack by land.

But she was not immune to misfortune. The Egyptian adventure ended in disaster in 454 with the loss of the original fleet plus most of another fifty vessel relief force and led to troubles in the empire (and provided the excuse for moving the Delian treasury to the Athenian acropolis). In 451 Argos backed out of her alliance with Athens and signed a thirty years peace with Sparta, but fortunately for the Athenians Sparta was willing to sign a five year truce, freeing Athens to deal with her imperial problems. Meanwhile, the

Great King, who had his own difficulties, was ready to be reasonable, and around 449 Athens and Persia initialed an agreement, the Peace of Callias, by which they promised to keep out of each other's way. Then, in 446 central Greece exploded. The Athenians lost the battle of Coronea and consequently all of Boeotia, with Spartan aid Megara returned to the League, and all the Athenian allies on Euboea revolted. But Pericles was in charge; he reduced the Euboean cities, which were an important source of grain for Athens, and wrote off the continental possessions, the control of which he had never supported.

Athens and Sparta were both now more than ready for peace, and in the winter of 446/5 they and their allies signed the Thirty Years Peace, which was pretty much a recognition of the status quo. Athens gave up Megara and central Greece, which she no longer controlled anyway, but kept Aegina as part of her empire. The two power blocks agreed not to interfere with one another's allies and granted the right of any neutral to sign up with either alliance in the future. The special position of Argos was recognized, and she was prohibited from joining either side. The Peace was realistic in that it accepted the world the way it was, but it did leave some problems unresolved. Athens and Sparta had every interest in maintaining peace, but there were those who did not. Aegina was certainly unhappy as a new subject of her age-old enemy, and the Corinthians now hated the Athenians, who had developed a stronger presence in the Saronic and Corinthian Gulfs, to the detriment of Corinth's trade. Thebes, now firmly in control of Boeotia, was apparently itching to use her new strength against her old enemy Athens. The Peace offered plenty of room for future friction.

For all her losses Athens emerged from the first Peloponnesian War in better shape than she had been previously. She now had a much tighter grip on her empire, and it had been recognized tacitly by the Great King and formally by Sparta. She had expanded her influence west into the Corinthian Gulf, and that old nuisance Aegina was completely under her control. And the war had discredited the policy of continental imperialism, to which Pericles had been opposed from the start, leaving our man even more firmly in the saddle. In fact, Pericles never again faced serious opposition to his leadership; that his political opponents found it necessary to attack his friends, such as the philosopher Anaxagoras and the sculptor Phidias (d. c. 430), bears witness to the security of his position. His foreign policy in the decade following the war was one of coexistence with Sparta and the peaceful development of the empire. There was no attempt to expand Athenian power beyond its present geographical limits, and the foundation in 443 of the Panhellenic colony of Thurii in southern Italy was less of an attempt to extend Athenian influence to the west than a clever reply to foreign and domestic critics of Athens' imperialism. The war had confirmed for Pericles the convictions that the development of Athenian hegemony should not be rushed and that there was little to be gained by provoking Sparta. Besides, Athens was a commercial state, and war was bad for business. The longer general peace prevailed in the Greek world, the stronger Athens would become relative to her potential adversaries. But it was not Pericles' intention that peace be preserved at any cost, and during the crisis and confrontation with Sparta in the late thirties Athens would demonstrate a firm resolve to defend her rights even at the risk of war.

The second Peloponnesian War, like many major conflicts in history, had its origins in seemingly unimportant events occurring in a distant and obscure locale. In 435 factional strife came to a head in Epidamnus, which being on the coast of modern Albania certainly qualified as distant and obscure from the Greek point of view. The democratic faction appealed to Epidamnus' mother-city, Corcyra (modern Corfu), which was, however, not interested in getting involved, preferring to let both sides in the civil war grind each other away before stepping in. The democrats then turned to Corinth, mother-city of Corcyra, and the Corinthians, delighted by the opportunity to get their fingers back into the lucrative Adriatic commercial pie, immediately sent troops and colonists. The Corcyraeans saw this as interference in their sphere of influence, and mother and daughter poleis were at war. As owner and operator of a fleet second only to the Athenian, Corcyra easily crushed a Corinthian expedition, but began to get nervous when Corinth began building a far larger navy and more threatening, calling on her Peloponnesian allies for help. A neutral state with no allies of her own, Corcyra decided it was time to obtain some and sent an embassy to Athens in 433.

The Corcyraeans pointed out to the Athenian assembly that an alliance would bring Athens economic benefits in the west and more important, the Corcyraean fleet. War between Athens and Sparta was coming sooner or later, they argued, and it was clearly better that Athens should add the Corcyraean fleet to her own rather than see it destroyed or captured by her enemies. Against this, the Corinthian embassy sent to counter the Corcyraeans could only mention past services and argue that an alliance would in fact bring on a general war. The advantages of a closer relationship with Corcyra did seem attractive to Athens, and after a hot debate the assembly voted a strictly defensive alliance, the first known of among the Greeks. Since Corcyra had been a neutral power the alliance did not violate the exact terms of the Thirty Years Peace, but this particular neutral was already at war with a member of the opposing block, so the Athenians moved cautiously. The alliance required them only to defend Corcyra itself, and the two squadrons they immediately sent west totaled only thirty ships. Towards the end of the year there was a full-scale battle between the Corcyraean and Corinthian navies at Sybota, near Corcyra, and the Athenian vessels interfered only at the last minute to prevent a Corcyraean defeat. The Athenians had acted properly throughout, but the bottom line was that they had fought Corinthians at Sybota, and Corinth was an ally of Sparta.

The Athenians knew full well that it took more than a few dead Corinthians to drag Sparta into a major war, but it seemed prudent in any case to see that everything in the empire was shipshape. Pericles looked about the Aegean and fixed immediately upon the city of Potidaea on the north coast. Potidaea was a tribute paying member of the empire, but she was also originally settled from Corinth and oddly enough still received her annual magistrates from her mother-city. In the circumstances this situation was not only bizarre, but also obviously potentially dangerous, especially in view of thinly veiled threats made by the Corinthians during the debate in Athens. In the winter after Sybota, then, the Athenians quite understandably asked the Potidaeans to tear down their walls and stop admitting Corinthian magistrates. Convinced by a secret Spartan pledge to invade Attica, Potidaea instead revolted, taking the unprepared Athenians completely by surprise. The promised invasion of course did not occur, but Corinth sent 2000 "volunteers" into Potidaea. Such unofficial action was necessary to avoid giving Athens formal grounds for declaring war, something Corinth certainly did not want until she had Sparta firmly behind her. (One is reminded of American "advisors" being sent into various countries.) The Corinthians are now beginning to realize that unless they are able to convince Sparta to back them up with the Peloponnesian League further confrontation with Athens and Corcyra could lead to disaster.

Later in 432 Athens took an interesting step; the assembly passed a clutch of decrees barring the Megarians, who had sent ships to Sybota, from the ports and marketplaces of the empire. This measure hardly ruined Megara's trade, since her merchants could act through agents, but it was a nuisance and something of an embarrassment for the commercialist oligarchy that governed the country. The point of the Megarian Decrees (which is hotly debated by scholars) seems to have been just that: to deliver to the Megarian leadership an annoying blow without committing an act of war. Pericles also wanted Corinth's Peloponnesian friends to understand that while Athens was not looking for a war, she was not to be trifled with, and in particular he had in mind the Spartans, since it was they who would ultimately decide whether or not Corinth could pursue her reckless course. With many friends at Sparta, including Archidamus II (469-427), the senior king, Pericles knew that there was strong support for Sparta's traditional conservative approach to war outside the Peloponnesus. His intention was to supply the conservatives with more ammunition by providing a gentle reminder of Athens' unprecedented economic power and making it perfectly clear that she was taking a strong stance. As it happened, however, Pericles' appreciation of the situation in Sparta was based on the older generation, which had experienced war with Athens back in the fifties. The younger generation, enthusiastic for war, read Athenian actions not as a warning, but rather as a challenge, and Athenian restraint as a sign of weakness.

In the summer of 432 Corinth, becoming desperate, joined the other Peloponnesian allies at Sparta in order to drum up support and influence the Spartans. There was clearly some sentiment for war at Sparta, but there was also a great deal of suspicion of the Corinthians, who after all had dragged Sparta into a scrap with Athens only twenty years earlier. Since Athens had not actually violated the Thirty Years Peace, which in fact required the current dispute to be arbitrated, Corinth could only harp on the general growth of Athenian power and how that was a threat to Sparta. She also hinted at seeking "some other alliance," but this was an empty threat, since Argos was the only significant neutral state and the Argives had shown no inclination to break their peace with Sparta.

The Corinthian charges were answered by Athenian ambassadors unofficially present at the meeting. They declined to debate specifics, but instead defended the Athenian Empire and its activities and generally delivered the Periclean line: "Think twice before you get involved with us!" This sentiment was echoed by king Archidamus, who warned the Spartans that confronting Athenian naval and economic power would be a mammoth task, one for which they were at the moment totally unprepared. Unlike most of his countrymen he understood the nature of Athenian power and her invulnerability to traditional methods of Greek warfare and spoke prophetically to that point: "For we must not bolster ourselves up with the false hope that if we devastate their land, the war will soon be over. I fear it is more likely that we shall be leaving it to our children after us." (Thucydides 1.81.6) And this is exactly what came to pass. Reason and caution were overcome by fear and resentment, and after stirring up these emotions with a rabble-rousing speech to the Spartan assembly the ephor Sthenelaides pushed a vote on the issue. By a large majority the Spartans decided on war.

Sparta later called an official meeting of the Peloponnesian League in order to convince her allies that they really did want to go to war, and she engaged in some last minute diplomatic maneuverings, designed, it seems, to buy some time and shift the blame for the war to the Athenians. She demanded that the Athenians "drive out the curse of the goddess," referring to a curse that had been incurred by the Alcmaeonid family back during he conspiracy of Cylon (another example of a ritual pollution). Pericles was an

Alcmaeonid, and the demand was a pathetic attempt to discredit him. Not to be outdone, Squill Head doubled the ante and demanded that the Spartans drive out the curse of Taenarus and the curse of Athena of the Brazen House, thus delivering a clever warning to the Spartans. Taenarus was connected with a helot revolt and the Brazen House with the anti-government conspiracy and death of Pausanias, victor of Plataea, and the curses thus served as a reminder of the unpleasant things that could happen to Sparta if she got involved outside the Peloponnesus. In what was probably the last gasp of Archidamus and the peace faction Athens was then informed that war could be avoided if she lifted the siege of Potidaea, rescinded the Megarian Decrees and granted autonomy to Aegina, but Pericles was not about to buy peace at the cost of allowing Spartan meddling in Athenian imperial affairs and the bid was refused. Sparta then laconically informed the Athenians: "Sparta wants peace. Peace is still possible if you will give the Hellenes their freedom." (Thucydides 1.139.3) This obviously signaled the end of any serious negotiations, and in the spring of the following year Archidamus led the Peloponnesian levy north.

Unlike Herodotus, Thucydides does not confuse the events leading to the outbreak of hostilities with the real cause of the war: "What made war inevitable was the growth of Athenian power and the fear which this caused in Sparta." (Thucydides 1.23.6) Well, the Athenian Empire in 432 was no bigger than it had been at the end of the last war, but it was in fact stronger. Athenian control of her subjects was much tighter, and the years of peace had allowed the accumulation of a huge financial reserve. Pericles had not pursued aggressive or expansionist policies, but events like the foundation of Thurii and the crushing of the Samian revolt in 440-439 made it easier to believe Corinthian arguments that he had. However peacefully Athens might be acting, the inescapable fact was that relative to Sparta and the other Greeks her power in the 430s was truly overwhelming, and Corinthian propaganda about the Athenian threat was readily swallowed. The Corcyraean alliance and the Potidaean affair, reasonable actions on the part of Athens, were portrayed as threatening to Spartan interests, and it took no great effort to depict the Megarian Decrees as an attack on the Peloponnesian alliance.

Blame for the outbreak of the war must be laid squarely at Corinth's door. Athenian conduct during the crisis was entirely proper and legal, if ultimately unsuccessful in preventing war, whereas Corinth blatantly violated the Thirty Years Peace by sending aid to Potidaea. More important, Corinth was reckless and selfish enough to drag Greece into a general war in order to settle her private quarrels. That she was dissatisfied with the settlement of 446 and running scared from Athenian commercial expansion perhaps explains, but hardly justifies her goading Sparta into starting Greece's version of World War I. True, there was apparently substantial enthusiasm for war in Sparta, but even had that not been the case Sparta would have had to come to the rescue sooner or later if Corinth continued on her current course. As in the previous war, she could not sit quietly by and watch her most important Peloponnesian ally go down to defeat; that would undermine the whole structure of the Peloponnesian League.

Is Thucydides correct in his explanation? Essentially he is. It was the actions of Corinth that brought about war in 431, but the growth of Athenian power created the atmosphere that made Sparta more receptive to Corinthian prodding. Obviously, it was not inevitable that war break out in 431; had there been no civil strife in Epidamnus, the whole chain of events would not have occurred. But the growth of the Athenian Empire pretty much divided the Greek world into two power blocks, and while Athens had no reason to threaten Sparta directly and Sparta traditionally had little concern for affairs outside the Peloponnesus, it was almost inevitable that friction should occur between their subordinates. Strife between neighbors had been a tradition for centuries, and while prudent behavior might prevent local conflicts from developing into a general war, the Greek polis was certainly never noted for prudent behavior. War was an accepted part of life in the polis, and lacking nuclear arsenals, Athens and Sparta were not scared into peaceful coexistence by the threat of mutually assured destruction.

###################

SUGGESTED READING

The best way of course to encounter Thucydides is to read some of his history, and Book I deals with the events discussed in this chapter. Far and away the best introductory book on Thucydides and his work is still John Finley, Jr., *Thucydides* (1963); I highly recommend this book for an understanding of not just Thucydides but also the war itself. W.R. Connor, *Thucydides* (1984) provides a good book by book examination of the historian. On the outbreak of the war go to Donald Kagan, *The Outbreak of the Peloponnesian War* (1969), an eminently readable and sensible account (even though I disagree with some of his analysis of the causes).

# # # # # # # # # # # # # # # # # # #

X. ATHENS IN VIETNAM

THE PELOPONNESIAN WAR

But the women won't even let us touch their pussy,
until we all establish a common peace
for all of Greece.

-Aristophanes *Lysistrata* 1004-6[23]

Now we can see it clearly – like the light at the end of a tunnel.

-General Henri Navarre

Athens began the war with immense advantages. Her control of the sea was virtually absolute, which meant that the enemy was going to have a hell of time just getting at her and her allies. The completion of the long walls linking the city with the port of Piraeus had turned Athens into a kind of artificial island, rendering her immune to the traditional strategy of laying waste the enemy's territory and forcing them to come out and fight. So long as the fleet could protect the grain ships sailing in from the Black Sea, the city itself would be secure. Offensively, the navy provided the Athenians with a big edge in rapid troop deployment and threatened the Peloponnesians with surprise raids on their coastal areas. Athens also had unprecedented economic resources from her imperial income and her trade and went into the conflict with something unheard of in Greece: a financial reserve. And finally there was the open and democratic nature of Athenian society, which had already made her preeminent in human resources, out-producing other poleis in leadership, talent and imagination. The democracy could, however, become a liability if the Athenians did not guard against the weaknesses of divisiveness and shortsightedness.

The Peloponnesians had but a single advantage over the Athenians – they were overwhelmingly powerful on land. In every other respect they were hurting. Any fleet they might scrape together would be dramatically outnumbered and out-rowed (the main pool of skilled rowers was within the Athenian Empire), and the alliance was financially unprepared to launch and maintain many more ships. And under the leadership of the Spartans, who did not even use coined money, that financial picture was not likely to change in the near future. Lack of an effective fleet meant that the Peloponnesians would not be able to stir up trouble among the Athenian allies, but it is unlikely that this concerned most Spartans, since they had never had any use for the sea and their notion of warfare did not extend beyond crashing hoplites. This suggests a further big disadvantage for the Peloponnesians: Spartan leadership. A system geared to the status quo and limited mental horizons only rarely produces leaders of more than plodding ability, and Sparta's traditional insularity and policy-bending paranoia about the helots might also be expected to hamper the war effort. But blinding many to these serious weaknesses was the centuries old Spartan reputation as the alpha male of Greece, and there was widespread belief that ships and money and newfangled ideas would not save Athens from the juggernaut of the Spartan led Peloponnesian levy.

Pericles knew better, and in this classic situation of a naval versus a land power he had a plan that would employ Athens' strengths and nullify the Spartan ground attack. He intended to fight a new kind of war, one for which only Athens was in any way prepared – a war of attrition. Pericles was concerned simply with the preservation of Athenian interests, not the utter defeat of Sparta, which meant that Athens could achieve her victory by remaining on the defensive. This he proposed to do by evacuating the population to the Athens-Piraeus fortress and temporarily abandoning Attica whenever the Peloponnesians invaded. Supplied from the sea and rich farmlands near the city, which could be ravaged only at great risk, Athens could theoretically hold out indefinitely, while the fleet conducted raids on the enemy coasts to remind them of the price of war. Pericles figured that after a few years of spending their summers in Attica and accomplishing nothing most of the Peloponnesians would lose whatever little interest they had in the first place, and the war would fizzle to an end.

Predictably, in the summer of 431 king Archidamus led two thirds of the Peloponnesian levy north and ravaged Attica, and nothing happened. Pericles' biggest problem in fact was preventing the outraged Athenians from marching out to meet the enemy, and the operations of the fleet around the Peloponnesus were as much to boost Athenian morale as to pressure Sparta's allies. Unable to think of anything better to do, the Spartans came again the following year and tore up more real estate, but this time the Athenians hardly noticed, because fortune had thrown them a curve in the form of the so-called plague. Possibly some form of epidemic typhus and/or cholera brought on by the urban crowding, the contagion ravaged the city and fleet and carried off perhaps as much as a quarter of the population. This was a heavy enough blow, but worse, in 429 the disease struck Pericles, and with his death came the demise of his careful plan for winning the war.

Would the plan have worked? Probably, had the Athenians stuck to it a few years longer. The strategy imposed a terrific strain on the finances and especially the morale of Athens, but by 429 the worst seemed to be past. Potidaea had finally fallen in 430, ending the biggest drain on the treasury, and the loss of life from the disease, which was in its last stages, apparently had not materially affected Athens' defensive posture. The initial demoralizing shock of the enemy devastation and the plague, reflected in 430 in a spurned peace offer to Sparta, had now been digested, and Pericles, who had actually been thrown out of office in 430, was back in charge. There was no sign that the Spartans, encouraged by the peace offer and the carnage in Athens, were about to quit, but in almost three years of war all they had accomplished was the destruction of a lot of Athenian produce. The Athenians had emerged from the ordeal of these initial war years with wall, fleet, empire and morale intact, and it was improbable that they would be so sorely tested again. There was nothing to prevent Athens from following the Periclean strategy for many more years, and it is hard to see how Sparta could sustain interest, especially among her allies, in a war that was making no real headway and bringing Athenian raids down on the Peloponnesus.

But we will never know, because Pericles died, and without his restraining hand Athens' strength, her democracy, gradually became her downfall. The cautious defensive strategy steadily evolved into an offensive one, and the goal of the war became the defeat of Sparta and the expansion of the empire. This would have been dangerous enough, but the democracy itself began to undermine the war effort, producing a new kind of democratic politician, the demagogues, men of mostly limited abilities who rose to power in the assembly by advocating a war of conquest. This led to a growing number of bad decisions and ill considered strategies and created threatening divisions in Athenian society, as the increasingly radical democracy struggled to manage a people becoming intoxicated with their own power.

The first phase of the conflict, from 431 to 421, is known as the Archidamian War, an ironic distinction for the Spartan king who had argued against it. In the wake of Pericles' death new leaders and policies quickly appeared, and in 426 Demosthenes, one of Athens' better generals, is leading a land expedition into Aetolia in western Greece, exactly the kind of thing Pericles wanted to avoid. It was a failure, but not a disastrous one. Demosthenes' aggressive strategy was supported by the first of the demagogues, the radical imperialist Cleon, whose political power lay in his control of the assembly rather than in the traditional mechanism of the generalship. These hawks were opposed by the wealthy conservative Nicias, a man of less than mediocre abilities, but utterly patriotic and very influential.

But Nicias wasn't influential enough to prevent a major escalation of the war in 425. An Athenian fleet on its way to Corcyra, where a bloody civil war was raging, was forced by weather into Pylos on the west coast of the Peloponnesus, and Demosthenes took the opportunity to seize and fortify the place, while the bulk of the fleet continued on. Sparta responded with attacks on Pylos and the incredibly stupid move of occupying the island of Sphacteria immediately to the south. When the Athenian fleet returned, it easily defeated a Peloponnesian squadron and blockaded the island. The Spartans immediately sued for peace, but under the influence of Cleon the assembly rejected the offer and sent the demagogue himself to capture the island's defenders. Chance then intervened once again: an accidental fire burned all the cover from the island, revealing the small number of the enemy and their location and making an assault feasible. The victory was actually Demosthenes' work, but Cleon got all the credit when the surviving garrison of 292 hoplites, 120 of them full Spartans, surrendered.

Yes, you heard correctly: *surrendered.* Never before in history had Spartans given themselves up, and Athens went crazy. Cleon was cemented in power, and the Athenians went on a roll, rejecting all peace overtures. Defensive war was forgotten, and in 424 they invaded Megara and Boeotia, reversing completely the policy of Pericles. The Megarian campaign was partly successful, but the Boeotian invasion culminated in a decisive defeat at Delium. And to make matters worse, in that same year a lone, uncharacteristically enterprising Spartan, Brasidas, engineered the revolt of several Athenian allies in Thrace (the area north of the Aegean) and captured Amphipolis, which guarded the land route to the vital Hellespont and Athens' food supply. This loss so frightened the Athenians that in the following year they agreed to a truce. They also incidentally ostracized Thucydides, who had been given inadequate forces to protect the entire northern coast and was now made a scapegoat for Cleon's failure in Boeotia.

The Spartans were ready for peace, despite the successes of Brasidas, who in fact excited envy and suspicion among his more narrow-minded countrymen. The Athenian base at Pylos was a magnet for revolting helots, and concern about the captives from Sphacteria was so great that the annual invasions of Attica had been called off. Cleon was probably right in urging that the Thracian situation be cleaned up first, since that would allow Athens to negotiate from a far stronger position, but in the wake of Delium the Athenians were beginning to think peace. During the year of the truce, however, affairs in Thrace deteriorated further, as Brasidas continued to act independently of Sparta, and in 422 Cleon and his inflated reputation as a general were sent north. In the ensuing battle for Amphipolis the Athenians and their inexperienced commander were routed, but in the course of the struggle both Cleon and Brasidas were killed, clearing the way for peace negotiations.

The Peace of Nicias, signed in 421, had about as much chance of success as the Munich agreement of AD 1938. Basically, the belligerents agreed to return to one another the prisoners and most of the places they had captured, especially Pylos and Amphipolis. But while Athens and Sparta were ready to beat their swords into plowshares, Sparta's strongest allies, Corinth, Megara, Elis and the Boeotian cities, were dissatisfied with the terms and refused to join the peace. To make matters more complex, Corinth, Elis and Mantinea formed a separate alliance with the Thracian cities that had revolted from Athens and with Argos, whose thirty year peace with Sparta had just expired. Meanwhile, the Spartans were realizing that returning Amphipolis, which they did not control, would be a tough proposition, and in order to prod the Athenians, who were understandably balking at filling their end of the bargain, they formed a defensive alliance with Athens. Nicias then foolishly surrendered the Sphacterian prisoners, the most valuable card in Athens' hand, and the Spartans could now breathe a little easier as they turned their attention to shoring up their crumbling alliance.

The next few years are a study in diplomatic confusion. Though now an ally of Athens, Sparta secretly reaffirmed her alliance with the Boeotians, who were still technically at war with the Athenians, who in turn allied themselves with Argos, Elis and Mantinea, thus driving Corinth and the Thracian cities back to Sparta. With the utter failure of the peace the war faction regained power in Sparta and Nicias was discredited in Athens, momentarily losing power to the latest hawk, Alcibiades, who urged a vigorous anti-Spartan policy in the Peloponnesus. The ultimate result of all this maneuvering came in 418 with the first battle of Mantinea, in which the Spartans virtually single-handedly defeated the Athenian coalition and thus restored overnight their injured prestige and their position in the Peloponnesus. The war was back on – in a way.

The primary reason for the allied defeat at Mantinea was insufficient support from the Athenians, who were having a hard time deciding between the policies of Nicias and Alcibiades. Athens was war-weary and the older generation in particular was getting fed up, but Nicias' failures and Sparta's successes had weakened the position of the peace faction, while the hawks had gained a most valuable asset: Alcibiades. Kinsman and protégé of Pericles, he was wealthy, intelligent, talented, beautiful and utterly amoral and self-interested – the perfect politician. He was a close friend of Socrates, and the device he bore on his shield was Eros, which provides some idea of his view of life. He was the darling of the younger generation, who enthusiastically supported his call for more war and the expansion of the empire, which he himself saw as the road to supreme power in the Athenian state.

After Mantinea Alcibiades got the upper hand, and in order to pump up war enthusiasm and convince the Athenians they were still "standing tall" (like Ronald Reagan's invasion of Grenada in AD 1983) in 416 he led the expedition against Melos described in the last chapter. The easy victory over the Melians coincided with a much more fateful development: an appeal for aid from the allied cities of Segesta and Leontini in Sicily. Since the middle of the sixth century the Sicilian Greeks had been struggling with Carthage, a Phoenician colony in North Africa, for control of the island and had won a decisive victory at Himera in 480 (see Chapter XIV). In the half century since then Syracuse had emerged as the strongest polis on the island an in 424 had declared a sort of Monroe Doctrine for Sicily and begun pressuring the Athenian allies. In response to the appeal the Athenians, now under the influence of Alcibiades and his imperial dreams, voted to send a massive force to capture Syracuse and the rest of the island. Nicias was far too clever in his opposition, and the assembly responded to his dire warnings by increasing the size of the expedition rather than canceling it. Incredibly, the same assembly then appointed Nicias a co-commander with Alcibiades and the political nonentity Lamachus, which was like teaming Ted Kennedy with John McCain for an invasion of Iraq. Panels of generals with equal powers were standard Greek practice, but this was a recipe for disaster if there ever was one.

In the early summer of 415, 134 triremes and a host of smaller vessels set sail for Sicily, carrying over 30,000 fighting men. And no sooner had they arrived at the island than Alcibiades was recalled to Athens to stand trial for impiety, charged with the mutilation of the Herms. These were short columns sporting a bust of Hermes and a phallus and stood on street corners and in front of temples and houses as symbols of good fortune. Just before the expedition had sailed, Athenians had awaked to discover all the Herms in the city had been mutilated, an outrage akin to the desecration of a church or mosque. Alcibiades certainly had few religious scruples, but the whole affair was clearly a political frame-up, and he well knew that with so many of his supporters in Sicily with the expedition he would surely be convicted by his enemies in Athens. So he fled to Sparta. There he advised the Spartans to reopen the war against Athens by sending a Spartan commander to Syracuse and establishing a fortified post in Attica, both of which were ultimately done. Who could know exactly what Alcibiades had in mind, but events suggest his goal was to help Sparta bring Athens to her knees and then return to his native city to lead her back to power. At any rate, that is the way things worked out.

Meanwhile, back in Sicily things went steadily sour. In his reluctance to go through with what were really Alcibiades' plans, Nicias wasted a great deal of time sailing back and forth before he began the siege of Syracuse, and then in 414 Lamachus was killed, leaving the fate of the expedition in the less than competent hands of its surviving commander. In 413 Athens sent out a relief force of another 73 triremes and perhaps 20,000 men under the command of reliable old Demosthenes. He took a final desperate shot at the Syracusan defenses, and when that failed he urged abandoning what was now a lost cause and immediately withdrawing. After some delay Nicias was finally convinced, but then the fateful eclipse of the moon occurred and the superstitious Nicias insisted on waiting the prescribed four weeks before moving. This delay gave the Syracusans time to defeat the Athenian fleet and force the expedition to attempt a retreat by land, its morale completely shattered. After great slaughter the army finally surrendered, and few survived the ensuing imprisonment in the quarries of Syracuse. Nicias and Demosthenes were executed.

Athens had certainly stabbed herself in the foot. Immediate action against Syracuse, even under the uninspired leadership of Nicias would have led to the capture of that city and almost certainly the entire island. Whether the Athenians could have held on to all this distant real estate is another question, but instead of gaining new imperial possessions, they created a disaster that led to the loss of the old. Back at home the war moved into high gear again, as the Spartans took Alcibiades' advice and fortified Decelea in Attica, thus putting the Athenians under year round pressure. This second phase of the war is variously known as the Decelean, after the fortified post, or the Ionian, after the fact that most of the action took place in Ionian waters.

In 412 the Syracusan bill came due. Emboldened by the disaster in Sicily, the allies began revolting in droves, and even worse, Sparta signed an alliance with Persia, which possessed a seemingly endless supply of money. Persian gold meant a Spartan fleet, which meant in turn a spread of the revolt and a threat to the security of Athens itself. The Persians may have been militarily helpless, but they were not stupid and knew that the defeat of Athens would almost certainly lead to the reestablishment of their power in Ionia. And the Spartans were of course prepared to sell the Ionian Greeks down the river in order to win Persian aid. In the midst of all this, incidentally, was Alcibiades, playing a double game as he negotiated not only with the Persians, but also the Athenians. The time was growing ripe for his homecoming, and in any case life in Sparta, uncomfortable at best, had become a little dangerous after his seduction of the wife of the absent king Agis II (427-399).

With the loss of so many radical democratic *thetes* (all those rowers) in Sicily and the absence of so many more, stationed with the surviving fleet at Samos, the conservatives in Athens were able to push for the creation of a limited democracy of 5000 citizens. Unfortunately, the extremists got the upper hand, and in 411 what Athens got in place of the radical democracy was a narrow oligarchy of 400. This was the darkest hour. Athens was on the verge of civil war, with the fleet and army at Samos hostile to the Four Hundred, almost all the empire except Samos was in revolt, and Persia was now funding the enemy effort. But characteristically Sparta took no advantage of the moment, and Alcibiades convinced the fleet not to sail against the oligarchs, who were overthrown after three months by the moderates. The unlimited democracy was restored in 410, and during these years Alcibiades, elected general by the Athenian forces at Samos, led the fleet to victory after victory, restoring almost completely the Athenian position in the Aegean. In 407 the one-time exile returned home, sailing into the Piraeus to a triumphant welcome.

But the Athenians seemed bent on self-destruction. They turned down peace offers from Sparta, and in 406 they threw out Alcibiades for some imagined failure. The Spartans, meanwhile, finally came up with a good admiral for their new fleet, Lysander, another of those rare Spartans of ability and imagination. Things turned against Athens again, and in 405 she lost her last fleet at the battle of Aegospotomi in the Hellespont and with the city under siege had no choice but to surrender in 404. Corinth and Thebes demanded her complete destruction, but Lysander realized Sparta needed some counterweight to Theban power in central Greece. So Athens survived, but stripped of her fleet, her walls, her possessions and even her democratic government. A group of oligarchic extremists, led by our friend Critias and remembered as the Thirty Tyrants, took over with the help of Lysander. The exiled Alcibiades, perceived as a danger by just about everyone in the eastern Mediterranean, was assassinated on Lysander's orders.

The Athenian democracy had failed. Despite an immense superiority in resources and talent Athens had found herself unable to put an end to the war and after twenty-seven years of struggle had lost everything, including her democratic government. How could this happen? For Thucydides the answer is clear. The way of life fostered by the democracy was a source of powerful forces, but it took a capable leader to control and direct these forces, to restrain the people and channel their energies towards realistic ends. Pericles was of course this kind of leader, able and patriotic, and Athens' misfortune was that after his death the democracy found no one who combined these two qualities. Nicias was utterly devoted to his country, but left a lot to be desired as an able leader. Alcibiades was one of the most talented men ever to capture the support of the people, but really cared about only one thing – Alcibiades.

The death of Pericles meant the death of his careful plan for winning the war and the beginning of Athens' troubles. "His successors, who were more on a level with each other and each of whom aimed at occupying the first place, adopted methods of demagogy which resulted in their losing control over the actual conduct of affairs. Such a policy, in a great city with an empire to govern, naturally led to a number of mistakes..." (Thucydides 2.65.10-11) Indeed. The prosecution of the war, the foreign policy of the state became more and more a reflection of internal politics, as Athens became the prey of demagogues, who rose to power by advocating a war of conquest. Time and again the Athenians passed up opportunities to end the conflict as winners in order to try instead for a vastly greater victory. And time and again these attempts to grasp more were ruined not by the strength of the enemy, but by the Athenians themselves, as the political feuding created dangerous cracks in the democracy. This domestic disunity was bad enough, leading ultimately to oligarchic revolution, but the cracks also showed themselves in the conduct of the war, in divided leadership of campaigns, inadequate support of expeditions and sudden reversals of policy. That this could be disastrous is amply demonstrated by the Sicilian adventure.

I am inclined to agree with Thucydides. Athens in the second half of the fifth century was simply under too much stress and faced with too many temptations to survive without the restraining hand of a leader like Pericles. And it was clearly a question only of guidance, for the democracy – the common people who voted every important policy decision – constantly showed itself to be perhaps the most aware and able body politic in history. It was after all Athens that lost the war, not Sparta that won it. Their own worst enemy, the Athenians bounced back again and again after each new disaster, revealing the nature of the human resources shaped by a democratic society. "And yet, after losing most of their fleet and all the other forces in Sicily, with revolution already breaking out in Athens, they none the less held out for eight years against their original enemies, who were now reinforced by the Sicilians, against their own allies, most of which had revolted, and against Cyrus, son of the King of Persia, who later joined the other side and provided the Peloponnesians with money for their fleet." (Thucydides 2.65.12) The Athenians and their experiences in the Peloponnesian War are a powerful testament to both the weaknesses and strengths of democratic government.

But before coming to conclusions concerning other democracies, one must bear in mind the particular nature of the Athenian version, which involved the direct and immediate participation of the citizen body. The Athenian people governed in the fullest sense of the word, and because of this they were very highly politicized. Our modern democracy is too big, too complex and too distant, and while, we, the people, ultimately have control, we really take no part in the government, especially at the national level. Consequently, we are not presented with the temptations of power, and our political assemblies and offices are for the most part filled with professionals, all of which adds a greater degree of conservatism and stability to our system. This of course has its own dangers. In Athens the problem was that the will of the people, enjoying complete control, would lead the state down dangerous paths; in our case it is that the government, no longer responding to the will of the people, will nevertheless lead the state down dangerous paths, as it in fact has.

While suffering the political difficulties, the Athenian democracy also underwent during the war a moral crisis, which was both cause and result of the political trials. This was the period when the radical sophists, men like Critias and Thrasymachus, were attacking the democracy and its egalitarian notions. Instead of the people they would see as rulers those who were by nature suited to rule – the "superior men" – and in place of the democracy they would have a narrow oligarchy. Well, after the disasters of the latter part of the war people began to listen to these characters, whose ideas on power had already influenced foreign policy, as Melos demonstrated. Reasonable and moderate men were losing faith in the democracy and becoming more attentive to these extremists at the other end of the political spectrum. Germany in the twenties and thirties saw a similar development, as moderate middle class Germans reacted to the perceived failures of the Weimar government and the threat from the left by paying greater heed to the far right.

As seen in an earlier chapter, the ideas of these sophists on the nature of justice – that might made right – fit perfectly with the growing will to power and empire among the Athenians. As the war continued the means slowly became the end for the Athenian people, as demagogic factionalism and the temptations of power combined to drive them to extremes. Pericles' simple defense of the empire was forgotten, and victory gradually became instead the grasping of more, the expansion of power and the total defeat of Sparta. Rather than what they might bring, success and power themselves became the real goal of the Athenians. At the same time the continuation of the war produced among the Athenians a growing sense of frustration because of their seeming inability to bring it to an end. When they were losing, the quality and strength of their national character compelled them to fight their way back, and when they were winning, that same character seduced them into reaching for more. Athens had the power and the resources to carry on the war, even after a disaster like Sicily, but she could not stop it. And this frustration further aggravated the problem, driving the Athenian people to seek even more urgently that light at the end of the tunnel, that final victory that would solve all their problems. It might be fair to label the response of Athens to this frustration, her continued and amplified operations of war, as acts of collective hysteria. This is the tragedy of a people being destroyed by their own greatness.

All of these things – the political turmoil, the frustrations, the national hysteria – were accompanied, perhaps inevitably, by a steady moral disintegration. As the war dragged on there was a growing loss of respect for authority and the moral traditions of the community, indications of a loss of faith in the society as a whole. The war certainly contributed to this moral breakdown, especially through the psychic conditions – the uncertainties, the alternating hopes and fears, the frustrations – it imposed on the Athenians, but the far more important cause was sophism. As you will recall, part of the impact of sophistic skepticism was the general erosion of accepted tradition and its authority, which of course undermined traditional morality. If it is all relative anyway, why necessarily accept the *nomos* of your fathers? Their values and standards of behavior may not be pertinent to your situation, and perhaps you should look instead to *physis*. Of course, the appeal to natural law can be mighty dangerous for the social fabric, as loathsome characters like Critias and Thrasymachus demonstrated.

This erosion of traditional morality in Athens can be seen reflected in the comedies of Aristophanes, who was clearly opposed to both the war and sophism. He makes his points by creating absurd, but familiar worlds in which traditional values fail and alienated heroes attempt to achieve antisocially what they cannot achieve socially. In the *Clouds* he of course attacks sophism head on with his wonderful image of Socrates and his Thinkery, but consider the hero of the work, Strepsiades. This Athenian fully recognizes the evils of the Thinkery and sophistic ideas, but nevertheless intends to learn sophistic rhetoric in order to argue his way out of his debts. Even before coming into contact with sophism Strepsiades had already been corrupted by a society losing its grip on traditional values.

Incidentally, Aristophanes' comedies highlight probably the most salient characteristic of Athenian society – its freedom. Always keep in mind that freedom has been the anomaly, not the norm in human society, and this applies especially to freedom of speech, the most basic and precious of all freedoms. For a society to allow untrammeled freedom of speech in wartime, when critical opinion is inevitably viewed as unpatriotic or even treasonous, is so rare as to be almost nonexistent. Here is a large part of the measure of Athenian greatness: in the midst of the agony of the Peloponnesian War and with no Constitution to protect him Aristophanes is producing popular comedies blatantly and stingingly critical of the war, the empire and the democratic leaders. In far less serious circumstances America has demonstrated a far less tolerant attitude

Finally, there is an aspect of the Athenian moral crisis that should be familiar to late twentieth century America – the development of something like a generation gap. Athenian society during the Peloponnesian War gave rise to what appears to be the first serious challenge of one generation by another in history. As with America in the sixties it was precisely the young, primarily young aristocrats, who were the focal point of the moral crisis in Athens, although their reaction was hardly one of protesting the war and using controlled substances. In fact it was generally the younger generation who were in favor of greater imperialist adventures. But Athenian youth of the period of the Peloponnesian War were like many young Americans of the Vietnam era in that the morality of their fathers, the inherited ethos of the society, was not necessarily valid for them. The extent of this challenge should not be exaggerated, being apparently essentially limited to aristocratic youth, but it did exist.

A generation gap had never occurred before this for the simple reason that only now had the ascendancy of the state and the individual so undermined the strength of the family that the ties binding one generation to the next had been loosened. With the stage thus set by the general social development of the polis conditions particular to Athens then prompted the generational challenge. First of all there was the democracy, which itself involved a certain rejection of tradition. The egalitarianism that was fundamental to democratic society eroded the authority of parents, of the previous generation, by stressing the importance of the individual and the equality of all. As an eighteen year old Athenian male, you are a full political person, with a vote in the assembly equal to that of your father, and in the assembly you might even become more influential than he. So why should you then obey him when the two of you differ back at home? Political freedom is not conducive to the passive acceptance of traditional authority.

Nor is an emphasis on reason, which only naturally tends to devalue authority based on tradition, and the growing respect for reason in fifth century Athens was causing many to question and sometimes reject traditional values. The focus of this was of course the sophists, whose rationalism was especially zeroed in on an attack on tradition, and they had quickly earned themselves a reputation as corrupters of the youth. It was not just their hostility to tradition, but also the simple fact that they existed, breaking the monopoly parents had held in the education of the younger generation. It is hardly surprising that the Baby Boom generation that was the first to seriously challenge traditional American values was also the first to go to college in massive numbers. Reason and doubt are deadly to knowledge based only on faith and acceptance.

The final factor contributing to this generational phenomenon was the social and political failure of the democracy during the war and the loss of faith in the established order that it incurred. We need only to look four decades into our own past to see the effect of such a failure on the young of society.

# # # # # # # # # # # # # # # # # #

SUGGESTED READING

The man to read on the war is obviously Thucydides, supplemented by Xenophon's *Hellenica*, which picks up where Thucydides leaves off in 411. Xenophon is a pale reflection of Thucydides, but you take what you can get. There are also Plutarch's live of Pericles, Nicias, Alcibiades and Lysander. I recommend once again Finley's *Thucydides*, and since Thucydides can certainly be a bit dry, for those who want a full account of the war I suggest another fine book by Victor Hanson: *A War Like No Other* (2005) and the other volumes in Kagan's excellent series on the war: *The Archidamian War* (1974), *The Peace of Nicias and the Sicilian Expedition* (1981) and *The Fall of the Athenian Empire* (1987). Mary Renault's novel *The Last of the Wine* is excellent, capturing well the flavor of Athens during the war; also focusing on Alcibiades and the war is Steven Pressfield, *Tides of War* (2000).

# # # # # # # # # # # # # # # # #

XI. ALL POWER TO THE PHALLOS

WOMEN, SEXUALITY AND DIONYSUS

Virginity, virginity, where are you gone, leaving me behind?
No longer will I come to you, no longer will I come.

-Sappho 114 (Voigt)[24]

Fine way you treat my son, you old stinker!
You met the boy coming home from the baths
and never fondled him, never even kissed him
or tickled his balls. And *you*, his daddy's pal!

-Aristophanes *Birds* 139-42[25]

The lot of women has hardly been great in any society, including our own, and the Greeks were no exception to the male rule of using the female's role in the bearing and nurturing of young as an excuse to make her a second class member of society. It may be said, however, that the Greek woman was at least spared the god-sent antifeminism that Christianity and Islam would later hammer into the fabric of European and Near Eastern society. And the open and healthy attitude of the Greeks towards sex kept her free of the additional burden of denying her own sexuality as a source of evil in the world. Greek males were on the whole no more liberated in their view of women than most, but they lacked the pious smugness of the Judeo-Christian-Islamic tradition and appear to have been the first ever to examine the role of women, even if they did nothing to change it.

As you might guess, there are severe limitations on what we can know about women and their sexuality, since our sources are almost exclusively male and thus uninterested and distorted. But it is possible to provide a general picture at least. The exact conditions of a woman's life and status varied somewhat throughout the course of Greek history, and the evidence of the epics suggests that noble women in the Mycenaean and early Dark Age worlds perhaps had a higher status and more influence than their later counterparts. Since kingship was the rule in these periods, a well placed woman often had the opportunity to exercise real power through a husband or son, and in any case through marriage she was politically important as the primary mechanism of alliance between families. Such would have especially been the case in the fluid social and political conditions of the early Dark Age, when the family was the basic unit of society, and the women of the *Odyssey* support this notion of greater freedom and involvement. The emergence of the polis and the concomitant disappearance of the monarchy and de-emphasis of the family brought an apparent decline in the position of women, and the golden age of Greece was something less than golden for those of the distaff persuasion. The return of monarchy and the general loosening of social bonds in the age after Alexander probably brought about some improvement for women, but certainly nothing of great significance. Bear in mind that despite these variations in status from period to period, a woman's primary role remained throughout what it has always been – producing and rearing children.

A woman was clearly a second class inhabitant of the polis, barred from political participation and possessing few legal rights. Such inferior status has of course been the norm around the world until recently, but in the case of Greek society the subordinate position of women was reinforced by Greek attitudes towards sex. Like just about everything else in Greek society, sexual relationships were also affected by *agōn*, and sex was often seen in terms of a competition, in which there was a winner and loser. Since it was a male dominated society and in any case the male was the one who mounted and penetrated, then he must be the winner, leaving the woman no option but to be the one who was dominated. Since it was inconceivable to the Greek mind that citizenship could coexist with such personal subordination to another, sex itself provided a further force against any political liberation of women. The very concept of citizen involved maleness.

From the very start a woman's life was not only more limited, but also at greater risks than a male's. She stood a far greater chance of being terminated at birth as a financial liability to the family, and it may be that girls in poorer families were not fed as well as boys. A young woman would be married in her early teens, typically to a man in his thirties or older (at least in the urban populations), and would begin immediately her career in baby fabrication. Bearing lots of children (in order to compensate for the high rate of infant mortality) is a serious strain on the body in any circumstances, but many Greek women suffered even more and risked their lives by giving birth when barely sexually mature. And indeed the evidence suggests that despite the wastage of men in warfare males normally far outnumbered females, one of the reasons for the tender age of the bride.

The average woman looked forward to a life of seclusion, shut away in the women's quarters of the house and meeting few males outside her close relations. Even the marketing was in the hands of slaves or a male, except for the poorest families, whose women not only went out, but even took jobs such as washing or nursing. This isolation was interrupted by funerals, sundry public festivals, some of which, like the Thesmophoria and Adonia, were specifically for women, and private religious practices, if the woman happened to belong to a cult like the Eleusinian mysteries. Added to this physical seclusion was the gulf between a man and a woman brought on by the difference in age, education, social status and freedom. This is not to say that Greek men did not love their wives, but beyond the production of heirs most everything that was important to them lay outside the house and with their male friends. Even in the area of heterosexual relations a man was likely to be inclined more towards the company of his female slaves or prostitutes, especially if his wife was pregnant.

Prostitutes were essentially the only sizable group that escaped the seemingly suffocating fate of the average urban woman. The life of a common whore was generally as wretched as it is today (and without the modern solace of drugs), but she certainly enjoyed more access to the public than her more respectable sisters and practiced a profession that although of extremely low status, was recognized as a legitimate and necessary service to society. At the top of the profession was the *hetaira* or courtesan, who was the rare Greek woman with an education. She sold not so much her body, as her wit and conversational abilities, and at the dinner parties she gave or attended she treated with men on a more equal footing than any other female in the polis. A successful *hetaira* had a good shot a earning and managing a substantial amount of wealth and might consort with the leading figures in society; Aspasia was a friend of Socrates and the mistress of Pericles. But prostitution was a career that few women actually chose for themselves, and most apparently became working girls for the same reason they do today – economic desperation. Prostitutes virtually never came from respectable families, and the famous *hetairai* were inevitably resident aliens.

Naturally the rules of the game were a little different for Spartan women. They were of course inferior to the men and were regarded primarily as the potential mothers of more Spartan warriors, but the unusual structure and goals of Spartan society provided them with a better than average situation. The Spartan mania for the production of healthy new Spartans led to a regard for the health of the mothers, and Spartan females not only received a better diet and began their child bearing at a more mature age, but were also physically fit, undergoing a female version of the infamous *agōgē*, which also freed them from the seclusion of the household. Adultery, which was viewed in the average polis as a serious crime because of the problems associated with illegitimate offspring, was treated more lightly by Spartan society with its emphasis on stealth and the creation of more babies. This helped contribute to a greater degree of freedom for Spartan women, who indeed had a reputation among other Greeks for being tough customers.

We know that lesbianism was popular among Spartan women, and given the general sexual isolation of females and Greek acceptance of bisexuality, it is probable that it was widespread in broader Greek society. Since Greek males did not choose to write about such things, little is known about female homosexuality, but the practice is clearly illustrated by many vase paintings. It is also suggested in the surviving fragments of Sappho (fl. c. 600), the famous poetess of early sixth century Mytilene on the island of Lesbos. Sappho was certainly a rare bird, an educated and at least semi-independent woman who was not a *hetaira*, but she was by no means unique among aristocratic women in the Archaic Age. And her significance must not be distorted: for all that she might be considered a relatively liberated woman, at least by Greek standards, so far as we know, she never expressed any interest in changing the lot of women in her world. Sappho was a fine poet, interested especially in female relationships, but she was not a feminist.

One would be pretty hard pressed to find a feminist anywhere in the Greek world. Certainly the images of women found in the literature are generally less than flattering. Granted, many strong and dominant women appear in the tragedies, inherited by the playwrights from the mythic traditions of the Bronze and Dark Ages, but most of these female characters are violent man devourers, like Clytemnestra. Perhaps the frightening females that inhabit tragedy represent some sort of repressed fear on the part of the socially dominant males or are the result of domineering mothers in households where the father was often absent? The fact is that it was a very rare Greek indeed who spoke for seriously altering the role of women in society. Even the Hellenistic philosophical schools, which challenged the social order and postulated basic equality among all human beings (see Chapter XVI), did not consider significantly different roles for women. Only Plato (c. 429-347), who admits women to the guardian class in the utopia pictured in his *Republic* (see Chapter XIII), suggested that women could perform tasks traditionally reserved for men, and even he felt that men were naturally superior in most areas.

For all this, however, we have no reason to believe that most Greek women were unhappy. Life was tough in many ways, but the citizen woman was protected legally and economically throughout her life by those same laws and institutions that confined her to an inferior status. The Greeks treated their women better than a lot of other societies in history, and in any case the Greek woman had nothing with which to contrast her lot. Being housewife, mother and generally second class had been the role of women in every civilized society before the Greeks and would continue to be her essential role in virtually every society that would follow. The average Greek woman knew no other role, and the finest minds of her time (which were of course all male) were telling her this was the natural order of things, so it is hardly surprising that she did not protest. Even today, with the knowledge that such is not the order of things and with the opportunity to affect change the Phyllis Shlafleys of the world not only accept the traditional role, but militantly defend it.

One of the factors that probably helped determine the attitudes of the Greeks towards women was their bisexuality. Because of deep-seated hostility in the Christian west to such practices, Greek homosexuality traditionally received little or no attention in the standard histories, and when it did, the account was typically distorted by the moral prejudices of the author. Otherwise competent scholars turned a blind eye to the evidence of widespread homosexuality, including the so obvious and explicit scenes found on pottery. (The Greeks depicted *every* sort of activity on their pots.) Only recently has classical studies turned to serious investigation of Greek sexuality, much of which investigation is unfortunately marred by new prejudices.

It should be noted right off that if modern terminology is to be used, Greek society was not homosexual, but rather bisexual. Homosexuality may be defined as the more or less exclusive sexual preference for members of the same sex and must be considered some sort of biological aberration (no offspring can be produced) affecting a minority in every society. Bisexuality is the willingness to entertain sexual partners of either gender and would appear to be in large measure a socially determined trait, unless we assume that the Greeks were somehow physiologically different from other people. Thus, while there was surely the usual homosexual minority, many urban Greeks, especially those of high social status, were apparently bisexual, seeking different things from the different sexes. In fact, to judge from the large numbers of female prostitutes and evidence such as the successful sex strike launched by the Athenian women in Aristophanes' *Lysistrata*, heterosexual relations were very important to Greek men.

Using modern terminology is in any case a dangerous practice, since there is the risk of also projecting into the past modern concepts that have a different or no meaning in ancient society. The terms "heterosexual" and "homosexual," which are only about a century old, are valid classifications for Greece only in the most superficial sense, that is, labeling a single different-sex or same-sex act. As more general characterizations they are useless because they group behaviors that the Greeks considered very different, the sex of the partner, for example, being almost a trivial concern compared to the all-important issue of social status. Dominance and issues of penetration and receptivity were frequently of far greater importance than gender, and certain areas of Greek society might be more appropriately described as phallocratic rather than heterosexual or homosexual, though this term as well is too restrictive and potentially misleading.

Why ancient Greece – or at least the upper levels of its urban population – should have been one of the very few openly bisexual societies in history is not perfectly clear. The origins of male homosexuality were seen by the Greeks in the sexual segregation of the Dorian military societies, and Plato in fact blames the Spartans and Cretans for spreading the practice. But while Plato may be reflecting an opinion generally held in Greece during the classical period, that opinion is not necessarily true, and there is no hard evidence for the diffusion of Dorian practices through the rest of Greek society. It is true, however, that the overwhelming male orientation of polis society, which resulted in a sort of sexual segregation, can probably be traced back to the warrior communities of the early Dark Age, a result of the Dorian invasions. The warrior hosts disappeared, but because of the endless intercity warfare, the polis was in many ways also a warrior society, and the absolute dominance of males continued.

The pertinent fact here is that outside of childbearing everything that mattered in the polis was in the hands of males, which meant in turn that outside of heterosexual relations everything that was of any concern to a Greek male involved other males. With very few exceptions women were completely uneducated and uninvolved in anything beyond the household and the odd cultic practice, and consequently, for meaningful companionship and a relationship with any intellectual content whatsoever a male normally had to turn to another male. Male relationships thus filled a basic social need. This situation of course does not necessarily lead to open homosexuality and did not in most other similar societies. Further, while it is perfectly clear that extreme sexual segregation inevitably leads to some degree of homosexuality (look at any prison population), it generally does not lead to open, socially acceptable homosexuality.

Why then the Greeks? An entirely satisfactory explanation is elusive, and I can only suggest a few reasons. First, the relatively high level of social and intellectual freedom in Greek society, due in part to the open nature of the constitutional polis and in part to the fragmentation of Greece into hundreds of separate political units, which encouraged some small measure of diversity. This resulted in a social atmosphere more conducive to change and acceptance of different practices. This is not to suggest that Greek society was wildly progressive – it certainly was not, even in the sixth century - but rather that the polis was at least marginally more inclined to accept nontraditional behaviors than the average pre-modern society. Much more important, the Greeks had no inherited prohibition of homosexuality, no command from god that erotic experiences between persons of the same sex was wrong, which would allow the homosexuality inevitably practiced in secret in sexually segregated societies to come out into the open. Finally, because sex was viewed as an important expression of status and citizenship, social position became much more important than the actual gender of the partner, producing an environment more open to sex between males. In short, the male dominance and sexual segregation fosters the bisexuality, and the relative social freedom and lack of any serious religious prohibition brings it out of the closet.

But let us not misunderstand Greek sexuality and think simply of cheap thrills and bathhouse promiscuity. Obviously, there were those who engaged in casual sex, especially with slaves and male prostitutes, but a serious relationship involving free males was bounded by a strict set of rules, and behavior that publicly violated those rules was socially unacceptable and sometimes criminal. An acceptable pairing involved an older male, the *erastēs*, who was the active partner, and a younger male, the *erōmenos*, who played a passive role. The *erōmenos* could not be too young, less than about twelve, and there would be talk if he were still playing the passive role much beyond the age of fifteen or sixteen ("when the beard was grown"). The pair could not openly engage in oral or anal sex, because that would compel the *erōmenos* to play a subordinate, female role and not only bring shame upon him, but also injure his future status as a citizen. Personal physical inviolability was one of the hallmarks of citizenship, and penetration of a male would place him in the category of slave and woman. The *kinaidos*, the man who allowed himself to be so used, was the negation of everything represented by the hoplite: manliness, citizenship and dominant status; the worst insult you could deliver to a man was to call him *euryprōktos*, "wide-assed." The acceptable practice was intercrural copulation, in which the *erastēs*, facing his partner, thrust his penis between his thighs.

Such at least was the social ideal, and some men maintained lofty attitudes regarding their liaisons, emphasizing the educational aspect of the relationship and their responsibility for the development of their *erōmenoi* as men and citizens. That the homosexual relationship sometimes served a valuable function in a society that had no formal educational apparatus and that may have strained the relationship between father and son is certainly true, but this must not be exaggerated. The evidence suggests that sexual attraction to and pleasure with adolescent males was the common motivation and that penetration was frequently practiced, for all that one never spoke of it in public. The Romans, incidentally, shared these attitudes, though unlike the Greeks they considered citizen youths out of bounds, and the distinction between penetrating men (permitted for virile males) and being penetrated by men (definitely not permitted) is still made among males in some Mediterranean and Latin American societies.

Free of any divine commandments to the contrary, the Greeks were able to develop a more open attitude about human sexuality, and I suspect their society was all the more psychologically healthy for it. The Greeks were more willing than most civilized peoples to recognize the inner nature of the human animal and squarely face what this meant in terms of human needs and behavior. This is not to suggest that the Greeks were completely successful in dealing with those needs; such obviously cannot be said about a society that was self-destructing through internal warfare. But there was a recognition, stated expressly by thinkers like Thucydides and Aristotle and implicitly through the general acceptance of orgiastic religious practices, that for all our powers of reason and moral reflection there remains an irrational, animal side to our character, one that is ignored only at risk. This is a fact of nature that most societies have resisted accepting, misled by the attributes that so radically separate humans from the rest of the animal kingdom or blinded by the presumption of a special divine creation.

Greek awareness and understanding of the animal within is most dramatically displayed in the *Bacchae* of Euripides (c. 480-406), first presented shortly after his death. The play takes place in Thebes, which is being visited by the god Dionysus, who has a special regard for the city, which was the home of his mother, Semele. Queen of Thebes, she had an affair with Zeus – always a dangerous business – and having tricked the god into revealing himself in his true form, she was blasted by his thunderbolts. The unborn child of the union, Dionysus, was rescued and raised by Zeus, and now he has returned, disguised as a mortal and spreading his cult. But the people of Thebes have refused him, and in return he has driven mad all the women, who are now up in the hills performing his rites. This infuriates the young and proper king, Pentheus, who mocks Dionysus and continues to resist acceptance despite obvious manifestations of the god's power. Finally, Dionysus touches Pentheus with madness and leads him in female garb to spy on the activities of the women in the hills. He is discovered and literally torn apart by the women, his own mother leading the pack, and she returns to Thebes with Pentheus' head, thinking it that of a lion. Dionysus causes her to see clearly, and as if this were not enough, he then deals out further harsh punishments to the Thebans, and the play ends.

The worship of Dionysus (or Bacchus) may have originated in Thrace, though the Greeks believed the god came out of Asia Minor, where in fact some Thracian tribes were living. "Far behind me lie/ those golden-rivered lands, Lydia and Phrygia,/ where my journeying began," (*Bacchae* 13-14)[26] says Dionysus in his opening speech. "Out of the land of Asia,/ down from holy Tmolus," (*Bacchae* 64-65) echoes his chorus of Bacchae (or Bacchantes or maenads), a band of female devotees that has followed him to Thebes. Maenads are always females and it is inevitably women who are pictured celebrating the Dionysiac rites, but with some restrictions men could also participate and experience the divine "madness." The cult was unusual in that it was not associated with a specific locale and thus took on a tremendous variety of forms, but in essence it revolved around ecstatic possession, the initiate seeking to share at least briefly the divinity of the god by practicing his rites. In theory the central ceremony involved consuming the flesh of a goat or lamb (possibly a man in its most primitive stage) that was supposed temporarily to incarnate the god. Having thus "eaten" the god, the believer partook of his divinity and entered into a state of ecstatic possession (*ekstasis*: "standing outside" yourself to make room for the god). This idea of consuming the deity as a mechanism of spiritual communion is a common one in religion, and the Christian Eucharist may be seen as a more sophisticated version of the Dionysiac rite. In actuality, however, virtually all the evidence for the consumption of the god is found in myth, and it is not at all clear how widely it was literally practiced in the cult, though the point of the rituals was clearly to infuse the believer with the god.

A Dionysiac gathering might be anything from a sedate picnic to a wild orgy, but the state of communion usually manifested itself in frenzied dances. "Blessèd is he who hallows his life in the worship of god,/ he whom the spirit of god possesseth, who is one/ with those who belong to the holy body of god./ Blessèd are the dancers and those who are purified, who dance on the hill in the holy dance of god," (*Bacchae* 72-77) sing the Bacchantes. The dance is a powerful form of religious expression, common to many societies, but not our own, since it has been absent from mainstream Christianity, which from the start rejected a practice associated with polytheist cults and orgiastic expression. We consequently think of the dance simply as a pleasant mechanism of social interaction, but in fact in its most essential form it is a strong and dangerous power, highly infectious and difficult to stop. We have accounts from the fourteenth to seventeenth centuries of dancing madness sporadically invading European towns, occurrences when a group would quite literally dance into town and otherwise sober and respectable citizens would feel compelled to join in and dance until they dropped from exhaustion. Such is a frightening experience for a society in which the dance has been secularized and its power defused.

The cult was also associated with wine, Dionysus in fact being credited with the invention of that beverage. This association has led to modern misconceptions about the nature of Dionysus, who is pictured as a happy-go-lucky god of wine, like the tipsy little fatso in the Beethoven's Sixth Symphony segment of Walt Disney's *Fantasia*. This was hardly the case. The connection between the god and wine was due to the effect produced by alcohol: it can create artificially – though in a very watered down sort of way – the kind of irrationality and release from convention that was the goal of the Dionysiac ecstasy. "For filled with that good gift,/ suffering mankind forgets its grief," (*Bacchae* 280-81) says the blind prophet Teiresias, suggesting perhaps the primary reason that ethyl alcohol is the chosen drug of the human race.

Dionysus is far from being the happy-go-lucky god of the grape. He is instead nature incarnate, *physis* in human form, and thus a powerful and dangerous amoral force, which may bring blessings, as to his Bacchantes, or destruction, as to Pentheus. He is the force of irrationality, the madness that brings release and communion with nature and that brings slaughter and destruction. He can be seen in the Theban women practicing his rites in the hills:

> Breasts swollen with milk,
> new mothers who had left their babies behind at home
> nestled gazelles and young wolves in their arms,
> suckling them. Then they crowned their hair with leaves,
> ivy and oak and flowering bryony. One woman
> struck her thyrsus against a rock and a fountain
> of cool water came bubbling up. Another drove
> her fennel in the ground, and where it struck the earth,
> at the touch of god, a spring of wine poured out.
> Those who wanted milk scratched at the soil
> with bare fingers and the white milk came welling up.
> Pure honey spurted, streaming, from their wands.

(*Bacchae* 699-711)

Such are the blessings of Dionysus. But when aroused, the women show the other side of the god, sweeping down upon the villages, killing and plundering: "And then/ you could have seen a single woman with bare hands/ tear a fat calf, still bellowing with fright,/ in two, while others clawed the heifers to pieces." (*Bacchae* 737-39) And of course there is the final gruesome dismemberment of Pentheus by his own mother. Such is the power of nature, of *physis*, of irrationality, of Dionysus.

It is into the arms of this power that the initiates of the cult throw themselves by consuming the god. They seek to immerse themselves in *physis*, to strip themselves of *nomos*, the conventions of civilized life. The experience they seek is essentially madness, to escape from themselves (*ekstasis* again) in a burst of irrationality and find emotional catharsis by letting it all hang out. In the Dionysiac frenzy there is at least momentary escape from the burden of responsibility each of us carries; there is a purging of all the irrational impulses that we collect in our daily lives. Greater sanity is sought through temporary insanity.

Confronting the awesome force that is Dionysus is the young king, Pentheus, ostensibly the representative of *nomos* and order, of civilization and rationality. But throughout the play Pentheus is accused by those around him of violating *nomos* because of his refusal to accept the new god. Indeed, by resisting Dionysus Pentheus is acting irrationally, and Teiresias tells him so in no uncertain terms: "You are mad, grievously mad, beyond the power/ of any drugs to cure, for you are drugged with madness." (*Bacchae* 326-27) His irrationality escalates when he ignores clear signs of Dionysus' power, the destruction of his own palace and miraculous release of the disguised god. When Pentheus asserts that he is the stronger, Dionysus' reply precisely defines the king's irrationality: "You do not know/ the limits of your strength. You do not know/ what you do. You do not know who you are." (*Bacchae* 505-6) Pentheus is without *sophia*, the all-inclusive wisdom that involves knowing oneself, especially one's limits and position in the universe. He is instead immersed in *amathia*, the precise opposite of *sophia*. (Over the entrance to the temple of Apollo – the antithesis of Dionysus - at Delphi were the words *gnōthi sauton*, "know thyself.") When he cuts the god's curls and attempts to imprison him, Pentheus does not indeed know the limits of his strength, what he is doing, who he is. Young and rash, he cannot see that he is struggling against an irresistible force. To resist Dionysus is not simply to defy a deity, but as the god himself puts it, to "rage/ and kick against necessity," (*Bacchae* 794-95) which is exactly what he is – the necessity that is nature. Dionysus can no more be ignored than gravity.

Pentheus' irrationality grows until he is in fact taken over by the god. Dionysus touches his mind with madness and instills in him a burning desire to spy on the Theban women, for which expedition he disguises himself as a female. And the god tells him "Your mind was once unsound, but now you think/ as sane men do," (*Bacchae* 947-48), which is certainly ironic, since Pentheus is no more rational now than he was before. The difference is that now his irrationality is derived directly from Dionysus, and consequently he has in a sense finally accepted the god. More than that, he has figuratively become the god, ready to be led up the mountain to serve as the sacrificial host and be torn apart by the frenzied maenads.

What in the end comes of all this is the simple fact that the irrational in man and his need to express it cannot be ignored and that to resist this force is to court ultimate disaster. The language of the post-Freudian world may be new – repression, id, superego, etc. – but the message is as old as Euripides: we dare not ignore the Dionysus that lurks within each of us (as did the super-advanced Krell in the movie *Forbidden Planet*). And the god is what you make of him, beneficial, as to his Bacchantes, or destructive, as to Pentheus, for nature is amoral and uncaring and can destroy as readily as it can nourish. Dionysus is the force behind both the religious ecstatic and the homicidal maniac; he drives both the frenzied dancers at a Rolling Stones concert and the lynch mob howling for blood. He is dangerous and must be given his due.

Euripides' conception of *physis* is perfectly clear: it is amoral, irrational, powerful, animal. The Dionysiac ecstasy is the religious manifestation of the sophistic idea of *physis*; it is the release of the animal within, the natural state for whatever it is worth. Thus are Dionysus and his initiates a perfect portrayal of the end result of sophistic cynicism and moral relativism – ethical nihilism. The maenads are beyond all law and morality, all *nomos*; theirs is the natural state, which knows no conventions or limitations, where the mother is blind to the murder of her own son. Such is the nihilism, the belief in nothing, the lack of any basis for a value system, and hard on its heels comes the fanaticism, the justification of anything born from the denial of everything. The Theban women turned Bacchantes become a raging flood of destruction, looting and slaughtering and finally dismembering Pentheus, not simply blind to their crimes, but fanatically driven, delighting in their service to the god, who is nature, which is themselves.

# # # # # # # # # # # # # # # # # #

SUGGESTED READING

Books on women in antiquity are plentiful these days, and many are filled with absolute nonsense. An excellent introduction to women in Greece (and Rome) is Sarah Pomeroy, *Goddesses, Whores, Wives, and Slaves* (1975), followed by Eva Cantarella, *Pandora's Daughters* (1987). For a more in depth look specifically at Greek women see Sue Blundell, *Women in Ancient Greece* (1995), which has illustrations, and Roger Just, *Women in Athenian Law and Life* (1989), which has a section on women and the *Bacchae*. Much more fun to read is James Davidson, *Courtesans and Fishcakes. The Consuming Passions of Classical Athens* (1997), which examines the Athenian pursuit of pleasure, in particular eating, drinking and sex. My vote for the best volume on Greek bisexuality is K.J. Dover, *Greek Homosexuality* (1978); this is a very readable book, unmarred by either the personal prejudices that attended this topic in the past or the Political Correctness and incredibly fuzzy thinking that attends it now. The plates also give you the opportunity to see some of the amusing erotic vases that are normally kept hidden away. E.R. Dodds, *The Greeks and the Irrational* (1971) is excellent, but a very serious read. Bennet Simon, *Mind and Madness in Ancient Greece* (1978) is certainly not as good, but it is interesting because it is written by a psychologist rather than a classicist. The literature on Dionysus is immense: you could begin with the sections on Dionysus and the Bacchic mysteries in Burkert's *Greek Religion*; for a fuller account Walter F. Otto, *Dionysus. Myth and Cult* (1965). Arthur Evans, *The God of Ecstasy. Sex-Roles and the Madness of Dionysos* (1988) explores the cult from the perspective of Euripides' play and ranges all over the historical and geographical landscape; interesting, but often very speculative reading. More sober and grounded, T.H. Carpenter & C.A. Faraone, eds., *Masks of Dionysus* (1993) is a comprehensive collection of essays covering every aspect of the god, but this involves some serious reading.

# # # # # # # # # # # # # # # # # #

XII. WHO'S ON FIRST?

THE FOURTH CENTURY

After this Lysander sailed into Piraeus, the exiles returned,
and the walls of Athens were pulled down among scenes of
great enthusiasm and to the music of flute girls. It was thought
that this day was the beginning of freedom for Greece. (404 BC)

Xenophon *Hellenica* 2.2.23[27]

In fact, there was even more uncertainty and confusion in Greece
after the battle (Mantinea) then there had been previously. (362 BC)

Xenophon *Hellenica* 7.5.27

This chapter is actually only about the first half of the fourth century, but the years between the defeat of Athens and the rise of Macedon form a distinct period in Greek history and for lack of anything better it is referred to as the "fourth century." This is not a pleasant time for the Greeks, as first the Spartans, then the Thebans, take their shot at establishing hegemony over Greece. Both fail, and the Greeks are treated to another forty years of almost continuous conflict, as Athens, Sparta and Thebes fight it out in a constantly shifting pattern of alliances, reminiscent of the endless war in Orwell's *1984*. And then comes Macedon and an end to the age-old struggles of the polis.

With the defeat of Athens in 404 Sparta was left the strong man of Greece and faced with two alternatives: liberate the Greek poleis, as she had promised, or take up the mantle of empire fallen from the Athenians. The problem with the first option was the Great King, who had been ceded the Ionian cities in return for his support against Athens; the Spartans had worried as little about the consistency of their propaganda and their actions as any modern state. Caught in the seductive web of their newly found power, the Spartans decided to reach for the imperial ring and rebuild the Athenian Empire under their own leadership. One could easily have predicted disaster.

In 404 Lysander, the victor of Aegospotomi, sailed among Athens' former dependencies, establishing Spartan rule. He set up narrow ten man oligarchies, called decarchies, and supported some of them with Spartan garrisons. The former allies of Athens now began to think wistfully of the good old days, as they groaned under their new puppet governments and heavy taxation. Not only was Spartan imperialism much more oppressive than the Athenian brand, but there was absolutely no justification for it, since the Spartans had appeased Persia by selling the Ionians down the river. But the ambitious Lysander had aroused envy back home and was recalled in 403, and his decarchies were undone with him.

The next move came from the Persians. In 401 Cyrus (d. 401), brother of king Artaxerxes II (405/4-359/8), decided that the empire would be better off if he were king and raised an army of Asiatics and 13,000 Greek mercenaries in Asia Minor, where he had been helping the Spartans fight Athens. The army marched inland, Cyrus and his Spartan captain, Clearchus (c. 450-401), keeping secret as long as possible the actual destination of the expedition, since Greeks were nervous about traveling so far from the sea. At Cunaxa, near Babylon, they met Artaxerxes and were on the verge of winning the battle when Cyrus took a foolish risk and was killed, rendering the whole affair pointless. Clearchus and his fellow generals then managed to get themselves treacherously murdered while negotiating with the Persians, leaving about 10,000 Greeks stranded in the middle of nowhere in the heart of the Persian Empire. Rejecting any idea of surrender, they formed themselves into an ambulatory polis under the leadership of the Athenian Xenophon (c. 430-c. 354), who later wrote a history of the expedition, the *Anabasis*. Fighting the locals all the way, they marched north through Armenia to the Black Sea and thence west along the coast to home. The Ten Thousand had saved themselves and had demonstrated to all just how seriously rotten the once great Persian Empire had become. Others would follow.

Meanwhile, in order to cause more trouble for his brother Cyrus had instigated a revolt of the Ionian cities before he left, and they had appealed to Sparta for help. Stirred by the success of the Ten Thousand, the Spartans sent an army to Asia Minor in 400, but nothing much was accomplished until the arrival in 396 of king Agesilaus II (399-360), one of the most energetic of the Spartan kings. Though born lame (!) and not in the direct line of succession, with the help of Lysander he had peacefully secured the throne when his brother Agis II had died, claiming that the rightful heir, his nephew Leotychides, was the illegitimate son of Alcibiades. Once in Asia

Agesilaus spent the next couple of years winning battle after battle against the Persians, but his strategic abilities did not match his tactical, and his victories brought the Spartans no solid gains. Further, the Persians responded by appointing an Athenian admiral, Conon, to command their huge fleet, and in 394 he destroyed Spartan naval power at the battle of Cnidus. This defeat made Agesilaus' position in Asia Minor ultimately untenable, and the Greek cities began slipping back to Persia. Cnidus must have been especially pleasing to Conon, since he had been responsible for the Athenian disaster at Aegospotomi, a resume item that had apparently not deterred the Persians.

The Great King had meanwhile taken another, traditional measure to get Agesilaus out of his hair – destabilizing mainland Greece, something that had never been all that hard to do. In 396 a Persian agent loaded with gold visited Argos, Corinth, Thebes and Athens, all the major states dissatisfied with Spartan supremacy for one reason or another. It did not take much persuading, and in 395 Thebes invaded Phocis in support of her friend Locris and was promptly threatened with a Spartan invasion. Athens then joined Thebes, and at the battle of Haliartus they defeated the invading forces, killing Lysander in the process. Argos, Corinth and a host of minor states now hopped on the bandwagon, and the Corinthian War was on. In 394 the Spartans restored their prestige by winning a big battle near Corinth, but failed to break the allied grip on the isthmus. Likewise, later in the year Agesilaus, who had marched his army all the way from Asia Minor, defeated the allies at Coronea in Boeotia, but failed to gain any strategic advantage. With Sparta still blockaded in the Peloponnesus, the war settled down into a string of small engagements around Corinth.

The Spartans finally succeeded in 390 in breaking the blockade at the isthmus, but by then their military prestige had been sorely damaged, especially by an incident in that same year. During the war the use of mercenary light troops called peltasts (from their small shield, the *pelta*) had been on the rise, and especially prominent were the peltasts under the Athenian mercenary captain Iphicrates (fl. 390-356). Equipped with a light shield, javelins, long sword and little or no body armor, the peltasts were turned by Iphicrates into Greece's first really effective light infantry force and played an important role in the operations around Corinth. In 390 they caught a detachment of 600 Spartan hoplites on the march and destroyed a large number of them with their hit and run tactics. Under this pressure the Spartans finally broke and ran, further injuring the already bruised reputation of the Spartan army. Light infantry had been very effective against Spartans on the broken terrain of Sphacteria back in 425, but now for the first time hoplites caught on favorable flat ground had been defeated, an ominous sign for the military class that had been the backbone of the polis.

The Spartans, who were also still at war with Persia, were now definitely considering peace, and they were supported by the Athenians, whose commerce was suffering from the war, which seemed to be bringing them little advantage. The other allies could not fight on without Athens, and negotiations resulted in 386 in the Peace of Antalcidas, also called the King's Peace because of his role in it. The Great King received the poleis of Asia Minor, but guaranteed the autonomy of the other Greek cities, which was favorable to Sparta since it broke up the union of Corinth and Argos created during the war and reduced Theban power by depriving her of the Boeotian cities. Of course no mention was made of Sparta's control of Laconia and Messenia. This was the ultimate humiliation for the Greeks, that the Great King of Persia, whose armies were obsolete and whose empire should have been dismantled long before, not only still controlled the Ionian cities, but was also dictating terms to the rest of the Greeks. Divide and conquer was certainly not an approach invented by the Romans.

The King's Peace did not turn out to be much of a peace. In 382 Sparta sent an army north to break up the Chalcidian League, an alliance formed by the cities in the Chalcidice (the three-pronged peninsula on the northwest coast of the Aegean) after their revolt from Athens during the Peloponnesian War. On the way through Boeotia the commander, Phoebidas, heard opportunity knocking, and with the aid of some Thebans he seized the Cadmea, the acropolis of Thebes, and installed a Spartan garrison and oppressive puppet government. Phoebidas was subsequently fined, but not disowned by the Spartan government, and Greece was outraged by this blatant violation of the Peace. The Spartans, meanwhile, went on to crush the Chalcidian League by 379.

Deliverance for Thebes came in the winter of 379/78. Disguised as women (no mean feat for the usually bearded Greeks), a group of exiles under Pelopidas (d. 364) infiltrated a banquet for the puppet rulers and killed them all. They then roused the populace, and probably to their surprise the garrison commanders capitulated without a fight. Athens had been a silent partner in this enterprise, but did not want to break her friendly relations with Sparta and so disowned the actions of some Athenian volunteers who had taken part in the affair. But the Spartans seemed determined to create another coalition against themselves. A Spartan garrison commander in Boeotia, Sphodrias, took it upon himself to attempt to seize the Piraeus by surprise after a night march; he failed utterly. He was not condemned by Sparta, and Athens promptly formed an alliance with Thebes for a new war against Sparta.

So endemic had war become in Greece that this one does not even have a name. It went on for eight years, during which time the Thebans successfully defended themselves against Spartan invasion and reestablished their hold on Boeotia, while the Athenians assaulted the Spartans at sea. By 371 Sparta, having suffered defeat after defeat, was ready to talk peace and found Athens willing to listen. Despite their successes and the formation in 377 of a Second Athenian League (a minor league compared to the fifth century empire), the Athenians felt they were carrying the burden of the war while Thebes increased her power at little cost to herself. With friction between the two allies increasing negotiations were opened with Sparta, and the result was the Peace of Callias, which was essentially a reaffirmation of the King's Peace. Athens and Sparta thus agreed formally to renounce their international organizations, except as voluntary associations, but at the conference the Theban representative, Epaminondas (c. 410-362), understandably balked at having the autonomy clause applied to Boeotia. His response to Agesilaus' demand to free the Boeotian cities was to ask "What about the Laconian towns?" and Agesilaus' reply was to strike Thebes from the peace treaty.

So a state of war still existed between Sparta and Thebes, and later in 371 a Spartan force under king Cleombrotus I (380-371) invaded Boeotia and found the Theban army at Leuctra. The Thebans were outnumbered by perhaps 11,000 to 6000, but Epaminondas had a surprise up his sleeve. Instead of forming the expected long thin line, he loaded up his left wing, which faced the Spartans themselves, packing it fifty rows deep instead of the normal eight or so. Here he also stationed a new unit, the Sacred Band, which was composed of 150 pairs of lovers, who could presumably be counted on to fight like hell for one another. In addition to the asymmetric line Epaminondas produced another innovation, the oblique approach, in which he advanced in echelon, leading, as it were, with his strong left hook, and in the ensuing battle the allies occupying the rest of the lines on both sides were apparently never seriously engaged. The first real tactical developments in some three centuries of hoplite warfare worked. The Spartans were overwhelmed by the Theban juggernaut, and king Cleombrotus was killed.

Leuctra was a shot heard around the Greek world. A Spartan army had been defeated in a set hoplite battle and by a force inferior in numbers. Never had this happened before. And not since Leonidas at Thermopylae had a Spartan king died in battle. Leuctra marked the beginning of the end for Sparta as a major power. Now it was Thebes' turn.

Events moved quickly in the wake of the Theban victory. A wave of anti-Spartan demonstrations swept through the Peloponnesus, especially Arcadia, the mountainous central region, which had never synoecized into a unified state. Most of the Arcadian cities now joined in a Pan-Arcadian union and erected a new city, Megalopolis, to serve as the federal capital. In 370 Sparta's oldest ally, Tegea, joined the new Arcadian organization, and in response Agesilaus led a small army north to tear up Arcadian real estate. His invasion had little effect beyond causing the Arcadians to appeal for outside help, first to Athens, which was not ready for a renewal of the war, and then to Thebes, which was just waiting for an invitation.

With Theban influence now paramount in central Greece Epaminondas was ready for a trip south to insure that the Spartans did not recover, and a pro-Theban unified Arcadia was just the ticket. In late 370 the Theban army invaded Laconia, but not Sparta itself, which had received aid from Corinth and a few other Peloponnesian states. Epaminondas then delivered a killing blow: he liberated Messenia and formed the independent and obviously anti-Spartan state of Messene. This act not only created a new foe for Sparta, but more important it also removed a considerable amount of land from the Spartan system, thus cutting the number of full citizens. Actually, the Lycurgean system was already seriously in decline due to internal breakdown and the influx of money and outside influences that came with the new imperial policies, and even before Epaminondas' invasion there were probably no more than 1500 full Spartan citizens. Now there were going to be even fewer. Having accomplished momentous things, the Thebans returned home in the spring of 369.

Now the Athenians, who had been nursing their own imperial ambitions, began to become concerned about Theban power and formed an alliance with Sparta. Epaminondas led a second expedition into the Peloponnesus later in 369, but accomplished little or nothing. Meanwhile, with Sparta almost eliminated as any sort of serious threat the Arcadians were beginning to make their arrangements independent of Theban wishes, and Epaminondas' third descent in 366 was intended to counter this annoying trend. He was apparently not too successful, because in the same year the Arcadians concluded an alliance with Athens, creating an interesting situation. Arcadia was now allied to both Athens and Thebes, who were at war with each other, while Athens was allied to both the Spartans and the Arcadians, who were also at war with one another. Only the Greeks could create a circumstance like this.

For the next few years there was a break in the action in the Peloponnesus while Thebes competed with Athens around the Aegean and looked after her interests in the north, establishing an hegemony over Thessaly. But in 362 the south beckoned again. The Arcadian League was coming apart at the seams and threatening to slide over to the Spartan side, and Epaminondas was compelled to make his fourth excursion into the Peloponnesus in order to support the Theban factions in Arcadia. At the second battle of Mantinea he met the allied army of Spartans, Athenians, anti-Theban Arcadians and sundry others and crushed it with a replay of Leuctra. Unfortunately for Thebes, however, Epaminondas was mortally wounded during the pursuit and died soon after. And with his death Theban power collapsed almost overnight. Not only had the Thebans lost their only great general, but they had also lost the linchpin of their empire, for as a statesman Epaminondas had serious failings. He had neglected to create the governmental machinery necessary to insure the survival of his policies and to allow imperial Thebes to function without a great leader. He had failed even to create a solid framework for turning Boeotia into a true national entity under Theban leadership, the necessary foundation for any stable Theban hegemony in Greece. Epaminondas was good, but he was a flash in the historical pan.

With the passing of Epaminondas Athens appeared to be in an excellent position. When the democracy was restored in 403 the Athenians had reformed their constitution, establishing new institutions and procedures to check the power of the people in the assembly and prevent the demagoguery and excesses that had led to the calamities of the Peloponnesian War. The law, and not the people, was to be supreme, and once again laws (affecting all and/or permanent) were distinguished from decrees of the assembly (affecting individuals and/or temporary or non-recurring). In the fourth century laws were passed by panels of *nomothetai* ("law-givers"), which were in many ways similar to the popular courts: the huge boards were randomly drawn from the annual pool of 6000 jurors (thus of "wiser" citizens thirty years or older) and followed procedures similar to those in a trial. Any law passed by the *nomothetai* could easily be challenged as "unsuitable," in which case it was subject to scrutiny by the popular courts, creating a two stage process that could be expected to curb excesses. The result was a much more moderate democratic government, one that despite the constant warfare and many defeats was stable until it was terminated by the Macedonians in 322.

Economically, however, Athens was not the state she once was. Her population had certainly declined as a result of the plague and the Peloponnesian War – the citizen body of the fourth century was stable at around 30,000, perhaps half that of the fifth century – but her commerce (minus the empire) and agricultural infrastructure had emerged intact. Nevertheless, the more or less constant warfare since 395 was a steady drain on the state, and the 350s were particularly hard times for state finances: the annual income was only 130 talents, compared to 400 talents just ten years later and 1200 talents in the peace that followed the battle of Chaeronea in 338. To be sure, during the sixties she had been rebuilding her second naval league and by 357 had recovered the Chersonese and Euboea and was hoping to regain Amphipolis, but in terms of money and power the fourth century league was a poor shadow of the fifth century empire. Moreover, her position in the eastern Aegean was being challenged by the rising power of Caria in southwestern Asia Minor. The Carian dynasts had served the Great King faithfully as satraps and were consequently allowed a free hand in building up their local power, which began to increase dramatically with the accession in 377 of Mausolus (377-353). He moved his capital to Halicarnassus on the coast and built a large navy, with which he could counter Athenian influence in the area. In 357 he convinced the important islands of Rhodes, Chios and Cos to desert the Athenian alliance, and Athens was unable to stop them; three years later they belonged to Caria. Meanwhile, to the north a far greater threat was growing.

The major trend of the fourth century should now be fairly clear: total instability. There were two ways peace could be won, and the Greeks could achieve neither. Either every polis was satisfied with what it had, which would obviously never be the case, or one polis was able to impose peace on all the rest, which also did not seem possible. Athens blew her chance in the fifth century by attempting to rush it and was not strong enough in the fourth; Sparta was simply not equipped with the necessary human and economic resources; and Theban supremacy had rested on the shoulders of Epaminondas. Instead of peace, the outcome was more or less constant war: the three major powers had been at war with one another for all but about twenty of the sixty-nine years separating the outbreak of the Peloponnesian War from the death of Epaminondas.

And this was not the restrained hoplite warfare of the Archaic Age. The emergence of mercenaries, specialized troops and professional military leaders and above all the development of protracted wars fought by coalitions of states had all led Greece away from the polite convention of the decisive hoplite battle with its severely limited damage. From the Peloponnesian War on the Greeks were increasingly practicing a more familiar and brutal warfare of long campaigns, destruction of military forces and devastation of territory, all of which meant an end to war as a relatively useful cultural mechanism and the beginning of war as a destructive burden the politically and economically fragile polis was ill-equipped to bear. The constant warfare aggravated in turn the other traditional weaknesses of the polis: financial and political instability. The war and economic devastation led to more poverty and social discontent, which led to greater political instability, which led to more conflict. The growing poverty and constant demand for soldiers bred more and more mercenaries, who in turn fueled the flames of war. And while ruining Greece internally, the constant warfare dragged her down on the international scene, allowing the increasingly decrepit Persian Empire not just to totter on, but even to meddle in Greek affairs. *Agōn* and the autonomy of the polis, so important to the constitutional and intellectual developments, were coming back to haunt the Greeks.

The Greeks were not completely blind to what was happening to their society, and there was at least an intellectual reaction, which of course had no impact on real affairs. The response was Panhellenism, which understandably sought a solution to Greece's problems in some sort of movement towards unification. The best known proponent of the Panhellenic movement is the Athenian orator Isocrates, who was born into a wealthy family in 436 and died in 338 – would you believe it – by suicide. With a life spanning the period from the Peloponnesian War to the Macedonian conquest of Greece Isocrates was perfectly positioned to observe the ills of Greek society, and having seen his family's wealth destroyed in the Peloponnesian War, he was hardly a dispassionate observer. Schooled in the realities of life, he was not interested in utopian visions, but wanted practical solutions to the problems of the polis.

Isocrates views the problems of the polis from the international angle, focusing on Greece's sorry relationship with the Persian Empire:

> We have gone so far in our passion to injure ourselves that, whereas it lies in our power to possess the wealth of the barbarians in security and peace, we continue to wage war upon each other over trifles, and we actually help to reduce to subjection those who revolt from the authority of the King, and sometimes, unwittingly, we ally ourselves with our hereditary foes and seek to destroy those who are of our own race. (*To Philip* 126)[28]

It was these wars over trifles that in addition to bringing Greece international humiliation were also leading to her domestic ruin, creating bands of men who "for lack of the daily necessities of life, are wandering from place to place and committing outrages upon whomsoever they encounter." (*To Philip* 120) It is hardly surprising then that Isocrates should seek solutions in an international context, Panhellenism, rather than in domestic reform of the polis.

Panhellenism was of course not dreamed up by Isocrates. For centuries it had been perfectly clear to any sensible Greek that life in the Balkan Peninsula could be more comfortable, if somewhat less exciting, if the poleis could peacefully settle their differences. While warfare was virtually a way of life for the polis, the Greeks, unlike the Romans, did not view it as a generally positive and profitable affair, and by the fourth century peace was an idea whose time had definitely come. Panhellenism was without question a racial idea, and the Greeks were hardly modest about it: they were quite simply better than everyone else. But perhaps the Greeks were a little too clever to be strictly ethnic about it, and although ancestry remained important in the question of polis citizenship, already early on the distinction between Greek and non-Greek hinged on language rather than ethnic background. Barbarians were simply all those who did not speak Greek (to the Greek ear all foreign languages sounded like "barbarbarbar"), and by the fourth century the notion had emerged that anyone, whatever his ethnic background, who learned Greek and adopted Greek ways became a Greek. Isocrates accepts this cultural definition, believing "that the name 'Hellenes' suggests no longer a race but an intelligence, and that the title 'Hellenes' is applied rather to those who share our culture than to those who share a common blood." (*Panegyricus* 50) A refreshing thought indeed, but the Greeks were not completely free from the silly racial prejudices that have plagued our species, and Isocrates, like most Greeks, also believes that most barbarians simply do not have the capacity to adopt Greek culture.

Isocrates first expresses his Panhellenic program in his *Panegyricus*, published in or about 380. The idea is a simple one: "It is not possible for us to cement an enduring peace unless we join together in a war against the barbarians, nor for the Hellenes to attain to concord until we wrest our material advantages from one and the same source and wage our wars against one and the same enemy." (*Panegyricus* 173) In other words, unite in an assault on the Persian Empire and all Greece's problems will solve themselves. There will be a finish to the seemingly endless conflict in Greece, because the poleis will be fighting together against an outside foe and this war will absorb all the restless individuals and energy now stirring up trouble for the Greeks. The crusade against the Great King, in addition to liberating once and for all the Greeks of Asia, will also cure the economic woes of the Greeks, enabling them to "bring the prosperity of Asia across to Europe." (*Panegyricus* 187) The conquered areas of the empire will not be assimilated, but simply subjugated, and the barbarians will be enslaved or removed and their lands given to poor Greeks. Thus, no more problems for the polis.

Isocrates was a Greek, so of course his vision of unifying Greece stopped at the gates of the polis, and what he is calling for is a league of autonomous poleis, not a Greek nation. Naturally enough, he sees Athens as the obvious leader of this league and praises the fifth century empire as a good model for all of Greece. The events of the decades following 380, however, soured Isocrates on Athens, or any polis for that matter, as possible leader of the coalition, while the rise of Macedonian power gave him a new idea. In his speech *To Philip* in 346 he restates his case for a Panhellenic crusade, but now invites king Philip II (358-336) of Macedon to become the leader of the alliance.

This must have been a tough decision for Isocrates. The Greeks identified kings with tyrants and associated them with barbarian peoples: "The Hellenes were not accustomed to submit to the rule of one man, while the other races were incapable of ordering their lives without the control of some such power." (*To Philip* 107) The fact that the Indo-European warrior kingship of Macedon was a far cry from the absolute autocracy of Persia was a distinction that the average Greek could not make, and selling Philip, who by 346 was a looming threat to the southern powers, was virtually an impossible row to hoe. Isocrates talks about effectiveness, which is what drew him to monarchy, and moderation and restraint and the Athenian monarch Theseus, who submitted to the law, but kingship will simply not pass muster. Fundamental to the concept of the polis was the rule of law, and in the minds of the Greeks a king was by definition above the law and thus incompatible with their way of life. (The Spartan kings, with their severely restricted power, were not recognized as true monarchs.)

Panhellenism, like world peace, was a grand idea whose benefits everyone could easily see, but whose implementation remained completely elusive. Even the smallest step towards voluntary unity meant that the polis had to surrender some of its autonomy, and several centuries of Greek history strongly indicated that this was not about to happen no matter how bad things got. The whole international approach of Panhellenism was wrong, for the problem was the polis itself, and so long as the polis was the autonomous political unit of the Greeks, they were doomed to strife. Even when Isocrates' Panhellenic dream came true, imposed upon the Greeks by Philip, even when the riches of Asia began to cross to Europe in the wake of Alexander's conquest, the poleis remained opposed to unity and ready to revolt at the first opportunity. Only as a province of the Roman Empire would Greece finally find harmony.

################

SUGGESTED READING

The main source for the first half of the fourth century is the Athenian general Xenophon, whose *Hellenica* picks up where Thucydides' history leaves off. He is supplemented by the Greek history of Diodorus Siculus (tedious) and Plutarch's lives of Pelopidas, Lysander, Agesilaus and Artaxerxes (amusing). By all means take a look at Xenophon's account of the march of the Ten Thousand, the *Anabasis*; it reads like an action novel (and apparently inspired the 1979 movie *The Warriors*, about a New York gang fighting its way back home). You would likely find Isocrates' speeches pretty boring. Among the few readable accounts of the period are Charles Hamilton, *Agesilaus and the Failure of the Spartan Hegemony* (1991) and L.A. Tritle, *The Greek World in the Fourth Century* (1997); a bit denser, but still readable is Raphael Sealey, *Demosthenes and His Time* (1993), which examines the entire century from the point of view of Athens. If you're interested in military affairs, try J.K. Anderson, *Military Theory and Practice in the Age of Xenophon* (1970).

# # # # # # # # # # # # # # # # #

XIII. THE HEAVY HEADS

PLATO AND ARISTOTLE

The children of the inferior Guardians, and defective offspring of the others,
will be quietly and secretly disposed of.

-Plato *Republic* 460C[29]

For when the unpropertied class without the support of a middle class
gets on top by weight of numbers, things go badly and they soon come to
grief.

-Aristotle *Politics* 1296A[30]

By the middle of the fourth century it was perfectly clear that the Greeks, who
were gradually battering themselves into oblivion, had serious problems, but
not even the Panhellenists, with their broader perspective, could deal with the
heart of the problem: the polis itself. The Greeks were seemingly ensnared in
their history, and even the two most towering intellects of the age, Plato and
Aristotle, were caught in the polis trap. When the two thinkers considered
the question of reforming the state and society, both unhesitatingly accepted
the polis as the starting point, positing new justifications for its existence as
the basic unit of Greek society.

The work of Plato and Aristotle, whose importance to western thought
can hardly be overestimated, covered many areas, but in keeping with the
major theme of this book I will concentrate on their political-social ideas. The
two men actually held many common assumptions regarding human society,
and the views of both are in part reactions to the moral and political failure
of the Athenian democracy. But they came from very different backgrounds
and developed entirely different intellectual methods, and consequently, from

the same basic assumptions they created two radically different visions of the ideal state.

PLATO

Plato was born into a wealthy and noble Athenian family sometime around 429, the year of Pericles' death. As an aristocrat he inherited a natural inclination away from democracy and towards oligarchy, but the flagrant terror of the Thirty Tyrants, two of whom were relatives, soured him on the far right. He was of course already unenthusiastic about the radical democracy, which he had watched destroy his country, but he was favorably impressed with the moderation of the democrats after their overthrow of the Thirty in the fall of 403. In 399, however, the restored democracy put to death his teacher and close friend, Socrates, and that was for Plato the last straw. He dropped out of active political life and devoted himself to philosophy until his death in 347.

Actually, in that half century Plato did on a couple of occasions step back into the real world. In 386 he founded the Academy, an association of scholars and students that was the first real school in Athens. While the curriculum of the Academy revolved about mathematics and philosophy, its goal was to train future statesmen, and many of its graduates are found drawing up law codes and constitutions and acting as advisors to rulers. Moreover, Plato himself attempted to put into effect his ideas about the philosopher-king. In 387 he traveled to Italy and then to Syracuse to instruct the tyrant Dionysius I (406-367), but that hard-boiled ruler was apparently so bored by the lectures on geometry, harmonics and the like that he sold Plato into slavery, from which his friends rescued him in 386. Plato tried again in the 360s with Dionysius' successor, Dionysius II (367-357, 346-344), but failed again and gave it up as a lost cause. One thing he did gain from the Sicilian trips, however, was contact in Italy with the Pythagoreans, a mystical sect organized by Pythagoras (fl. 2nd half 6th cent.) in the sixth century. While Pythagoras and his followers did a lot of solid work in basic mathematics, especially number theory, they were also caught up in all sorts of religious foolishness like numerology and the transmigration of souls, and Plato was contaminated by their number mysticism.

Plato's experiences of Athenian politics in the last decades of the fifth century soured him on both democracy and oligarchy as they existed. In his words:

> ...finally, looking at all the States which now exist, I
> perceived that one and all they are badly governed; for the

state of their laws is such as to be almost incurable without some marvelous overhauling and good-luck to boot. So in my praise of the right philosophy I was compelled to declare that by it one is enabled to discern all forms of justice both political and individual. Wherefore the classes of mankind (I said) will have no cessation from evils until either the class of those who are right and true philosophers attains political supremacy, or else the class of those who hold power in the States becomes by some dispensation of Heaven, really philosophic. (*Epistles* 326A-B)[31]

Thus, Plato abstained from traditional political activity and set about instead to define justice and the ideal state, to describe society as it ought to be.

In order to understand the utopian state that Plato presents in his *Republic* it is necessary to understand a bit of his metaphysics. Plato is heir to the tradition of Parmenides and Heraclitus and believes that the world around us, the world we know through our senses, is not true reality, but only a shadow. In fact, he uses an analogy involving shadows to get his point across. We are, he says, like people tied up in a cave, facing a wall and unable to turn around. Behind us are moving figures and behind them a fire, which casts shadows of the figures on the wall before us. Unable to turn because of our bonds, we can see only the shadows and thus assume that they are reality, when actually reality is behind us and true knowledge is outside the cave altogether. So too are our senses a sort of imprisoning cave, leading us to the false assumption that the world they reveal is reality.

Where is true reality then? It is beyond our senses, in a metaphysical world that we can only get at with our mind. There one finds a variety of "Ideas" or "Forms," each of which is created by god and is an absolute and unchanging template for some thing or concept found in our ever-changing sensory world. There, for example, exists the Idea or Form of the essential chair, and every chair that exists in this world or in our minds is simply a reflection, an emanation, an echo of that Idea. This doctrine of Ideas covers abstract notions as well as concrete objects, and the ultimate Idea, the one from which all the others in some way derive their existence, is that of the Good. Understanding these Ideas, especially that of the Good, is the only path to true knowledge, and the serious lover of wisdom sets his sights on the Ideas and ignores the illusions of sensory data. If some of this seems a little vague, it is because Plato is. He assumes that reality and the Good are equivalent, so that to understand his Ideas, which constitute reality, is to understand the Good. There is more than a little Pythagorean mysticism in all this.

This doctrine of Ideas is at least partly Plato's reaction to the later sophists, who denied that there were any such absolutes in the universe. Plato feels that there are absolute objective truths and that they can be known through deductive thinking. The physical sciences are of course of no concern to him, because they deal with the shadow world of the senses and consequently do not lead to the Truth. There is little point in studying the physics or chemistry of shadow chairs, which will provide only "opinion," when you can go right to the heart of the matter by understanding the Idea of the one real chair, from which you gain true "knowledge."

Plato's doctrine of Ideas is mankind's first shot at dealing with the philosophic problem of universals, and there is consequently much that is wrong with it. How far do the categories go? Is there an Idea of dirt or saliva? If there is a single Idea of the line, how can there be an Idea of the triangle, since it is composed of three lines? If the Ideas are eternal, how could they have been created by god? And so on. On the other hand, the work is ground-breaking, and in some ways Plato with his insubstantial archetypical Ideas has come closer to describing the "reality" revealed by post-Newtonian physics than the atomists like Democritus. The ultimate building blocks of reality, such as quarks and other subatomic entities, are as insubstantial as Plato's Ideas, mere shadows expressible only as mathematical symmetries. The mathematical mysticism that Plato inherited in part from the Pythagoreans strikes an oddly familiar chord with the physicists of the relativistic, quantum mechanical universe. And then again, Plato's doctrine is an excellent example of "So what?" philosophy: the world around us may be an illusion, but so what? We have no choice but to live in it anyway.

What is the connection between this otherworldly philosophy and politics, which after all deals with this sordid shadow existence? In order to practice well his art or craft an artist or craftsman must know the end or good of his particular craft; in order to make good pots you must have some idea of what constitutes a good pot, what its end or purpose is. Some crafts are "architectonic," that is, they involve subsidiary crafts, and politics, the art or craft of ruling, must be *the* architectonic craft, since it deals with all of society, which of necessity includes all other crafts. And if politics is thus at the apex of the pyramid of all arts and crafts, then its purpose or good must also be at the apex. It must be the ultimate good, which by definition is the Idea of the Good. Only true philosophers can understand the Good, therefore only philosophers can practice well the craft of politics. Therefore the well-run society requires philosopher-rulers, who, guided by their knowledge of the Good, will make the laws by which the rest of society will order their lives.

Thinking like this, Plato cannot of course even begin to consider democracy as a valid form of government, since by assuming that every man has some ability in the art of politics, democratic theory runs completely counter to his philosopher-ruler idea. For Plato men are clearly unequal in their ability to rule, just as they are obviously unequal in their ability to do other things. This inequality among men is in fact at the heart of Plato's definition of justice and the structure of his ideal state. Each man has a particular thing he does best, and for each man to do his particular thing to the best of his ability is the proper aim of society, since anything else would be wasteful and unfair to the society. For the individual then the attainment of virtue means performing his proper role in society and leaving other roles to others. And this becomes Plato's definition of justice: "...in our state one man has to do one job, the job he was naturally most suited for...justice consists in minding your own business and not interfering with other people." (*Republic* 433A-B)[32] Thus, "do your own thing," except that in the case of Plato's state your own thing is determined not by your desires, but by your natural abilities and the needs of the society. You might feel that playing the guitar is your thing, but if the state determines that you can screw dome lights into Chevettes better than anyone else, you get the job. And that is justice.

The population of this ideal state is divided into three groups, reflecting three basic roles in society. There are the workers, who are the craftsmen and farmers, the productive element in society, and the guardians, composed of the auxiliaries, who defend and police the society, and the philosopher-rulers, who govern the society. This tripartite division of the state corresponds to the three elements into which Plato divides the human soul. The workers parallel the appetitive element, which is all the basic instincts and desires, the forces that drive the human being, as the workers power the state. The rulers are of course the rational element, which controls and directs the energies produced by the appetitive, and the auxiliaries are matched by the spirited element, which includes those things that are not strictly appetitive or rational, such as honor and courage. As the auxiliaries would side with the philosopher-rulers in guiding the workers, so does the spirited side with the rational element in managing the urgings of our instincts. The rational, spirited and appetitive elements of Plato's soul might, with a little stretching, be compared to the ego, superego and id.

This correspondence between the state and the soul emphasizes how for Plato the state is a natural entity, a product of *physis*. This is also in opposition to the later sophists, who claimed that the state was simply a human construct, a product of *nomos*. Plato hearkens back to the traditional view that the polis – and Plato, good Greek that he was, automatically accepted the polis as the natural societal unit – grew out of basic human needs, not out of compacts and conventions. It was a macrocosm of the soul, as the soul was a microcosm of the state. Its aim was the ordering of human life towards the realization by each individual of his particular virtue and the realization by society as a whole of the concept of the Good.

Of course, in so tightly structured a society as the one Plato envisages the state must have absolute control over education. A close relationship between the polis and education (in the sense of moral and political education) was in fact a facet of traditional Greek political thought, but Plato goes to extremes. All children would be educated to their capacity, but only that far, so that by the time the elementary education was completed at age twenty, most would have reached their limit and would become workers. The rest would continue on with a philosophical and political education and become guardians, the very best becoming the philosopher-rulers. So Plato is creating a state ruled by an aristocracy of intellectual talent, and while he divides society into classes, those classes are not fixed castes and individuals will apparently rise or fall according to their abilities. He actually nowhere states that the children of workers will be educated in this fashion, but he strongly implies it and not doing so would waste potential human resources.

Religion and the arts would be reduced to being subordinates of politics and play their role in educating citizens, instilling them with the proper virtues for the functioning of the state. The myths and beliefs of the Greeks would need to be sifted to allow only those stories useful to the society, and some "magnificent myth" would be created to justify, especially to the workers, the class divisions. Plato apparently sees no inconsistency in stressing education and the pursuit of truth (as he understands it), while allowing the government to lie to the people. Literature and art would be censored to allow only that which contributed to the desired social virtues, and the arts would have a moral and political, rather than an aesthetic purpose. And if Stalin, Mao and socialist realism are any indicators, this would likely mean the death of any real art in Plato's ideal state.

For the guardian classes Plato takes further steps to avoid conflict and promote harmony. The dramatic and usually negative impact of economic interests on political stability in the polis was obvious to any thinking Greek, and Plato concluded that private property could only corrupt the governing class and interfere with their service to the society. Consequently, the guardians will have absolutely no personal property whatsoever - common meals, common quarters, common everything. This might be considered a sort of Platonic communism, but unlike your garden variety Marxist-Leninism, which is concerned with economic power and the whole of society, Plato's aim is purely political and limited to a small group,

It was further clear to Plato that family loyalties could be very divisive and harmful to the interests of the state, so the guardians will have no families. They will not marry, but in order that valuable resources not be lost to the gene pool they will procreate, not as they please, but in matches determined by the state according to eugenic principles. The offspring of these unions will be raised by the state and thus never know their parents or siblings. Plato's hope is that they will regard the entire older generation as their parents and all those of their generation as siblings, thus forging new bonds of harmony. This may be starting to sound like an SS fantasy, but Heinrich Himmler and company were concerned with superficial physical characteristics, while Plato is interested primarily in the mind. The idea of selective breeding for humans will strike most people as repugnant, but there are certainly aspects of the notion that might be considered, such as refusing those with genetic diseases the right to reproduce.

All these measures would be confined to the guardian classes, and the workers would have more or less normal families, private property and differences in wealth. Far more interested in the philosophical pursuits of the rulers, Plato is very vague on the whole topic of the workers, but presumably they would be closely watched by the auxiliaries in order to insure that their more normal life-style did not lead to conflict. Like the proles in George Orwell's *1984*, the workers are compensated for their total lack of political power by being allowed a more traditional, less severe existence than the guardians, whose lives are completely dedicated to the state.

In his desire to use the human resources of the society in the fullest possible fashion Plato, incidentally, becomes the first real spokesman for the liberation of women. The poetess Sappho has received all the publicity in this area, but she in fact has nothing to say about changing the lot of women in Greece. Plato is intelligent enough to realize and open-minded enough to admit that females have talents and capacities that are being wasted because of the traditional practice of keeping them shut away in the house. He believes that males are generally superior, but suggests that many women are better than men in many areas and proposes that they be given equal education and access to serving the state as members of the guardian class.

Such, briefly, is Plato's utopia, an ideal place, if you happen to think as he does, valuing the harmony and unity of the state above the individual and chasing after his brand of metaphysical wisdom. For most of us, I suspect, it is an appalling community, a totalitarian nightmare. It was in fact not so appealing to the average Greek either, despite the fact that the Greeks had a far stronger sense of community than we. Basic to the traditional idea of the polis was the notion that authority in the state derived from the people, and while that notion is not explicitly rejected by Plato, the nature of his utopia effectively eliminates it. Whatever they might claim, the authority exercised by the guardians comes from above, perhaps not from heaven, as in the oriental monarchies, but from a metaphysical vision nevertheless. The philosopher-rulers might as well be oriental despots, for they are not subject to the rule of law like the mass of workers, but to a *physis* that they themselves are constantly defining. They may be pursuing their idea of the Good, but so were Khomeini and Kahane and the Ku-Klux Klan.

ARISTOTLE

The circumstances of Aristotles' life forged a mind of a temperament utterly different from that of Plato's. He was born into a family of Ionian background in 384 in Stagira, a town in the Chalcidice, and from 367 to 347 was a student in Athens at Plato's Academy. When the master died he moved to Assus in Asia Minor, where a group of Academy graduates had established a kind of Platonic think tank. They had been given the town by the local tyrant, Hermias (c. 355-341), whose niece Aristotle married, bringing him an inside look at autocratic government. In 344 Aristotle was off to the island of Lesbos to work as a marine biologist, but his researches were interrupted about two years later when the call from Macedon came. Aristotle's father was chief sawbones at the Macedonian court, and through his influence his son was appointed tutor to prince Alexander (336-323), soon to become the Great. Aristotle seems to have had little influence on Alexander, and though he may have taught the lad some moderation and stirred a scientific curiosity that was probably already there, none of his political views rubbed off, and Alexander would go his own way in dealing with the Asiatics (see Chapter XV). The celebrated association lasted until 335, when the student had become the king of Macedon and the teacher returned to Athens to establish his own school, the Lyceum. There he remained until 323, when Alexander's death stirred Athens to revolt against Macedon and to look unfavorably upon former tutors to the king. Aristotle fled to Chalcis, and there he died the following year.

It would be surprising if Aristotle did not look at the world differently from Plato. In Athens, where he spent most of his life, he was a foreigner, free of any attachments to the traditional politics of his adopted home. Middle income in origin himself, he also lived in the Athens of the conservative, bourgeois fourth century democracy and missed the antics of the radical democrats and oligarchs that were so much a feature of Plato's youthful environment. Not only could Aristotle look at politics more dispassionately than his teacher, but he also had no cause to despair of realistic reform and flee into utopian dreams.

Further, Aristotle's temperment and his father's medical profession turned his mind early on to the physical sciences at which Plato had sneered and instilled in him a commitment to observation and inductive reasoning, at least in his study of marine biology and political science. In doing biology or geology or whatever you examine many individual cases or facts and then inductively arrive at a generalized truth; you move from the specific to the general. Plato thought deductively, moving from the general to the specific; he began with some grand truth or axiom and from that deduced the particulars. In short, Aristotle employed the scientific method – some of the time at least – and his *Politics* is the result of bringing that method to bear on the questions of political science. The *Republic* is based on speculation; Plato sat down in a comfortable chair, poured himself a cup of wine and began thinking: "The state is natural and must therefore reflect the human soul, which is divided into three parts, so the state ought to be likewise divided, etc." Not so for Aristotle the scientist. The *Politics* is based on hard data, gathered from the examination of the constitutions of 158 actual states, both Greek and non-Greek. Like a good doctor Aristotle studied the morphology and pathology of human society before recommending a cure.

Like Plato, Aristotle accepts the polis as the basic unit of society, which is in a way ironic, since Aristotle was above all an observer of the world around him, and even before Alexander there were signs that the world was moving towards social-political units larger than the polis. And even more ironic, he was for six years tutor to the man who would almost single-handedly put an end to the polis as the dominant political type in the Greek world. But Aristotle was a Greek, and his belief in the polis was almost genetically determined.

Also like Plato, Aristotle has a teleological view of things, which is to say he believes there are immanent in nature purposes that have nothing to do with the human will. Everything is determined towards some particular end in a way that goes beyond simple mechanical causation. Aristotle's teleology is wrapped up in his ideas on matter and form, which hold that everything develops from the potential of unformed matter to the actual of the formed matter. Take, for example, the teleology of the oak. In the acorn there is the matter (metaphysically speaking) of the oak, but as yet only the potential of the tree. In order for the actual to be achieved the matter must take on its form by developing in the proper environment, in the case of the acorn one of soil, sunlight and water.

Aristotle applies these ideas to develop his concept of man and the state. The state is natural because man is a "political animal," that is, he can find his full development only in the context of a state. Like Thucydides, Aristotle recognizes that there exist in men primitive antisocial instincts or inclinations, the kind of uninhibited drive to self satisfaction seen in small children and in adults in anarchic situations. These urges are part of the *physis* of the human being, but they are only the unformed matter, the potential of the fully developed man. For man to achieve his full development, for the matter to take on form, he must be placed in the proper environment, and since he is a political animal, that environment is human society, as embodied in the polis. The man raised alone in the woods is incomplete, and his basic instincts rule his life, leading him to no greater accomplishment than satisfying his thirst, hunger, lust, etc. Only in the state can these impulses be controlled and the complete man be developed, as the political craft – *nomos* – shapes the basic human nature – *physis* – into its developed form. Thus, the state is natural because it is necessary to the teleology of the human being. Besides, says Aristotle, alone among the animals man has the power of "reasoned speech," which is meaningful only in the political context, so he was clearly designed for life in the polis.

How does the state come about? It arises from the natural impulse to partnership, most obvious at its primary stage, the attraction of male and female. They create a family, which ultimately generates more families, which will be drawn together to form a larger association, the village. Ultimately a number of villages will combine to form the polis, at which point the process stops, because the polis represents a stage at which self-sufficiency is reached. No further development is required to satisfy man's intellectual and material needs. True to the traditional view of the polis, Aristotle also insists that the state has a moral purpose: "So we must lay it down that the political association which we call a state exists not simply for the purpose of living together but for the sake of noble actions." (*Politics* 1281A) He believes the state must, through its laws, shape virtuous citizens, and he thus also holds to the traditional notions of a close relationship between the state and ethics and the state and education. This all fits in with his general teleological ideas – the state is the nurturing environment that shapes the unformed human matter into its final form, the civilized, virtuous citizen.

The law that Aristotle has in mind when he speaks of shaping the virtuous citizen is not quite what we or the Athenian democrats would think of. He has an older vision of law as a sort of body of guidelines, hallowed by time and changing only very slowly. It is distinguished from specific decrees of the assembly, which he feels are not law, but destructive to it, an idea reflected somewhat in the structure of the fourth century democracy in Athens. Unlike Plato with his absolutes, Aristotle is enough of a realist to recognize and admit that society and its laws cannot be static, but he says virtually nothing about the acceptable mechanisms for change.

Justice for Aristotle is obedience to the laws, and in the state where the laws are morally correct justice is equivalent to virtue. This is his grand definition of justice, but he also recognizes two forms of particular justice: corrective and distributive. Corrective justice is familiar to us; it is the criminal and civil law that acts to restore the proper structure of society by punishing the wrongdoer and providing the injured with an avenue for the redress of his grievances. Distributive justice is the notion that the state distributes its honors or offices according to the contributions of its citizens. In a democracy this theoretically means little, since the contribution of each is the same: being a citizen. For Aristotle, who believes the creation of virtue to be the goal of the state, the standard of distribution is virtue, so that the virtuous man will be better rewarded by the state. Like Plato, Aristotle emphatically believed in the inequality of men, even to the point of asserting that many men were by nature best suited to be slaves. This is reflected in his definitions of the best constitutions, both of which deprive large segments of the population of the citizenship.

Aristotle discusses his ideal state in Books VII and VIII of the *Politics*, but actually has little to say about it. Most of his time is spent discussing education, and he supplies only the barest sketch of the state's actual structure. Agriculture and commercial activities would be in the hands of non-citizens, while the citizens would serve as soldiers when young, rulers when older and priests when retired. State directed education will play a major role in the life of the citizen, and the state will regulate marriage and procreation, though not so thoroughly and coldly as in Plato's utopia. Aristotle's cursory treatment of his ideal state demonstrates how different he is from Plato. Speculation about utopias is fine, but the real meat for the political scientist is found in an examination of existing states, and the best part of the *Politics* is found in Books IV-VI, where Aristotle analyzes the nature and problems of existing constitutions. Drawing from the results of this analysis, he presents his semi-ideal state, the constitution most likely to suit realistically the majority of men and conditions.

For Aristotle the best all around state is one broadly based on the middle class, which he observed to be "the steadiest element, the least eager for change. They neither covet, like the poor, the possessions of others, nor do others covet theirs, as the poor covet those of the rich." (*Politics* 1295B) They lack the drive to power of the wealthy and the political lethargy of the poor and are less susceptible to the extremes of tyranny and anarchy. They are accustomed both to governing and to being governed. In short they are the perfect balance, the political mean between rich and poor, and they thus fit Aristotle's general doctrine of the mean, which prescribes the middle way and moderation in all things.

In this constitution, which Aristotle calls a polity, the middle class must form the bulk of the citizen body, so the lower classes, the small farmers and artisans, will be disenfranchised. Like the *metics* in Athens, they will have private rights and be protected by the law, but they will not be citizens and will hold no property. This is a moderate, middle class democracy, similar in fact to the constitution Athens actually had for a time after the death of Alexander. And similar to many other constitutions in the Greek world, which is partly why Aristotle arrived at it. His examination of existing states revealed that limited franchise democracies, in which the middle class wielded the most power, were generally the most stable and least prone to factional strife. Within this polity there were the virtues of oligarchy and democracy without the extremes of each; there was both quality and quantity in government. In coming to these conclusions, incidentally, Aristotle was breaking new ground in political science, becoming, so far as we know, the first to think of societies and political structures in terms of combinations of socio-economic groups, rather than just constitutional forms.

Plato and Aristotle shared a great deal in their political thought, at least in terms of basic assumptions. They both had a teleological world view and believed in the basic inequality of men. They both accepted the polis as the natural unit of human society and felt that the state must play a positive moral role in shaping its citizens. They consequently both postulated a close connection between the state and education and saw *nomos* and *physis* as complementary rather than antagonistic. But their different modes of thought, stemming from their different backgrounds, produced from these same basic assumptions two entirely different visions of society. Plato, the deductive idealist and mathematical mystic, dreams up the revolutionary and visionary utopia of the *Republic*; Aristotle, the inductive realist and logical scientist, assembles the entirely workable middle class polity.

# # # # # # # # # # # # # # # # # # # #

SUGGESTED READING

The basic readings are obvious: Plato's *Republic* and Aristotle's *Politics*, to which should be added Aristotle's *Nicomachean Ethics*, which examines fundamental issues discussed further in the *Politics*. As you might suspect, these are not works that will keep you at the edge of your chair. Once again I refer you to Kagan, *The Great Dialogue*, whose chapter on Plato also includes discussions of his political thought in the *Politicus* and the *Laws*. There are countless books on Plato and Aristotle; I recommend an oldie but a goodie, Ernest Barker, *The Political Thought of Plato and Aristotle* (1906); his *Greek Political Theory* (1918) is also excellent and includes material on the Greek state, the pre-Socratic philosophers and the sophists as well as Plato and Aristotle.

# # # # # # # # # # # # # # # # # # # #

XIV. THE TIMES THEY ARE A-CHANGIN'

MAGNA GRAECIA, PHILIP II AND THE RISE OF MACEDON

(Philip) was so overcome with drink and with rage
that he tripped and fell headlong. Alexander jeered at him
and cried out, "Here is the man who was making ready to cross
from Europe to Asia, and who cannot even cross
from one table to another without losing his balance."

-Plutarch *Alexander* 9.5[33]

About the time that the Theban supremacy was evaporating and the Athenians were learning the limitations of their second naval league a new power was stirring in the far north of the Balkan Peninsula, one that would change the face of Greece. Before attending to that dramatic story, however, some attention needs to be given to the Greeks of Italy and Sicily. Apart from the odd contact like the Athenian expedition of 415-413 the western Greeks were generally peripheral to the main thrust of Hellenic history, but they are Greeks and they certainly played an important role in the development of the two western superpowers, Rome and Carthage. Consequently, a quick review of the action in the wild west is warranted before getting on to the higher profile Macedonians.

MAGNA GRAECIA

Magna Graecia, that is, the Greek cities of Sicily and southern Italy, was settled during the great colonization of the eighth through early sixth centuries. Because of powerful Italic tribes in the interior, settlement on the peninsula was confined to the coastal areas, and Etruscan power in central Italy meant that Cumae, about one hundred miles southeast of Rome, was the northernmost penetration. But even this limited presence was enough to have a dramatic impact, and it is hard to exaggerate the importance of these poleis, most especially Cumae, to the history of Rome. Almost from its birth Rome was being overwhelmed by the more developed culture and institutions of the Greeks, which is why so much of Roman culture – military forms, gods, art, etc. - seems to be Greek material translated into Latin. In fact, the Latin alphabet you are reading at this very moment is a product of that cultural assault, as the locals adopted and modified the Greek script for their own use.

On Sicily the Greeks found native Sicans and Sicels, who were easily driven into the interior, and the mysterious Elymians, who shared the western end of the island with a far more important group, the Carthaginians. Carthage (on the Tunisian coast) was founded in the late eighth century by settlers from the Phoenician city of Tyre (on the Lebanese coast), and by the arrival of the first Greeks on Sicily they had established trading stations on the western coast. Busy building a commercial empire that stretched from north Africa to Spain to southern France, Carthage had little concern for the Sicilian Greeks until the early sixth century, when Greek colonists appeared in the western part of the island. This aggressiveness led to a major Carthaginian expedition and Greek defeat on the island in the middle of the century, while at the battle of Alalia in c. 535 a joint Carthaginian-Etruscan force broke the back of Greek naval power in the western Mediterranean.

Untroubled by the Carthaginians for the next half century, the Sicilian Greeks indulged themselves in intercity warfare and tyrannies, the most important of which were those of Gelon (485-478) of Syracuse and Theron (c. 489-473) of Acragas. Then, in 480 Carthage invaded Sicily again, almost certainly acting in consort with the Great King of Persia, who was himself busy trying to conquer the Balkan Peninsula. Gelon and Theron met Hamilcar (d. 480) and his Carthaginians at Himera and crushed them, and six years later Gelon's successor, Hieron (478-467), helped destroy Etruscan naval power at the battle of Cumae, thus freeing the western Greeks from their two major threats. Cumae and her Latin allies had already defeated the Etruscans at Aricia in c. 505, securing in the process the independence of the new Roman Republic, which would ultimately absorb the entire Greek world.

With the death of Hieron in 467 Sicily's age of tyrants essentially came to an end, and republican Syracuse gradually became the dominant power on the island, in effect declaring the island off limits when imperial Athens began nosing around in the 420s. Syracuse successfully resisted the massive

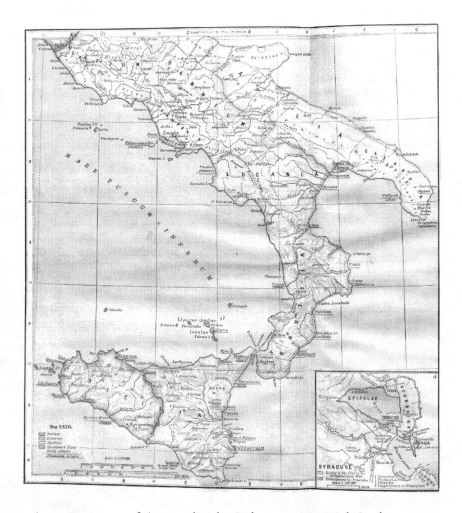

Athenian invasion of 415-13, but her exhaustion tempted Carthage to try again, and in 409 Hannibal, grandson of Hamilcar, invaded Sicily, setting off four years of Greek-Carthaginian warfare on the island. The conflict provided the circumstances for the emergence at Syracuse of a new tyrant, Dionysius I, who in 405 concluded with the Carthaginians a peace that left them in control of roughly the western half of the island. Dionysius, whose tyranny would last almost forty years, then consolidated his hold on the Greek part of the island and in 398 set out to conquer Carthaginian Sicily, squeezing the Carthaginians into the northwestern corner of the island by 397. A second Punic (from "Poeni," Latin for Phoenician) war in 392 only confirmed the outcome of the first, and the tyrant then spent the 380s extending his empire into southern Italy.

In 367 Dionysius was succeeded by his weak son, Dionysius II, who was initially under the influence of his father's most trusted advisor, Dion (c. 408-353). With lofty ideals and designs for reforming the state Dion convinced the new tyrant to invite Plato to Sicily for a second time, but the visit only led to troubles between Dionysius and his advisor, who was driven into exile. Dion returned in 357 and captured Syracuse, which led to a decade of strife in the city and empire and a growing threat from Carthage. In 344 Corinth, mother city of Syracuse, sent out a tiny force under a native son, Timoleon (d. c. 335), who restored order on the island, retired Dionysius and established democracy in Syracuse, bringing in sixty thousand Greek immigrants to repopulate the city. He then decisively defeated a massive Carthaginian invasion in 339, but beset by enemies on the domestic front, he had no opportunity to finish the job by throwing the Africans off the island altogether. Having defeated the Carthaginians and freed Syracuse and most other Sicilian cities from tyranny, this remarkable man simply retired, refusing the power that typically seduced most men of his ability and accomplishments.

When Dion began his war with Dionysius II, the Syracusan empire in Italy collapsed immediately, and the Greek cities were soon threatened by the local Italic tribes in the interior. Following the lead of Syracuse, in 343 Tarentum (or Taras), Sparta's only colony, appealed to her mother city, which having been reduced to a minor player in Greece, was free to send king Archidamus III (360-338) and a band of mercenaries. Unfortunately, Archidamus was far less successful than Timoleon, getting himself killed in 338, and in 334 Tarentum invited in king Alexander I (342-330) of Epirus, uncle of Alexander the Great. Alexander was successful against Italian barbarians, but not his own ambitions, and his attempt to build an Epirote empire in Italy ended with his assassination in 330.

All this action in Magna Graecia was about to come to an end, however, as the new kid on the block, Rome, grew stronger and stronger. Syracuse was seized in 316 by a new tyrant, Agathocles, who ruled until his death in 289/8, which ushered in a period of instability until Hieron II (c. 271-216) seized power in c. 271. Back in Italy, in order to meet the threat from Rome Tarentum in 281 invited in a second Epirote king, Pyrrhus (307/6-272), who defeated the Romans in two battles (but with heavy losses - your original "pyrrhic" victories), intervened in Sicily and returned to Greece in 275, leaving the Italian Greeks to their fate. Meanwhile, in Sicily Agathocles' one-time barbarian mercenaries, the Mamertines, now under pressure from Hieron, made an alliance with the Romans, whose installation of a garrison in Mamertine-controlled Messana brought on the First Punic War between Rome and Carthage in 264. With the end of the war in 241 Carthage would surrender all claims to Sicily, and henceforth, the western Greeks would be part of Roman history.

MACEDON

North of Thessaly and the Olympus range and west of the Chalcidice, Macedon was a country generations behind the poleis to the south. The Macedonian heartland, the area immediately to the northwest of the Theramic Gulf, had never synoecized, and while there were Greek cities in the region, Macedon itself was not a polis, but a kingdom. The Macedonian monarch ruled over the coastal region directly, but his control over the upland districts to the north and west was limited to a loose overlordship, if that. The highland tribes were mostly non-Greek, and in their desire to remain independent they were accustomed to invite in their barbarian cousins, the Illyrians to the west and the Paeonians to the north. The Macedonian king was thus kept busy trying to control his own vassals, while fighting off barbarian incursions and increasing interference from the Greeks to the south.

The Macedonians were of Greek stock and spoke Greek, but they were regarded by their southern cousins as semi-barbarians at best. Except for the language the Greeks to the south could find little to distinguish the Macedonians from the barbarian tribes that surrounded them: they had a warrior monarchy instead of a legitimate constitutional government, they had virtually no real cities and they were constantly armed and fighting one another. (The Greeks were being more than a little hypocritical here.) And they drank their wine neat, when any civilized person would of course cut it with several parts of water. Some progress in Hellenizing the kingdom had been made, especially by king Archelaus (413-399), who imported artists and intellectuals, such as Zeuxis (fl. c. 425) and Euripides (the *Bacchae* was first produced there), and moved the capital from ancient Aegae to Pella on the coast, providing easier access to the wider Greek world. But the stigma remained, and it may be that Alexander's special treatment of a constantly double-dealing Athens stemmed at least partly from the desire to be accepted as a real Greek by the city that in many ways defined the term.

Constantly occupied with fending off their neighbors and trying to keep their own house in order, the Macedonians had had no opportunity to do more than occasionally pop on and off the stage of Greek history. They had been compelled to submit to the invading Persians, and the kings of the fifth and early fourth centuries had been forced to step lively in order to avoid, not always successfully, becoming pawns of the major powers to the south. This all changed in 359, when king Perdiccas III (365-359) was killed, along with 4000 of his troops, in a battle with invading Illyrians. He was succeeded by his son Amyntas III (359-358, d. 336) who was however only a child, so his brother Philip was appointed as guardian and regent. The twenty-four year old Philip faced a truly daunting task. The Macedonian army had just been annihilated, Illyrians occupied the western part of the land, a Paeonian army threatened from the north, a horde of Thracians was approaching from the east and a variety of pretenders were parading around drumming up support, especially in the south.

Philip's first move was to buy some breathing space. He scraped together the money to buy off the Paeonians and Thracians and eliminated any pretenders he could get his hands on. Then, during the winter he put together an army of 10,000 and in 358 smashed both the Paeonians and Illyrians, employing some new ideas on tactics. While in the west, he helped out Epirus, the area south of Illyria and a valuable ally, and took as his wife a wild Epirote princess, Olympias (d. 316). With Macedon thus secured he immediately began a push to the east, into Thrace and towards the gold mines of Mt. Pangaeus, which brought him into conflict with Amphipolis. In 357 he took that city, and in the following year gained an alliance with the Chalcidian League in order to keep them and the Athenians off his back while he pushed further east. By 353 he had secured his grip on Thrace and with the exception of the Chalcidice now controlled the north coast of the Aegean east to the Chersonese. His general Parmenio (c. 400-330) had meanwhile crushed the Illyrians a second time.

During this period Philip was also engaged in uniting Macedon and building a new model army, two jobs that he fused into one. He incorporated the tough highlanders into his new army and turned them into professional soldiers with a stake in the fortunes of Macedon, thus beginning the process of turning them into Macedonians. It was the revenues from Thrace that allowed him to pay these and the rest of his soldiers and create the first national standing army in Greece (if the Spartans are not counted). The Macedonian army would thus be composed of paid professionals, as skilled as mercenaries, but loyal to the Macedonian state rather than to some temporary paymaster. As a sop to tribal identity and pride, Philip initially needed regiments organized along tribal lines, but by the end of his reign they had been abandoned, as the highlanders came to think of themselves as Macedonians first.

This professional force alone would give Philip an edge over the citizen armies and mercenaries of the south, but he also applied some new ideas on tactics. He opened the phalanx formation up a bit and gave the heavy infantry a smaller shield, suspended from the neck, and a true, two-handed pike, anywhere from thirteen to fifteen feet long. More important, working with Epaminondas' idea of the knockout punch, which he had learned as a teenage hostage in Thebes, he became the first Greek general to integrate the various types of arms under his command. Until now cavalry and light and medium infantry had essentially been used independently, and the big battles had more or less been hoplite shows. Philip's new tactics saw the different parts of the army working together, and his common approach in a set battle was to engage and grind away with the phalanx until a weak spot appeared in the enemy line, at which point the Companion cavalry were sent in to blow open a hole. The Companions, at the head of which Alexander would be accustomed to ride, are often described as heavy cavalry, but they were not actually such. True heavy cavalry puts all the momentum of the charging horse behind the blow of the lance, and the ancient world lacked two key pieces of equipment for this: a saddle with a high cantle and even more crucial, the stirrup, which did not appear in the west until the eighth century AD. A Greek horseman hitting a target with a couched lance like a medieval knight would simply be knocked off the back of his horse.

The young Philip had accomplished an impressive amount in this first phase of his rise. Macedon's frontiers were secured, and she now enjoyed a steady income from her control of Thrace. The country was well on the road to becoming truly united, with the upland tribes serving as a new source of strength rather than a constant disruptive force and hassle. The new Macedonian army was quickly emerging as a formidable organization, and for the first time in her history Macedon could expect a little respect from the poleis to the south. Philip had done this through incredibly adroit diplomacy and his talent for military innovation and leadership. He was in fact so good that only a year after he took over from his dead brother the Macedonian people under arms (i.e., the army) set Amyntas aside and elected him king Philip II. A survival of the Dark Age and the epic world of Homer, this is the old Indo-European kingship in action – the warrior leader elected by the warrior host. His was the legitimate line now, and his first son, Alexander, born in 356, would follow him – if of course he could handle the job.

For the next several years Philip was busy with operations in Thrace and Illyria (being unable to appreciate power in the abstract, barbarians must be taught a lesson every other year; ask the Romans about this) and in Thessaly, where in 352 he defeated a huge force of Phocian sponsored mercenaries and won control of the forces of the Thessalian League. This control was formalized later in 342 when the Macedonian king was made permanent archon or *tagus* of the League, creating a personal union between Macedon and Thessaly that lasted until the Roman conquest. With all his other marches secured, in 349 he finally attacked the Chalcidian League, which fell the following year and was incorporated into Macedon. Virtually everything north of Thermopylae was his.

During this second phase Philip was also involved in an increasingly open war with the Athenians, whose interests in the north he was definitely injuring. He had stirred up trouble among their allies, raided their grain ships and most important threatened the Chersonese and the Athenian food supply. The spirit of the resistance in Athens was the orator Demosthenes (384-322), who had perceived early on the threat Philip posed to Greece, but the Athenians were tired of war, especially war at a distance, and Athenian efforts, such as aid to the Chalcidians, were mostly ineffective. The Athenian navy, however, was very effective in keeping Philip away from the Hellespont, and he decided to wait upon developments in central Greece before pushing further in the east. And so in 346 the Peace of Philocrates was signed and Philip and Athens became allies, the former guaranteeing the security of the Chersonese and the latter finally renouncing her claims to Amphipolis.

There was one final move in this second phase of Macedon's rise to power. In 356 the Third Sacred War had erupted in central Greece when the Phocians illegally occupied the Delphic sanctuary and had war declared upon them by the Delphic Amphictionic League, an ancient cultural and religious association of the central Greek states. Normally a military light-weight, the Phocians looted the Delphic treasuries to hire a mercenary army of unprecedented size, with which they were able to hold off Thebes and the Amphictionic forces for most of a decade. It was this army that Philip had decimated in Thessaly in 352, thereby dooming the Phocians to ultimate defeat, and by 346 they were on their last legs. But one of those legs was a garrison in the pass at Thermopylae, and when Phocis was expressly excluded from the Peace of Philocrates, the garrison commander despaired and in exchange for the safe conduct of his troops handed the pass over to Philip. Without lifting a sword Philip had gained possession of the crucial gateway to central Greece. He also gained Phocis' votes on the Amphictionic Council, which along with the Thessalian and other seats he controlled provided him with the dominant voice in the affairs of the Amphictionic League. Macedon was now the paramount power in the Balkan Peninsula.

For the next few years Philip is again out smashing barbarians in Illyria, Epirus and Thrace, where he carried Macedonian arms all the way north to the Danube. The southern powers were meanwhile finally waking up to the reality of Macedonian strength, and Demosthenes was in the political ascendancy in an Athens now preparing for war. Looking to bring the war on, he engineered the revolt of Byzantium (Istanbul) from the Macedonian alliance in 341, and when Philip laid siege to this key to the Black Sea the following year, Athens abandoned the Peace and sent her navy into action. Essentially helpless against naval power, Philip was forced to withdraw and went north to the lower Danube to deal with a big invasion of Scythian barbarians.

Blocked in his eastward expansion because of his lack of a serious navy, Philip looked again to the south, and incredibly, in 339 the Greeks themselves invited him in. In that year the Amphictionic League, as it had earlier against Phocis, declared war – the Fourth Sacred War – against western (or Ozolian or Amphissan) Locris for a sacrilege committed against Apollo. Thebes, a traditional friend of Locris (they both hated their common neighbor, Phocis) abstained from the voting and was followed by Athens, which under the influence of Demosthenes was doing everything possible to get an alliance with the Thebans against Macedon. Left wide open to the influence of Philip, the Amphictionic Council appointed him commander of the League forces, and in early 338 he showed up in central Greece with the Macedonian army. The Thebans realized that the crunch had finally come and took the Athenian deal, which included recognition of their claim to Boeotia. This alliance was the final triumph of Demosthenes, who had managed the well nigh impossible feat of convincing the Athenians to forget two hundred years of hostility towards their neighbor. But it was too late.

In August of 338 at Chaeronea in Boeotia the king brought his 32,000 Macedonians against perhaps 35,000 Boeotian, Athenian, allied and mercenary infantry and humiliated them. Philip suckered the Athenians, who were facing him on the right of his line, with a feigned withdrawal, which both put the pursuing Athenians into disarray and also opened up a gap in the allied line. He then turned and crushed the disorganized and surprised Athenians, while the eighteen year old crown prince Alexander drove the Companion cavalry into the gap, rolling up the Boeotian hoplites. The Theban Sacred Band died almost to the man, and after the battle Philip, ever the warrior king, was found weeping over their bodies.

In the wake of the battle the allies surrendered, and a parade into the Peloponnesus brought the submission of the rest of the Greek states, excepting Sparta. Philip apparently decided that this pathetic remnant of a once great power was of some value independent, a menace to keep the other Peloponnesian states aligned with him. It is customary to say that Greek freedom died on the field of Chaeronea, but this is not quite accurate. What expired at Chaeronea was the autonomy of the polis. Except for the fact that they would not be spending nearly as much time killing one another, for most Greeks life would go on pretty much as it had before. The poleis would continue to exist until the Roman conquest some two hundred years later, and some would manage to stay relatively independent, one of them, Rhodes, even playing a significant role in Mediterranean affairs. But essentially

Chaeronea meant the end of the polis as the dominant political unit in the Greek world. It was time to move on to bigger things.

In late 338 Philip organized the Greek states, except Sparta, into the League of Corinth, a federal union of theoretically autonomous poleis, pledged to maintain the peace and security of the Greek world. It had a council of representatives, the *synhedrion*, that determined policy to be carried out by the League under its permanent hegemon, the king of Macedon, and in its first meeting in early 337 the League immediately declared war on the Persian Empire. The Panhellenic dream was realized - in a way. One could not but help notice the Macedonian garrisons in Thebes, Chalcis, Corinth and Ambracia, and League policy seemed to be pretty much whatever Philip was interested in. The League of Corinth was in fact a mechanism by which Macedon could exercise an hegemony over central and southern Greece, not so much to control and exploit these states as to prevent them from threatening Macedon or distracting it from other business, like conquering the east. The Greek states in question were certainly not amused. They planned a revolt at the news of Philip's death, they did revolt at a rumor of Alexander's death and they revolted again when Alexander did die. The idea of autonomy in the polis died very hard, and even over a century later Athens still presumed she could deal with the Romans as if she were a significant power.

In 336 Philip sent Parmenio and Attalus (d. 336) with 10,000 men across to Asia Minor to prepare the way for a full-scale invasion. Philip was to bring the rest of the forces later in the year, but he never made it. At the wedding ceremony in the theater at Aegae for his daughter and the king of Epirus he was killed by a dagger thrust delivered by a disgruntled noble named Pausanias, who was himself immediately dispatched by the king's bodyguard. With the assassin dead before he could be forced to talk suspicions of a conspiracy abounded, and accusing fingers were pointed at Parmenio and other officers, at Olympias and even at Alexander.

We will of course never know, but it may well be that Pausanias, who did indeed have a personal grudge against Philip, was the cats-paw of a conspiracy. In recent years Attalus had been especially honored and elevated by Philip, who in the previous year had taken Attalus' niece Cleopatra (d. 336) as his seventh wife, and nobles like Parmenio and Antipater (c. 397?-319) may have felt threatened. Already at odds with her husband (this was a seriously dysfunctional family), Olympias might well have seen Cleopatra, a full-blooded Macedonian, as a challenge to her status as queen, and even Alexander may have wondered what threat Cleopatra's infant son posed to his position as crown prince. Both aggressive and headstrong men, Philip and Alexander manifestly did not get along, and the impetuous Alexander must have been becoming increasingly impatient with his father's rule, which might well continue for decades. On the other hand, assassinating the king was risky business and could easily plunge the kingdom into civil war and undo the work of twenty years, and there was certainly no guarantee that Alexander would inherit the throne. But the Macedonian barons had never been known for excessive caution.

A great man was dead, and history was already conspiring to deliver Philip an even lower blow that Pausanias' dagger. Almost all we know about Philip comes from his enemies, especially the eloquent Demosthenes, and the picture thus drawn is hardly a flattering one. Worse, Philip was cursed by having a demigod as his son and successor, and while the entire human race has heard of Alexander, how many people know anything about his father? Though condemned forever to remain in the historical shadow of his son, his achievement is nevertheless magnificent. He inherited an almost nonexistent country, defeated, occupied and surrounded by enemies, and in twenty years he created a strong and unified Macedonian state, in control of Thrace and the entire Balkan Peninsula and in possession of the finest army the world had yet seen. Himself cheated of the crowning glory by an assassin, he laid the foundation from which his fair-haired boy would assault Asia. Despite Alexander's incredible achievement, Philip was remembered by the Macedonians as their greatest king, and they deified him, but not his son. Alexander and his ideas were to prove too big and too modern for his people, but Philip the Great was the perfect king of Macedon, both the sophisticated statesman and general, building the state into a world power, and the simple Homeric hero, weeping over the bodies of his slain enemies.

##################

Richard M. Berthold

SUGGESTED READING

On the western Greeks see A.G. Woodhead, *The Greeks in the West* (1962) and J. Boardman, *The Greeks Overseas*[3] (1980); Plutarch has lives of Dion, Timoleon and Pyrrhus. Our main sources for Philip are the history of Diodorus Siculus and the speeches of Isocrates and Demosthenes, none of it especially exciting reading; see also Plutarch's life of Demosthenes. On Macedon a couple of books stand out: R.M. Errington, *A History of Macedonia* (1990) and N.G.L. Hammond, *The Macedonian State. Origins, Institutions and History* (1989); the latter is much heavier going, but Hammond, who fought in the Greek civil war, probably knew more about Macedon than anyone else ever has. On Philip specifically see J.R. Ellis, *Philip II and Macedonian Imperialism* (1976), George Cawkwell, *Philip of Macedon* (1978) and Ian Worthington, *Philip II of Macedonia* (2008) ; M.B. Hatzopoulos & L.D. Loukopoulos, *Philip of Macedon* (1980) is a collection of articles by prominent historians, but is more noteworthy for its lavish illustrations.

################

XV. HE'S FAST, HE'S COOL, HE'S ALEXANDER THE GREAT

ALEXANDER AND THE CONQUEST OF THE EAST

Higgledy-Piggledy Philip of Macedon
Cursed Alexander, his famous papoose:
"Why should I try to be philoprogenitive?
Everyone thinks that his father was Zeus."

-Anonymous

Alexander III was now king of Macedon at the age of twenty. Of necessity his reign began with executions, including those of Attalus, his niece Cleopatra and her son (the latter two killed by Olympias, a woman of extreme vengeance) and Alexander's cousin, the former king, Amyntas. Alexander lived in a hardball world, and the removal of these and other dangerous people was absolutely vital to the security of himself and the state he now headed. The loose nature of the Macedonian monarchy demanded that possible rivals for the throne be eliminated without hesitation. Excepting the half-wit Philip Arrhidaeus, who was allowed to live, Alexander was the eldest legitimate son of Philip, which made him king in theory; that he had the support of his father's officers, especially Parmenio and Antipater, made him king in fact. True, Alexander was already known and trusted by the rank and file of the army, but much more so were these two commanders, and the new king would have to tread carefully for a while.

If Alexander's position in Macedon was a bit insecure, his position outside the homeland was threatening to crumble completely. Where his father might have moved slowly and cautiously, he displayed the speed and boldness that would characterize his career. Leaving Parmenio in Asia and Antipater in Macedon, he hustled south and caught Thebes and Athens before they could actually revolt. He reorganized the League of Corinth, which now swore allegiance to him, and in 335 rushed back north again to deal with trouble in Thrace. Several battles against the barbarians and a brief foray to the north bank of the Danube secured the entire area, and then it was off to the wild west, where several Illyrian tribes were celebrating Philip's death by marching on Macedon. Alexander intercepted them at Pelion, and in his first really serious campaign as king (Thracian barbarians do not count) he won a decisive victory at the cost of extremely light casualties, beginning what would be the greatest love affair ever between a general and his troops. Word had meanwhile been received that the Thebans, thinking Alexander killed, were in open revolt, and the army took off straight through the mountains of central Greece a feat that was thought close to impossible. Alexander not only did it, but covered some 250 miles in two weeks, a phenomenal rate of march even in good terrain. Caught by surprise, Thebes was quickly captured, and by vote of the League the city was leveled (excepting the temples and the house of the poet Pindar [c. 518-c. 438?]) and the surviving inhabitants enslaved. Alexander has been criticized for this act, but the example of the strongest

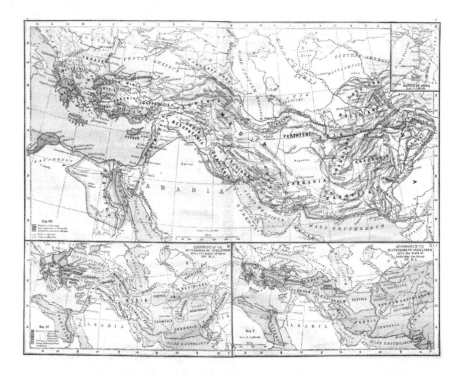

military power after Macedon disappearing overnight certainly had the desired effect. Peloponnesian forces at the isthmus withdrew, Athens hastened to submit to Alexander and all thoughts of revolt evaporated. Instead, the League voted Alexander troops and ships for the expedition against Persia.

The great crusade finally got rolling in the spring of the following year, as Alexander crossed to Asia Minor with 32,000 infantry and 5100 cavalry. The enthusiasm of the Greeks may be judged by the fact that the king left Antipater behind with almost half the Macedonian army, and the League troops with the expedition saw little action, serving mostly as hostages. Aided by dynastic troubles at the Persian court in far off Susa, Parmenio had been able to clear the way for the invasion and liberate some Greek cities, but he had recently been checked by local forces under the Greek mercenary general Memnon (d. 333). With the arrival of Alexander Memnon advised retreating south and destroying all supplies, hoping to draw the Macedonians into overextending their lines of communication, but his suspicious and arrogant Persian co-commanders refused and he reluctantly took up a defensive position on the river Granicus.

Alexander could not leave a hostile army in his rear and in any case wanted to keep them from doing just what Memnon had suggested, so he took his 13,000 Macedonian infantry and all the cavalry and raced to the Granicus. There he discovered the Persians had lined up their 10,000 excellent cavalry on the river back *in front* of their infantry. The value of cavalry is in its mobility and shock value, and the Persians had pretty much surrendered both by stationing their horse in a defensive position. Charging across the stream, Alexander was able to break the enemy horse and expose the 5000 or so Greek mercenaries, who surrendered after a sharp resistance. The surviving mercenaries were sent home in chains as traitors to the Greek cause, but subsequent Greek captives were simply hired, mostly to fill the ever growing need for garrison troops.

The victory at the Granicus uncovered the way south, and by winter Alexander had captured the coast as far south as Halicarnassus and improved immensely his money and supply situation. This helped forestall the danger from the Persian fleet, which outnumbered his own puny navy (which was mostly Athenian) by almost three to one and which had finally begun moving northward. In order to avoid the risk of a naval defeat and the great expense of maintaining the ships and crews, Alexander disbanded his own fleet and determined to defeat the enemy navy by seizing all its ports. The onset of winter marked the end of the sailing season anyway, and with the naval threat momentarily neutralized he sent Parmenio and the bulk of the army inland to seize the central Anatolian plateau, while he took a smaller force southeast along the coast to capture the Lycian cities. After some tough winter mountain warfare he moved north through Pisidia and met Parmenio at Gordium in the spring of 333. Leaving Antigonus the One-eyed (c. 382-301) behind to guard this vital point in his communications, Alexander took the army southeast through Cappadocia and the Taurus mountains by way of the undefended Cilician Gates and reached Cilicia and the Mediterranean.

Alexander had freed the Greeks and conquered most of Asia Minor in little more than a year, succeeding where Agesilaus had failed by carefully depriving the enemy of bases while building up a supply system of his own. Probably because of Agesilaus' failure, the new Great King, Darius III (336-330), was not unduly alarmed by this new invasion and thus failed to employ immediately his strongest weapon, the Persian fleet. The sea was Alexander's obvious weak spot, and Darius' navy could have hindered, if not prevented the crossing to Asia. During the winter of 334/3 the Great King finally woke up to the magnitude of the threat and appointed Memnon supreme commander in the Aegean, providing him with 300 warships. But before Memnon could do either of the two things that would cause serious trouble – attacking the Hellespont and Alexander's communications with Europe and stirring up revolt in Greece – he died, leaving the fleet in far less competent hands. Memnon's death was a major break for Alexander, for it not only took the real sting out of the naval threat, but also deprived Darius of far and away his best general.

Knowing that Darius was now marching west with an army, Alexander, who was for a while incapacitated with a fever, sent a force east to secure Issus, where the coast turns south, while he campaigned in Cilicia after his recovery. When these operations were completed, he reunited his army at Issus and began moving south, aware that Darius was now just on the other side of the Amanus range, which parallels the coast. Darius, meanwhile, unaware of Alexander's illness and Cilician campaign, was wondering what was taking the Macedonians so long, and with growing supply problems he took the initiative and crossed the mountains and seized Issus. Delighted to discover the entire Macedonian army to the south of him, he set up his forces in a defensive position along the Pinarus river, which flows out of the Amanus into the Mediterranean.

Darius' move across the Amanus brings up a subject that ancient authors unfortunately rarely say anything about, because their readers found it boring: logistics, which are as important a factor in the movement of ancient armies as is strategy. The cardinal point here is that a large army cannot stay very long in one place unless that place happens to be a port, because an army eats *a lot* of food; just 30,000 men will require forty-five tons of grain per day, and if there are horses the figure grows even larger. Unless they are near a city with huge stocks, food will have to be carried in, and the only efficient way the ancient world could deliver large quantities of goods was by ship. Alexander or someone on his staff must have been a logistical genius, because although his increasingly large army moves through some of the most inhospitable places in Asia, there are almost never any serious supply problems. This is in many ways as impressive an achievement as the actually military victories.

Darius' arrival on the coast came as good news and bad news to Alexander. The good news was that he would now fight Darius in the cramped area between the Amanus mountains and the sea, where the Persian superiority in numbers and cavalry could not be effectively exploited. The bad news was that the enemy was sitting right on his line of communication, which meant that if he did not win a decisive victory, he and his army were probably doomed. This was just the kind of high risk situation Alexander liked, but it is improbable that he had purposely tried to create it. He moved his army back north.

At the Pinarus he found the enemy in a mile and a half long line, stretching from the foothills to the sea. Darius had placed most of his cavalry, probably more than 20,000, on his right wing, while the center was held by as many as 15,000 Greek mercenaries, who were in turn flanked by an unknown number of cardaces, who were an unsuccessful attempt at creating Asiatic heavy infantry. A huge mass of light infantry backed up the line, and Darius was stationed behind the mercenaries, towards the left. Allocating what he hoped would be enough horse to stem the Persian onslaught along the shore, Alexander loaded up his right with the Companion cavalry and medium infantry and placed the phalanx and sundry hoplites in the center. His forces only numbered perhaps 25,000 infantry and some 5000 cavalry, but it was enough. On the left Parmenio held out against the avalanche of Persian cavalry long enough for Alexander on the right to punch through and begin mowing down from the rear the mercenaries, who had been giving the Macedonian infantry a hard time. At this point Darius fled, and that was the signal for the collapse of his entire army. As expected, the confined battlefield had worked against the Great King; because of the narrow front much of his cavalry and all of his light infantry never participated in the battle, except to be slaughtered in the pursuit.

This time Alexander sent no spoils back to Greece, probably because among the captives he found Athenian, Spartan and Theban envoys, who had clearly been intriguing with Darius. He also found in his possession the Persian military treasure, which ended his money problems for the moment, and Darius' mother, wife and children, whom he treated with great respect. These royal hostages probably had something to do with Darius' next move, which was to offer Alexander an alliance and by implication possession of Asia

Minor. Alexander of course refused, informing Darius that he, Alexander, was now the Great King and did not make alliances with subordinates.

The general rules of strategy suggested that Alexander now take off east after Darius, striking at the heart of the enemy and ignoring the periphery. But Alexander needed to secure his rear against the Persian navy, and that meant moving south along the coast to deprive the fleet of all its bases. He spent the next year doing that, and only the island fortress of Tyre and the desert citadel of Gaza refused to open their gates, probably to Alexander's delight, since he loved a good challenge. Well, they were certainly challenges, the siege of Tyre lasting half a year, but they both fell, and the Persian fleet evaporated. Egypt surrendered without a fight, and Alexander became the latest Pharaoh, a step necessary to legitimize his rule in the eyes of the locals. While there he visited the oracle of Amon at the Siwah oasis in the western desert, mainly, it seems, because no other ruler ever had, and in the western delta he built a new port for the Nile valley, Alexandria. As Alexander hoped, this Alexandria quickly grew to be one of the major metropolises of the Mediterranean, unlike the dozens of other Alexandrias he found all over his empire. These cities, with their core populations of retired vets and sundry Greeks, made administration easier, particularly in the eastern boondocks of the empire, served as focal points for the spread of Greek culture and functioned as live-in garrisons.

In the fall of 331 Alexander was finally ready to move east and crossed the upper Euphrates river in northern Syria with 40,000 infantry and 7000 cavalry. Rather than follow the usual route south along the Euphrates, he moved north and east and crossed the upper Tigris. Darius meanwhile had moved his new army north from Babylon and waited between the towns of Gaugamela and Arbela just to the south of Alexander. With him he had perhaps 6000 Greek mercenaries, more than 20,000 excellent cavalry and some unknown, but certainly huge number of Asiatic infantry, probably in the vicinity of 60-70,000. This time he also had the proper battlefield, an endless featureless plain, and he improved upon nature by creating in front of the army smoothed runways for his 200 scythed chariots. Yes, a chariot corps! These Bronze Age leftovers were intended to break up the enemy formations with their charge, creating gaps into which the horse could be sent.

With nothing upon which to anchor his flanks Alexander had to take steps to protect his numerically inferior army from being engulfed. Behind the phalanx he formed a second line of 18,000 heavy infantry, giving them orders to face about if the army was encircled, and off each flank he stationed extra formations of cavalry and light infantry, which in the worst case scenario could form a defensive square with the front and rear lines. As usual, the right wing was to deliver the punch and was loaded with cavalry, including the

Companions. In accordance with this arrangement Alexander had the entire army move to the right as it advanced, and in order to stop this and protect his left flank Darius began sending units of cavalry against the Greek right wing. Alexander responded by slowly feeding in his own horse, and a general cavalry engagement developed. Darius then ordered a general advance, and while the chariot charge was a total failure (the horses were killed by missile fire and the pikes of the phalanx), Alexander's weaker far left wing was soon in trouble with the enemy cavalry. Before they were forced to give way, however, the movement of cavalry on Darius' left had finally caused a gap to appear in that wing, and Alexander promptly charged in with the Companions and a brigade of medium infantry. When Darius observed the Macedonians beginning to chew their way towards him through his left wing, he fled, and once again this was the cue for all his men to take off.

Alexander had done everything right to compensate for his disadvantages in the battle, and Darius had helped him by surrendering the initiative and by delaying and then not pressing home his assault on Alexander's weaker and more exposed left flank. More vigorous and coordinated action (units that did penetrate the Greek flank headed for the baggage) by the Persian right wing would have changed the complexion of the battle, but the Persian commanders, unlike their Macedonian counterparts, were hampered by their lack of operational independence. The result was not just a defeat, but a humiliation. Alexander lost no more than a couple hundred killed, while the slaughter of the unprotected Asiatic infantry must have been in the tens of thousands. But the biggest prize got away. Alexander and the Companions pursued Darius for seventy-five miles, but lost him nevertheless.

The Macedonians now proclaimed Alexander king of Asia, which appeared indeed to be the case. Darius was still at large, but he was clearly not going to be given the time to assemble another large army. Alexander immediately moved down the Tigris and in the course of the next year occupied the heart of the empire, Iraq and western Iran, and captured all the centers of Persian power: Babylon, Susa, Ecbatana and Persepolis, where Xerxes' magnificent palace was burned down in symbolic revenge for his invasion of Greece. This campaign involved only minor operations against Persian rear guard forces and rebellious locals, and Alexander was in fact already reorganizing the army for the small unit and mountain warfare he expected to meet in the far east. By this time the Macedonian military establishment, including the troops under Antipater (who in 331 crushed an army of Persian financed mercenaries led by king Agis III [338-331] of Sparta), numbered about 150,000, of which perhaps a quarter were Macedonians. Supporting this army was costing Alexander an arm and a leg, but he now had arms and legs aplenty; in the Persian capitals he found over 7000 *tons* of gold and silver.

Richard M. Berthold

Alexander considered the Panhellenic crusade to be now over and sent home those allied Greek troops who chose not to enroll in his army. The empire east of the Caspian Sea and the Persian Gulf was in fact territory of questionable value, mostly unproductive mountain and desert, undeveloped, with poor communications and only marginally ever under the control of the Persian central government. But Alexander needed to catch Darius or at least deprive him of any possible base of operations, and in any case Alexander was Alexander, always looking for the challenge. He thought that the ocean that surrounded the world was just to the north and east of the frontiers of the Persian Empire and was determined to carry his power to the very edge of things. But these campaigns would not be led by the hegemon of the League of Corinth, but by the new Lord of Asia.

Leaving Parmenio with half the army to pacify the districts south of the Caspian, Alexander hurried east in an epic pursuit of Darius, but what he finally found in that summer of 330 was Darius' corpse. The last Achaemenid king had been murdered by one of his satraps, Bessus (d. 328), who escaped the pursuit and later assumed the regalia of kingship, at a rather inopportune time, one would have thought. Whether or not the assassination of Darius was good fortune for Alexander is not clear, since the ex-king of the empire might prove an asset in the new administration as king of Persia. On the other hand, a live Dairus could turn out to be a real danger, serving as a focal point for Iranian resistance. In any case his death made things simpler and enabled Alexander to display himself as heir to the imperial throne by executing Bessus as a traitor and pretender when he was captured. Before chasing Bessus, who fled northeast into Bactria, Alexander headed southeast into Areia and Drangiana (western and southern Afghanistan), in order to pacify these wild areas. Then it was back north through Arachosia to Kabul, where the army passed the winter of 330/29. On the way north Alexander was joined by the rest of the army, which he had ordered to come up from Ecbatana. It was dangerous to leave the centers of Persian power so denuded of troops, but events that had occurred while he was in Drangiana made it imperative that Alexander reestablish personal control over the forces he had left behind with Parmenio.

You will recall that Alexander's seat on the Macedonian throne had initially been insecure and dependent upon the good will of his father's top generals, especially Antipater and Parmenio. His incredible success and unmatched popularity with the Macedonian rank and file had obviously greatly strengthened his position, but his emerging policy of playing the Great King and involving the Persians in the administration and military was extremely unpopular, especially with his father's generation. Sitting back in Macedon with an army of his own, Antipater was a serious danger, but

Alexander had apparently made some sort of deal with him (as part of the conspiracy that killed Philip?), and in any case Olympias, who was never to be underestimated, was there to keep tabs on him. Parmenio was a different story. He was with Alexander and a constant thorn in his side, and he had an entrenched position in the army, where he was second-in-command and had many adherents in high posts. By 330 Parmenio's position had weakened somewhat. His youngest son, who had commanded the medium infantry, had died, while another, who had commanded the light cavalry, had been kicked upstairs to be satrap of Lydia. Parmenio's own reputation had suffered from being stuck in the major battles with the thankless task of holding with the left while Alexander got all the glory at the head of the Companion cavalry on the right. But for all that he was still a danger, especially now that Alexander was more openly developing his unpopular Asiatic policy and was about to push off into the comparative unknown of the far eastern reaches of the former Persian Empire.

But opportunity apparently came knocking in Drangiana. Parmenio's son Philotas (d. 330), who commanded the Companion cavalry, got wind of a plot against Alexander, a common enough occurrence, but supposedly decided it was too insubstantial to trouble the king with. Alexander meanwhile heard of the conspiracy and had Philotas arrested for complicity. As was long tradition with treason cases, Philotas was tried by the Macedonian army and despite the absence of any real evidence was condemned and executed. Ancient Macedonian law called for the execution of immediate relatives in treason cases, and agents were sent hurrying back to Ecbatana, where Parmenio was killed by senior officers who had switched their loyalty to Alexander.

It appears that there was in fact some sort of vague plot against the king, but Philotas' actions make absolutely no sense if he was involved in it. I suspect that he was entirely innocent and that Alexander probably knew it, but seized the opportunity to put a frame around him. Condemning Philotas provided a way to get rid of Parmenio, who was the real target. Given Parmenio's position in the army, especially sitting back in Ecbatana, the key to the west, Alexander dare not arrest him for no reason at all, and the Philotas frame provided him with a legal reason that in effect had been approved by the army in Drangiana. Alexander could thus present the Ecbatana army with a *fait accompli* and lessen the risk of mutiny. It worked, but Alexander felt compelled to order the Ecbatana force to join him in order that he might reestablish his personal control by turning his apparently considerable charm on them.

In spring 329 the grand army marched north out of Kabul and made the difficult crossing of the Hindu Kush to operate in Bactria and Sogdiana (northern Afghanistan and Tadzhikistan, later the site of fabled Samarkand).

The area initially submitted, but then revolt broke out and Alexander was forced to spend the next two years subduing the region. He carried Macedonian arms north to the banks of the Jaxartes (Syr Darya) river, which was to be the northern frontier of his empire, and even crossed the river to destroy an army of Scythian cavalry that had taunted him. The pacification of Bactria and Sogdiana involved the Macedonians in their toughest campaigning yet, as they struggled with inhospitable terrain and a seemingly endless number of fortified towns and rocks, but Bessus was captured and executed and the area secured by early 327.

Alexander established numerous cities and forts in the region in an attempt to unite the more civilized populations against the constant pressure of the Scythian nomads coming out of the steppe, and he took as his wife a Sogdian princess, Roxane (d. c. 311). Though Roxane was said to be the most beautiful women in Asia, the marriage was surely political, intended to bind this remote region more closely to the king and symbolize his policy of union between Europe and Asia. Since the death of Parmenio Alexander had been more openly demonstrating this policy, adopting Persian court dress and customs for the benefit of his Asiatic subjects, and the reaction of his Macedonians was hardly enthusiastic. One evening in 328 Alexander and his Companions got into a drunken brawl over the issue, and the king ended up murdering a close friend, Cleitus the Black (d. 328), who had saved his life at Granicus. Needless to say, Alexander was appalled at what he had done and never again let his drinking get the better of him. In 327 an assassination plot by the royal pages was discovered, and Alexander took the occasion to execute the philosopher Callisthenes (d. 327), a nephew of Aristotle who had been in charge of the pages' education and increasingly vocal in his criticism of Alexander's Asiatic policy. With the removal of Parmenio Alexander was no longer tolerating any objections to his plans for the empire.

In 327 the army recrossed the Hindu Kush to the Kabul valley and then moved east to the Indus watershed (Pakistan), the main body under Hephaestion (d. 324) and Perdiccas (d. 321) traversing the Khyber pass, while Alexander took a force through the mountains to the north. The reunited army, some 75-80,000 strong, crossed the northern Indus in spring of 326 and moved southeast into the kingdom of Porus (d. 318), the man in charge of most of the north Indus valley. Porus was lined up on the far side of the Hydaspes (Jhelum) river with perhaps 30,000 infantry, 4000 cavalry, some chariots and as many as 200 elephants, all of which made it a little tough to cross the river at this spot. Leaving Craterus (d. 321) and the bulk of the army with orders to cross only if the elephants were moved, Alexander got across sixteen miles to the north with 10,000 infantry and 5000 horse and headed south to meet Porus.

The Indian king set up a standard formation with his cavalry on either wing, but the 200 elephants lined up in front of the army prevented Alexander from employing his usual tactics, since cavalry not trained to face the pachyderms will go nowhere near them. So Alexander put all his cavalry on the right and moved his army to the right as it advanced, thus threatening to turn the Indian left flank. He meanwhile sent out a thousand horse to the left across his front in order to pin down the Indian cavalry on the right as long as possible. Predictably, as the Indian army moved left to compensate a gap opened up between the infantry and the left flank horse, and while Alexander's main cavalry force hit the Indian cavalry from two sides, the squadron sent to the left suddenly wheeled right and took them in the gap. The left flank was thus annihilated before the Indian cavalry from the right could join it, and the whole left wing of the Indian army was thrown into confusion, at which point the phalanx hit them. The elephants were a real test of the discipline of the phalanx, but Porus was doomed and finally surrendered after all his officers and two thirds of his army were killed or captured. He should have posted scouts on the far side of the Hydaspes to watch for the end run, and when it came to battle, he should have anchored his left on the river. Not that this mattered, however, since Alexander promptly gave him his kingdom back to rule as a vassal king.

Thinking the edge of the world near, the army moved east, but by the time they reached the Hyphasis (Beas) river it was becoming clear that India was perhaps a little bigger than expected, and the men refused to go on. It was hard to imagine a more attractive commander for a professional soldier than Alexander, but it had now been almost a decade since his veterans had seen home and they were tired of it all. For the first and only time, Alexander's usual tactic of sulking in his tent did not work, and so the army turned back, to head down the Indus valley instead. A fleet of 1800 boats was built, and the army, now at 120,000, split into four columns, one of them riding with the fleet. It took Alexander about half a year to conquer the Punjab and Sind and reach the Indian Ocean, and this was in many ways his most brilliant campaign. He had to deal with unfamiliar and difficult terrain, a population of urbanized, but unusually warlike peoples and a huge multiracial army, of which now only about a quarter was Greek. The heavily urbanized Indus valley was to be his eastern frontier, with the river providing excellent communications for the commerce he hoped to develop between India and the Tigris-Euphrates and the Red Sea.

It was time to go home. In summer of 325 Craterus was sent with the larger part of the army north and west to subdue northern Gedrosia (Baluchistan), while Alexander left a couple of months later along a much more difficult route along the coast. The southern Gedrosia expedition was partly because of the challenge (even Cyrus the Great had lost an army here), but mainly because Alexander was sending a fleet from the Indus delta to the Persian Gulf and needed to establish supply depots along the coast. The march, especially a 150 mile stretch through the Kolwa depression, turned out to be the toughest Alexander ever made, but though the sources speak of tremendous losses, it was apparently the camp followers who suffered. The 12,000 soldiers of the primarily Macedonian force seem to have come through with little loss, saved by their discipline and Alexander's leadership. They linked up with Craterus in Carmania (southern Iran) and marched northwest towards Susa. Meanwhile, Nearchus (fl. c. 336-312), who left with the fleet a couple of months after Alexander, also had a tough time, but made it to the gulf, and the whole army was reunited near Susa in early 324.

After exploring the Tigris-Euphrates delta Alexander took the army north of Babylon to Opis, where he quelled a mutiny of Macedonians, and then moved in the autumn to Ecbatana, where Hephaestion died suddenly of an illness. Hephaestion was Alexander's Patroclus, his closest friend and perhaps his lover, and Alexander went crazy, spending on the funeral 10,000 talents, some twenty-five times the annual income of the fifth century Athenian Empire. He sent the army to Babylon under Perdiccas, while he spent the winter working off his grief by smashing hill tribes to the southwest of Ecbatana. In the spring of 323 he was in Babylon, dealing with administrative problems and preparing for an expedition around the Arabian Peninsula, but there were to be no more marches. At the end of May he came down with a fever, probably malaria (he had suffered recurring bouts of fever ever since Cilicia, which was known for malaria), and on 10 June 323 Alexander died, not quite thirty-three years old.

The conquest of the Persian Empire had been overdue for at least a century, and in some ways Alexander was simply the first to have the opportunity to give the job his undivided attention and take advantage of the Persian weaknesses: an obsolete and poorly led military, a tottering administrative structure and a central government beset by increasing instability. Very likely any competently led and adequately supported Greek army could have begun the job of dismemberment long before Alexander arrived on the scene, but he had some particular advantages. He had as his instrument of conquest not just any Greek army, but Philip's legacy, the finest military machine the world had yet seen, and his opponent was not just any Great King, but Darius III, one of the least competent monarchs of the Achaemenid house. And there was of course Alexander himself, a tactical, strategic and logistical genius, who never lost a single action, from guerilla skirmishes to the huge set battles. He was a winner, whose men quite literally loved him, not just for winning, but also for sharing all their hardships and being more careful with their lives than any other of the great captains in history. Other commanders could have toppled the Persian Empire, but only Alexander could have done it in so spectacular and rapid a fashion.

Alexander also had a fine administrative sense, a quality that usually eludes the great conqueror, and he realized that the administration of his huge empire would require him to be something more than a standard Macedonian king. His Asiatic subjects were accustomed to the oriental monarch, absolute in his power, distant from mortals and surrounded by ceremony, and in order to convince them of his authority Alexander was compelled to adopt some of the dress and ritual of the Persian court and take up the fifteen hundred year old kingship of Babylon. He adopted the Persian policy of respecting local traditions and governing through native forms at the local level, while appointing satraps at the provincial level. All this would have been annoying enough to his Macedonians, but Alexander went further, appointing Iranians to high governmental posts and gradually admitting Asiatics into the army, even into Macedonian units. It was a question of supply; there simply were not enough Macedonians or even Greeks to fill the administrative and military needs of the empire. Be that as it may, the Macedonians had trouble appreciating this and at Opis in 324 actually mutinied over the issue, but Alexander shamed them into submission by discharging them all and telling them he would rely on his Asians.

Alexander was not merely attending to immediate needs, but was in fact pursuing a long-term policy of fusion of east and west. He encouraged thousands of his men to take Asian brides and settle in Asia, and he and his officers took wives from the highest rank of the Iranian nobility. He set in motion a plan to train 10,000 young Iranians to fight in the Macedonian fashion, and at a magnificent banquet at Opis in 324 he celebrated the brotherhood of Persians and Macedonians. It is, however, going too far to suggest that Alexander was chasing some proto-Stoic vision of the brotherhood of all races, because although he was opening the army to all, the ruling aristocracy would be limited to those of Greek and Iranian stock. And for all his radical policies Alexander remained a Greek, convinced of the utter superiority of Hellenic culture, and he was uninterested in that of Asia. But this is visionary enough, especially for a Greek. Even Aristotle, his tutor and the greatest mind of the age, could not break the confining bonds of Greek prejudice towards non-Greeks, and it is to Alexander's credit that he did not accept the lesson of Hellenic narrow-mindedness.

In short, Alexander was indeed Great. He was one of those very few characters in history about whom one could argue that the man made the history rather than the history calling forth the man. The collapse of the Persian Empire was an historical inevitability, but Alexander did not simply destroy the empire of the Great King. In little more than a decade he changed forever the shape of Greek civilization and the face of the Near East. He was on his way to creating what appeared to be a successful multiracial community, something the modern world has not had much luck at, and had he lived a normal lifespan and trained a competent successor, the whole of Mediterranean and western history might well have been very different. But culturally perhaps not; the values passed on to Europe by the Roman Empire encompassed those of Alexander.

Alexander's men thought he was a god, and for all his ruthless realism he may well have suspected that they were right. As a child he was constantly told by his mother that his father was Zeus, not Philip, and then as a young man he destroyed overnight the two hundred year old Persian Empire. He conquered what he thought was half the world, never lost a battle, survived wounds (a punctured lung in India!) that could normally be expected to kill a man and lived in a world where the dividing line between mortal and divine was indistinct. He might well have begun to believe himself a demigod. Perhaps he was.

# # # # # # # # # # # # # # # # # # # #

SUGGESTED READING

Easily our best and most accurate and sober source for Alexander is Arrian, who preserves the lost eyewitness accounts of Ptolemy and Nearchus; he is supplemented by Plutarch's life. For the other side of the coin look at Curtius Rufus, who represents the "vulgate" or National Inquirer tradition of Alexander sources, the growing body of romantic nonsense and fiction that most readers preferred to the truth. There are a million biographies of Alexander, ranging in their interpretation from candidate for sainthood to just another mass murderer; an excellent middle-of-the-road account is Ulrich Wilcken, *Alexander the Great* (1967). For a more romantic view see W.W. Tarn, *Alexander the Great* (1948), possibly the most influential biography of our hero, and for a more cynical picture see Peter Green, *Alexander of Macedon* (1974). More recent and also very good is N.G.L. Hammond, *Alexander the Great. King, Commander and Statesman* (1980). Go to J.F.C. Fuller, *The Generalship of Alexander the Great* (1958) for that aspect of the man, and Donald Engels, *Alexander the Great and the Logistics of the Macedonian Army* (1978) is a fascinating book. There is a highly amusing "what if" essay: Arnold Toynbee "If Alexander the Great Had Lived On" in *Some Problems of Greek History* (1969). Harold Lamb, *Alexander of Macedon* is an entertaining biographical novel, and Mary Renault, *Fire From Heaven* is a plausible account of Alexander's youth. Her novel about Alexander the adult, *The Persian Boy*, presents a different (and I believe incorrect) view of the conqueror. Finally, I recommend a novel by L. Sprague de Camp, *An Elephant for Aristotle*, in which a group of soldiers are assigned to transport an elephant all the way across Alexander's empire to Greece.

# # # # # # # # # # # # # # # # # # # #

XVI. WAITING FOR THE ROMANS

The Hellenistic Age

Fortune's like a barmaid mixing us a drink,
Putting in one measure of good liquor and adding three of bad.

-Diphilus 107[34]

Ever the winner, Alexander had nevertheless failed in one vital regard: he had neglected to produce a successor. True, he probably thought he would have more time to think about it, but it was the king's duty to produce and train an heir as quickly as possible. The Macedonian monarchy was a high-risk business, and the lack of a clear-cut successor could be dangerous for the state. It certainly was for the empire.

When Alexander died, those closest to the king and most influenced by his ideas, the Bodyguard and the Companions, chose as the new lord of Asia Roxane's unborn child. They guessed right, and in late 323 little Alexander IV (323-310?) was born. But the rank and file of the army, for all their love of Alexander, were true Macedonians, and they selected as king of Macedon Philip Arrhidaeus, who owed his survival as Philip's only living son to the fact that he had the mind of a child. Perdiccas was chosen as regent, since Alexander had given him his signet ring before he died, a gesture to which Perdiccas' colleagues and future competitors attached far less significance than he. This arrangement was a clear recipe for disaster, even if the two choices had been competent adults, and the various factions in the grand army almost came to blows just settling on this questionable compromise. It is very likely that all the major players were already thinking in terms of their future interests, and the next forty years are one long struggle among

Alexander's generals for control of first the entire empire and then various parts of it. This was the age of the Diadochi, the Successors, and it is a lively time for the Greeks, packed with action and almost constant war.

Upon hearing the news of Alexander's untimely demise, Athens and a number of other poleis of course revolted and were of course crushed the following year by Antipater, who, incidentally, ended the long run of the Athenian democracy by installing a moderate oligarchy. Antipater then became regent in 321, when a coalition defeated Perdiccas, who was killed invading Egypt, which had been seized by Ptolemy, who subsequently established a ruling dynasty as Ptolemy I Soter (305-283). Antipater died of old age in 319, leaving his son Cassander (d. 297) to struggle for control of the Balkan Peninsula with sundry competitors, including Olympias. She captured and killed the hapless Philip Arrhidaeus in 317 and was herself caught and executed by Cassander, who later also put away Roxane and Alexander IV, thus bringing an end to the Temenid (or Argead) dynasty that had ruled Macedon for three hundred years. An old legend predicted the dynasty's end should a Macedonian king not be buried at ancestral Aigai; his corpse hijacked by Ptolemy, Alexander was interred in Alexandria. Meanwhile,

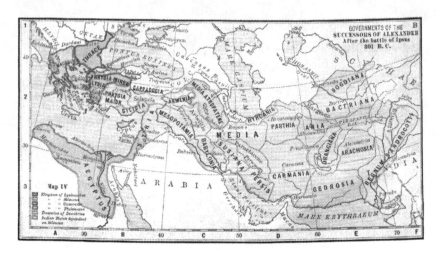

Antigonus the One-Eyed and his son Demetrius (336-283) won the Asian scramble and had a shot at the whole empire, which of course caused all the other players to combine against them, and their hopes and Antigonus' life were ended in 301 at the battle of Ipsus, which involved some 150,000 men, the largest all-Greek battle in history. Before being captured in 285 Demetrius managed to get his son Antigonus Gonatus (c. 277-239) on the Macedonian throne, establishing a new Macedonian ruling dynasty, the Antigonids. To the east, meanwhile, another young general, Seleucus (301-281), picked up the Asiatic pieces of Alexander's empire and founded the Seleucid dynasty. Ptolemy died in 283 and Seleucus in 281, and the last of Alexander's marshals thus passed from the scene.

So ended the Age of the Successors, and the Greek world settled into an uneasy stability for the next eighty years. The Ptolemies (or Lagids) ruled Egypt and parts of the Aegean, the Seleucids ran an Asiatic empire that shrank constantly westwards and the Antigonids controlled Macedon and more or less of the Balkan Peninsula. Throughout most of the third century these three monarchies remained in a precarious balance of power, two ganging up against the third if it became too strong. The traditional poleis simply could not compete with these giants, and most were little more than pawns, though two multi-polis organizations, the Aetolian and Achaean Leagues, emerged to hassle the Antigonids in Greece. Only one polis was able to maintain its independence and play a meaningful role in Greek affairs – the island republic of Rhodes, whose commercial might and cutting-edge navy made her a valuable ally and a state not to be trifled with. Finally, in the far east an independent Greek-run kingdom arose in Bactria, and cut off from the west by the emergence of the Parthian Empire in Iran, it expanded into India, penetrating as far east as Patna on the Ganges near the frontier of Bangladesh. Greek rulers thus held sway over Afghanistan, Pakistan and northwestern India until well into the second century, but their cultural impact was minimal because they were cut off from the heart of the Greek world and the supply of new Greeks. The last Greek kings in these regions were finally overwhelmed by hordes of nomads, particularly the Sacae, and they have been almost completely forgotten by history.

It was said of Prussia in the early nineteenth century AD that it was not so much a state as an army with a place to stand, but the Prussian army at least had a connection with its territory, the homeland from which its soldiers were drawn. Excepting Antigonid Macedon, the Greek monarchies of the Hellenistic Age (323-30) had absolutely none. The administration and armies of the Seleucid, Ptolemaic, Bactrian and minor kingdoms were almost exclusively Greek, drawing only economic support from the local populations, and the frontiers of these states were defined simply by the territory controlled by the army at any given time. Rarely has history seen such a collection of completely artificial states, run by people politically sundered from their homeland. It gives Hellenistic history even more of the flavor of a great game than is often found among competing monarchies, as minorities of Greeks played out their history on a board that mostly belonged to others.

It could not last forever. By the end of the third century the balance of power among the three great monarchies was crumbling, and a weakling

Ptolemaic Egypt appeared to be on the verge of dismemberment at the hands of Antiochus III the Great (225-187) of the Seleucid Empire. The Antigonid king, Philip V (221-179), had meanwhile challenged Rhodian power in the Aegean, and with no one else to turn to the Rhodians appealed in 201 to the new kid on the Mediterranean block, Rome. Within little more than a decade of this appeal both Philip and Antiochus had been defeated, and there was left no Greek power that could face the Roman legions. Greek history was finished, even though Rome would not begin creating provinces in the east until the second half of the second century. Ptolemaic Egypt turned out to be the last independent Greek state of any significance, surviving through Roman sufferance until the death of its last ruler, Cleopatra VII (51-30).

Alexander had utterly destroyed the old Hellenic political order, completing the work begun by his father on the field of Chaeronea. The polis had been forced to give way to the Hellenistic monarchy as the primary political unit in the Greek world, and constitutionalism had succumbed to autocracy. And the world had been dramatically expanded, as Greek language and culture were carried all over the eastern Mediterranean and Near East, and the polis became the cosmopolis, the "world polis." The far eastern areas were soon lost to the Greeks, but the Hellenization of the western parts of the old Persian Empire stuck, and Anatolia, Syria, Palestine and Egypt retained at least a veneer of Greek civilization for the next thousand years, until the Arab conquest.

This explosive expansion of Greek civilization, this Hellenization of the east could hardly fail to have important effects on Greek society and culture. For one thing, Greek rationalism now confronted eastern mysticism eyeball to eyeball, and the unfortunate result was the general erosion of the rationalism, though the meeting of the Greek and Hebrew religious traditions would produce something of profound importance – Christianity. Generally what happened was that Greek culture was diluted, becoming for most non-Greeks a kind of skin-deep affectation, convenient for the propertied classes in the Hellenistic states. In an attempt to secure greater control and unify their kingdoms the Greek monarchs pursued a policy of Hellenization, and the upper classes generally cooperated, learning Greek and adopting Greek ways and building gymnasia and suchlike, becoming "culture-Greeks." But nowhere did this new popular Greek culture, detached from the polis that had shaped Greek values for centuries, run very deep, and the lower and rural classes, the great mass of native populations, were apparently little affected. And one group in particular steadfastly refused Hellenization – the Jews. Their monotheistic religion, which permeated every facet of their society, made them virtually impossible to assimilate into a polytheistic world, and the result was constant friction and finally the revolt of the Maccabees from the Seleucid ruler Antiochus IV Epiphanes (175-164), who certainly receives less than fair treatment in the biblical account. The Romans would have exactly the same problem, but stronger than the Seleucids, they would crush their two Jewish revolts.

Greek culture seemed to be drying up, losing the intense creativity that characterized the incredible cultural outburst of the poleis of the sixth, fifth and fourth centuries. Art lost the restraint and elegance of the classical period, and though an increasing naturalism produced new and impressive work, there was also a tendency toward ostentation and gigantism, especially in the service of the monarchs. Literature became mundane and vapid. As the tragedy typified the fifth century, so did the romance characterize the third. This was Hellenistic soap opera; boy seeks adventure, meets girl, loses girl to pirates, has more adventures, recovers girl, etc. As for the realm of comedy, the biting social and political satire of Aristophanes would obviously not be welcome in the more restricted political atmosphere of the monarchies nor of much interest to the apolitical masses. New Comedy, as it is called, was situation comedy, and throughout the Greek world *Saturday Night Live* gave way to *I Love Lucy*. The plots were standard and inoffensive: mistaken identities, lovers' intrigues, discovery of long-lost children; and the characters were stock: the wily slave, the shrewish wife, the braggart soldier, the star-struck lover. Only one complete example of Greek New Comedy is extant, Menander's *Dyskolos*, but the Roman comic writers Plautus and Terence produced many Latin translations that do survive.

In a way Greek intellectual activity entered a second stage in the period after Alexander. This was the great age of Greek scholarship, and generally the emergence of the scholars is a sure sign that creativity is past. The artistic and intellectual inheritance of the classical period overwhelmed Hellenistic thinkers and became the subject of scholarly scrutiny, diverting attention from original work. The mythic traditions, for example, were chronologically organized, accents were added to written Greek (to make it easier to learn!), older authors, like Homer and Herodotus, were divided into books and endless commentaries and derivative works were written. Established in the 280s by Demetrius of Phaleron (c. 350-c. 283) with the patronage of Ptolemy I and the future Ptolemy II Philadelphus (282-246), the great Library and Museum at Alexandria collected more than a half million rolls and became a magnet for academic types, rivaling and in many way surpassing Athens as a center of intellectual activity. Greece had become the captive of its own past.

This was also the great age of Greek science and engineering, which were stimulated by the expansion of the Greek world and the increased commerce and manufacture and exchange of ideas that came with the explosion of

Hellenism. A prime example of the Hellenistic scientist is Archimedes (c. 287-212/1). He was primarily a mathematician, but is popularly remembered for his engineering exploits – "Give me a point of support (a lever and fulcrum) and I shall move the world." While slipping into a full tub at the public baths, Archimedes noticed the water overflow and suddenly had the solution to a problem he had been mulling over. He had discovered specific gravity, and in his excitement and eagerness to work on the idea he supposedly ran home naked through the streets of Syracuse, shouting "Eureka!" ("I have found it!") Obviously one of the few mathematicians to become a legend in his own time. But though Greek science in the Hellenistic Age seemed often to be on the verge of great discoveries, to be approaching the threshold of a scientific revolution, it never crossed over that threshold. Scientific thought remained distinctly inclined towards the speculative and nonmaterial, which did indeed lead to huge strides in mathematics. Sometime around the beginning of the third century, for example, Euclid (fl. c. 300) produced his compendium of plane and solid geometry, the *Elements*, which in the next two millennia would be second only to the Bible in the study it would receive. Archimedes' work on the surfaces and volumes of solids would not be superseded until the invention of the calculus in the seventeenth century.

Physics and chemistry languished, however. Few practical technological advances emerged from the basic ideas, except perhaps in the area of weaponry, an understandable development given the heavy royal patronage of thinkers in the period. For example, Archimedes, who was in Syracuse during the great siege by the Romans in 213-211, spent a lot of time devising machines to disable the enemy warships attacking the harbor. Many basic principles, such as the expansive power of steam, were understood, but never developed into anything beyond toys. The west would not have as good a chance for a scientific revolution again until the modern period, and many important discoveries, such as Aristarchus' (fl. c. 280) heliocentric theory, were in fact subsequently lost. Incidentally, proposing that the earth (the circumference of which was measured with an error of about five percent by Eratosthenes [c. 285-194]) spins on its axis and along with the other planets revolves about the sun was bold enough, but bolder still was Aristarchus' acceptance of the dramatic consequences of the heliocentric idea. If the earth is moving in a huge path around the sun, but the stars display little or no parallax shift, then the stars must be incredibly far away. Aristarchus accepted without hesitation this million-fold expansion of his universe, demonstrating an openness of mind rare among human beings.

Why the failure? The basic problem lay in the Greek intellectual tradition, so powerfully pulled away from observation and experimentation by the early dominance of philosophy. Even the work of Aristotle could not break this contempt for what was considered manual labor, and the scientist who experimented and the engineer who built were looked down upon by those engaged in pure theory as mere craftsman, part of the same inferior class as merchants. And because of this the best minds tended towards philosophy, and science never developed the mechanisms and methodologies of empirical demonstration that would allow the Greeks to test their theories even had they been inclined to do so. The domination of philosophy is also reflected in the disinclination towards or complete lack of certain attitudes and conceptual tools basic to science. The Greeks preferred absolutes over relatives, patterns over randomness, qualitative evaluation over quantitative measurement and were committed to a vision of the cosmos as a living organism or set of beings that directly affected men on earth. When Aristarchus proposed that the planets moved about the sun, he naturally assumed that the orbits were circles, since the heavens were perfect and since Greek astronomers had a tradition of thinking geometrically rather than dynamically. The observational data of course did not fit this hypothesis, but I suspect that if Aristarchus had postulated the actual elliptical orbits, his theory would have been rejected nonetheless. The ellipse is an imperfect figure, and in any case the notion of a heliocentric universe contradicted centuries of popular belief in and, more important, intellectual support for (including Aristotle) a geocentric theory, in which divine spheres revolved about a fixed earth.

Because of the economic environment, largely shaped by traditional attitudes towards money and labor, there was also little stimulus for applied science and the development of new technologies. The Hellenization of the east had created a huge area that operated on a money economy with a common standard, but the conquering Greeks were still subject to archaic economic ideas that revolved around social status and warfare rather than the free market. Heroic age aristocratic suspicion of change and contempt for commerce survived the heady progress of the sixth and early fifth centuries and remained a disabling feature of Greek society. Stability, not growth, was the economic goal, and the only socially acceptable mechanisms for increasing wealth were plunder and the natural growth associated with agriculture. Working for another, in whatever capacity, was ultimately demeaning and limited freedom, and a Greek gentleman, like his counterpart in eighteenth century Europe, lived from the rents supplied by his lands. Even among merchants the idea of investing in production never made a serious appearance, and virtually all loans were short-term and for the purposes of consumption. It was not just the abundance of cheap labor, both slave and free, that provided no incentive for the invention of labor saving devices, but also the ingrained upper class fear that allowing the poor any break from the constant struggle to survive would lead them immediately to revolution.

And keeping the poor poor in the interests of social stability further stifled invention and industrialization by preventing the development of any real market for mass-produced goods.

The Hellenistic Age was certainly a strange one. As we have seen, there was a tremendous urge towards seeing the reality of things, as the scientists attempted to describe the world, the artists committed themselves to naturalism and the men of letters depicted everyday life. But at the same time there was an equally tremendous urge to escape from that reality, for like the Archaic Age, the Hellenistic was one that filled the individual with insecurity and anxiety. It was a time characterized by upset and change, by continual war and the constantly shifting frontiers of states that had no identity beyond the figure of the reigning monarch. It was a time that coupled increasing poverty for most Greeks with unprecedented riches for a few, and fortunes were rapidly won and lost in the scramble for wealth and power. It was a time of great opportunity and great confusion, in which the hand of Fortune loomed large in the life of the individual, who was cast from the snug, secure world of the polis and set adrift in the wide and capricious universe of the cosmopolis. Greeks were suddenly faced with a new rootlessness, as the identity created by the community-based relationships of the polis was shattered.

The reaction of most to this harsh reality was to emphasize personal relationships and substitute private associations for the lost public institutions of the polis and to escape into the refuges offered by religion and philosophy. For the masses it was magic and the mystery cults, which with their developing salvationist ideas and their detachment from the polis were a perfect fit for the age. Their number and variety were expanded by the creation of the cosmopolis and the contact with a plethora of non-Greek cultures and mystical traditions. One of the most popular mystery cults of the age (and on into the Roman Empire) was that of Isis and Serapis, a kind of Greco-Egyptian hybrid that grew out of Greek control of the Nile valley under the Ptolemies. In a very real way Greek thought was preparing the Mediterranean world for the arrival of Christianity, which in many aspects would be the ultimate mystery religion.

For the intellectual elite solace was found in philosophy, which abandoned the traditional search for truth and became primarily escapist and religion-like in its concern for the spiritual well being of the individual. The road to this sea change in philosophy was paved by fifth and fourth century thinkers, but most especially Plato, who in many ways provided the final synthesis of reason and religion. The assault on traditional religion by the Ionians and the sophists had finished the anthropomorphic gods of Homer and Hesiod, at least as far as the intelligentsia was concerned, but atheism was as unpalatable to them as it was to the masses and new interpretations of the old beliefs were forged. The result: by the beginning of the fourth century the educated man believed the stories of the poets to be untrue literally but to contain a subtext of truth, and he was willing to tolerate traditional civic religious practices as socially useful and as a reflection of a deeper piety. He believed in a kind of cosmic deity or mind, whose existence was demonstrated by the order inherent in the universe and by the mind of man, which was itself a spark of this universal intelligence (Plato's Idea of the Good). This notion of a cosmic religion would be inherited by the Stoics, but it was ultimately doomed by its emotional emptiness and its intimate connection to a cosmology that was simply wrong. It also eliminated all the humor and fun found in the traditional beliefs.

The loose philosophical sect known as Cynicism actually had its origins in the later fourth century, but in its concern for individual happiness and its attack on polis society it was a harbinger of Hellenistic thought. The ideas basic to Cynicism were developed by Antisthenes (mid-5th-mid-4th cent.) an associate of Socrates, and then applied to everyday life by the famous Diogenes (end 5th cent.-c. 324). Antisthenes believed that traditional social classifications were invalid, that all were alike – rich and poor, slave and free, man and woman, Greek and barbarian. He asserted that happiness lay in fulfilling natural needs in as simple a manner as possible and that any natural act was not obscene or shameful and could thus be performed in public. This sort of thing was hardly well received by the average citizen, and when Diogenes began practicing Antisthenes' teachings, he quickly became known as the "dog" (*kuōn*), from which the Cynics got their name. The Cynics were ostentatious slobs, proto-hippies, slapping society in the face with their rejection of traditional values and life styles. They tried to exist as free from material possessions and as shamelessly as possible, living in public places and begging for spare change. Diogenes himself lived in a tub.

Some of this might sound good, specifically the notion that we are all the same under the skin. But the Cynics carried this idea to the extreme, and to them *all* distinctions were invalid. All personal value and ability were rejected, and everyone was as good as everyone else. Virtue required only commitment, the will to live as the Cynics did, rejecting society and traditional standards of behavior and hygiene. To most it is perfectly obvious that whatever transcendental equality there is among men, on the face of this earth we are clearly not equal, but to the Cynic there was no difference between an illiterate boob and an intellect like Aristotle. Intelligence was thus of no value, a manifestly absurd proposition. The Cynics essentially said: "Do your own thing; it's as good as anybody else's." And if your thing is living in a tub or copulating in the street, it was exactly as valuable or invaluable as composing a symphony or healing the sick. The Cynics were hypocrites to boot, living as parasites on the society they had supposedly rejected. What they really rejected was everything that made human beings something more than animals.

Cynicism was never widespread enough or stable enough in its doctrine to be called a "school" of philosophy, and although there were a handful of notable Cynics, who rejected the grosser aspects of the sect, it apparently attracted mostly losers. More important were Skepticism, Stoicism and Epicureanism, all of which were distinct products of the Hellenistic environment and established philosophical schools. Skepticism, founded by Pyrrho (c. 365-275), simply expanded and formalized the doubts that had bothered the Greeks right from the start, maintaining that absolutely nothing was beyond doubt, including ethics. Not only did this assault the basis of deductive logic, by denying the existence of self-evident axioms, but it also suggested that whatever behavior was convenient was correct, since there were no certain grounds for choosing one way over another. This second consideration gave Skepticism some appeal for the uneducated, suggesting that they knew as much as the intellectuals, but the appeal was never very great because the philosophy offered nothing positive. Stoicism and Epicureanism were more successful because they did, aiming not at the traditional philosophical goal of the discovery of truth, but rather at the satisfaction of a more practical need in the Hellenistic Age – the happiness of the individual.

The Stoic school was established in Athens at the end of the fourth century by Zeno (335-263), a Semite from Cyprus, who was influenced by the Cynics. He delivered his lectures in the Painted Stoa, a sort of colonnaded mall, and thus inadvertently gave the philosophy its name. Like Zeno himself and his successors Cleanthes (331-232) and Chryssipus (c. 280-207), Stoicism ultimately has eastern roots and was in fact one of the results of the meeting of Greek rationalism and eastern mysticism; it was a union of philosophy and religion for which Plato had prepared the way. The Stoics envisaged the universe as one great city, the cosmopolis, ruled by one supreme power, which could be called by many names – Zeus, Amon-Ra, Destiny, Yaweh, Chronosynclastic Infidibulum, whatever – but was actually *physis* or natural law set up as a kind of god or divine mind. The design of the universe was thus purposeful and good, and everything that existed, including the soul of man, was derivative of this god, was part of it. This was pantheistic universalism and was in part a result of syncretic tendencies already present early on in Greece and the eastern Mediterranean.

Like the Cynics, the Stoics believed all men to be equal, despite outward appearances; they were all sparks of the supreme power and thus brothers and citizens of the cosmopolis. Men had reason, so free will must be part of the divine plan of things, but how could this be if the universe is determined?

Well, the Stoics were a little vague on this one and sidestepped the issue by emphasizing the concept of duty. It was the duty of the good Stoic to employ his free will to approximate the divine will, to see the natural way and move along with it. But of course that left a problem of ambiguity: was the worst tyranny sanctioned by the simple fact of its existence or was trying to overthrow that tyranny part of the divine plan? You could go either way, depending upon how you understood natural law. Many Stoics played the political game, especially Roman Stoics much later, but there was built into Greek Stoicism a definite tendency towards accepting things as they were and espousing the Philosophy of the Drift.

The main goal of Stoicism was to find happiness and freedom for the individual, and the approach it took was a negative one. Rather than facing the complex problem of describing what constituted happiness, the Stoics simply defined it as the absence of unhappiness. Since unhappiness came from not having what you wanted, like a new car, and not wanting what you had, like terminal acne, a clear route to happiness was to accept what you had and not want what you did not. The basic idea was acceptance of your lot and the avoidance of all passions, which were a sure cause of unhappiness. Even the positive passions or emotional highs must be avoided, since as the great twentieth century philosopher Johnny Carson often observed, you can't have peaks without valleys. There is inevitably a down side to every high, so the proper course is to maintain a kind of mental and emotional equilibrium, a passion flat line or permanent cool, which the Stoics called *apathē* ("without passion"). But if happiness is avoiding passions and hassles, then you would certainly want to think twice about involvement in social and political affairs. Indeed, the ideal Stoic was the man who could do what he felt was his duty to society in the light of his understanding of natural law (the divine plan), yet go about it with complete detachment, totally cool. Do this, and you are also truly free, even if your body happens to be in chains.

So Stoicism had a sense of responsibility to society, but that commitment was undermined by the possibility of simply accepting what was as the way things ought to be, because that was the master plan. And in any case your primary concern was your own happiness, and since by the Stoic definition that had nothing to do with the outside world, there was even less reason to get involved in society. Later Roman Stoics, with their greater sense of duty and responsibility to society, would stay politically involved, but most of us would find it hard to emulate the dedication and emotional detachment of a Marcus Aurelius. Stoicism was a kind of intellectualized cop out, a sort of mysticism in philosophical clothing. As in many religions, happiness was internalized, and the good Stoic could find his peace within. He could convince himself that he had true happiness and freedom no matter what was happening to the world around him. He could watch society crumble and chalk it all up to the divine mind.

Epicureanism was a variation on the Stoic theme. The big variation was that Epicurus (341-270) was for all practical purposes an atheist, who despised religion and consequently rejected the pantheism and divine mind of the Stoics. His universe was an uncaring machine, formed from the randomly crashing atoms of matter proposed by Democritus and Leucippus (fl. 2ⁿᵈ half fifth cent.) back in the fifth century. There was no divine design, no immortal soul, and if the gods existed, they certainly did not care about human beings and their affairs. The Epicureans did not accept the absolute natural law of the Stoics, but were instead *nomos* men, believing that all laws were artificial and relative. So society and political systems were not the product of *physis*, but of human desires, and there were no absolutes in justice and morality, only expediency. With no gods and no moral absolutes the Epicureans were blatant materialists, for whom virtue was individual happiness and happiness was the pursuit of pleasure. The Epicureans were not, however, total party animals; by pleasure they meant intellectual pleasure, which for them was a state of being undisturbed, the absence of pain and passion. They called it *ataraxia* ("impassiveness"), but it was the same as Stoic *apathē*. Happiness was internalized and negatively defined, and the Epicurean idea of a roaring good time was endlessly discussing such matters.

So, although Stoicism and Epicureanism differed absolutely in their vision of the universe, their provisions for the individual were identical. Virtue was the happiness of the individual, and that happiness consisted of the avoidance of pain and passion. This meant a certain rejection of society and the avoidance of political affairs, and though the Stoics had a concept of duty, that duty could easily be interpreted as simply accepting what was. Both philosophies thus tolerated the emergence of the Hellenistic monarchs and erosion of Greek constitutionalism. The Stoic could accept the king as part of the divine plan, while the Epicurean would grant obedience to any power in order to escape the hassles of political involvement. Epicureanism, incidentally, never had very wide appeal, probably because Stoicism satisfied the same individual needs in the same manner and had the added attraction of a god and a purposeful universe. Men were not and still are not ready for a completely godless cosmos. Stoicism, on the other hand, did find wide acceptance among the intellectual elite and ultimately became the ruling philosophical idea of the Roman nobility in the Principate.

Stoicism and Epicureanism were an answer to an insecure world, one in which happiness and social justice were frequently hard to find. They represent a typical human reaction to conditions that overwhelm the psyche – escape. The avenues of escape from the hard realities of the world and society are many. You can remove yourself physically, like Christian monks or those who go off to live in communes in the wild. Or you can remove yourself mentally or spiritually, like the Stoics and Epicureans. Or you can remove yourself by simply erasing reality, like the alcoholic or junkie. In all cases it is an escape into the self, and it comes inevitably when times are hard. What is sought is negative freedom in a world where positive freedom is in short supply or too difficult to manage. Freedom becomes the freedom not to struggle, the freedom to drift with events, no matter what, the freedom to do nothing. Stoicism, Epicureanism and their kindred philosophies are all manifestations of the great Doctrine of Sour Grapes. They all proclaim: "If I can't have this or that happiness or pleasure, then I really didn't want it anyway. What I really want is what I already have, no matter what it is." Happiness and freedom are reduced to simple acceptance. This is submission, the philosophy of defeat.

Such an approach to the world might be good for the peace of mind of the individual, but it is terrible for society and humanity as a whole. It is an assertion that there is no cause to worry about society, to try to improve the human condition and solve the mysteries of the cosmos. Better to worry only about your individual happiness and escape the pains and passions that are the inevitable lot of humanity. This kind of thinking points directly towards the ultimate escape – suicide, for in death you truly feel no pain or passion. And this is the ultimate defeat of the human spirit.

This then was the spiritual inclination of the Hellenistic world. The masses who sought the solace of the mystery religions could hardly be blamed for seeking spiritual relief from the inescapable and frequently harsh realities of their lives, but the intellectual vanguard who turned to Stoicism and Epicureanism betrayed the promise of the Ionian discoveries four hundred years earlier. For them the world and society were simply no longer worth caring about, and the tools of rationalism were useful only for justifying these conclusions. Struggle, competition and protest were not worth the trouble, and instead there was escape. This was the worst sort of intellectual cowardice and perhaps fittingly, certainly sadly, marks the exhaustion of the incredible Greek cultural experience.

##################

SUGGESTED READING

A good introduction to the Hellenistic world is Michael Grant, *From Alexander to Cleopatra* (1982); a better and more detailed book is W.W. Tarn, *Hellenistic Civilisation* (1974); but far and away the best book on the era is Peter Green, *Alexander to Actium: the Historical Evolution of the Hellenistic Age* (1990). Do not be scared off by the massive scale and scholarship of this tome (almost 200 pages of notes!); the text is not only filled with historical insight, but also written in a witty and entertaining style that should be accessible to anyone who can make sense out of this book. If you want to go to the sources, look at Diodorus Siculus, the appropriate lives of Plutarch and for the period of Roman involvement Polybius, the best ancient historian after Thucydides. There are a wide variety of books on the various Hellenistic kingdoms and monarchs; look in the bibliographies of the works mentioned above. For the militarily inclined I recommend highly W.W. Tarn, *Hellenistic Military and Naval Developments* (1930), an excellent and readable work. On the fascinating (well, to me at least) topic of the far eastern Greek kingdoms try George Woodcock, *The Greeks in India* (1966); the last word on the subject is W.W. Tarn, *The Greeks in Bactria and India* (1966), but this is pretty thick going. And of course for the exciting history of Rhodes the standard book is now R.M. Berthold, *Rhodes in the Hellenistic Age* (1984), a fascinating and penetrating work. On Hellenistic science George Sarton, *History of Science Vol. II* (1959) will tell you everything you could possibly want to know. A thorough, if wildly unexciting introduction to the philosophies is A.A. Long, *Hellenistic Philosophy: Stoics, Epicureans, Sceptics*[2] (1986). The third volume in Mary Renault's Alexander trilogy, *Funeral Games*, deals with the wars of the Successors. Finally, for a taste of Hellenistic New Comedy (in its Roman guise) watch *A Funny Thing Happened On the Way to the Forum*.

# # # # # # # # # # # # # # # # # # #

EPILOGUE

THE GIFTS THE GREEKS BEAR

The significance of the Greeks should now be clear. The physical remnants, the surviving art and literature, are wonderful, but most every society has the capability of creating beauty. Rather than these artifacts, it is the ideas inherent in them that are truly important, for it is with their ideas that the Greeks have shaped western and ultimately world civilization. Other societies in other places have caught glimpses of these vital ideas, but nowhere else are they so confidently pursued and nowhere else do they have such a profound and extensive influence beyond the circumstances of the society that discovered them.

And it is no single, particular achievement, not the invention of democracy or the discovery of history or the development of philosophy, but rather the underlying ideas, the basic concepts utterly necessary to a mature civilized society. It is constitutionalism, the notion that law is at the foundation of the social organization and that the people, not kings and gods, are the source of authority. It is rationalism, the will to doubt and wonder, to think and examine the universe according to the patterns of logic and evidence, rather than faith and fantasy. It is humanism, the greatest idea of them all, the conviction that man, rather than god, is at the center of things, that he is what is most important in our world. In sum it is the idea of the individual, the curious notion that the individual human being has a value and a dignity quite apart from the group and the gods. These are the gifts the Greeks bear, their legacy to the human race, unmatched by any other.

Greece in the roughly four hundred years of the Archaic and Classical Ages was one of those rare moments in the often sorry history of humanity when society was ruled by law rather than kings, when reason was celebrated over faith, when men were more important than gods, when the individual stood before the group. The moments come rarely because the gifts are fragile and in fact dangerous. True constitutionalism is a delicate bloom, continually assaulted by the forces of greed and political ambition and constantly undermined by the demands of national security, the fear of social disorder and most recently, the lure of enforced equality. Humanism and rationalism lead inevitably to a colder and more lonely universe, one in which the individual must essentially bear alone the burden of his existence and find his way bereft of divine guidance. Freedom and truth are quite often frightening; they demand an individual responsibility and surrender of personal security that for many is too high a price to pay. The Greeks taught the human race to stand and walk alone, but even two and a half millennia later the steps are still hesitant and unsteady.

Athens, Sparta, Thebes and the rest are gone, but the Greek polis is with us still. It had always been as much a state of mind, a collection of ideas, as it had been a place or an institution, and it continues to exist wherever those ideas survive. It lived in the meetings of the English Parliament and grew in the classrooms of the medieval university. It flourished in the workshops of Renaissance Italy and was encapsulated in the American Constitution. It was the polis ultimately that sent Magellan around the earth and Apollo to the moon. Wherever there are people wondering about the cosmos or crying out for freedom, there is the polis.

###################

CHRONOLOGICAL TABLE

(Kings and tyrants are dated by reigns.)

c. 3000	Beginning of the **Bronze Age** on Crete ("Minoan") and in Balkan peninsula ("Helladic").
c. 2000-1700?	Indo-European invasions.
c. 1700-1400	Great age of Minoan Crete.
c. 1400-1200	Great age of Mycenaean Greece.
late 13th-mid 11th cent.	The **Catastrophe**; destruction of the Hittites; Dorian invasions.
c. 1000	Iranians (Medes and Persians) move into western Iran.
mid 11th-mid 8th cent.	**Dark Age**; beginning of the **Iron Age**.
mid 8th cent.-479	**Archaic Age**.
late 8th-6th cent.	**Age of Colonization**.
c. 700	Introduction of the hoplite phalanx.
mid 7th-6th cent.	**Age of Tyrants**.
c. 650	Phraortes unites the Medes.
650-550	Median empire.
594/3	Solon's reforms in Athens.
559-530	Cyrus II (the Great) unites the Persians, conquers the Medes (550), builds the Persian empire.
546-527	Peisistratus tyrant of Athens.

c. 545	Persians capture the Ionian Greeks.
530-522	Cambyses; captures Egypt (525).
527-510	Hippias tyrant of Athens.
522-486	Darius I.
c. 512	Persians occupy Thrace.
c. 507	Cleisthenes' reforms in Athens.
499-493	Ionian revolt.
490	Persian expedition to Marathon.
486-464	Xerxes I.
480	Xerxes' invasion of Greece; failure at Tempe; battles of Thermopylae, Artemesium and Salamis; Carthaginian invasion of Sicily.
479	Battles of Plataea and Mycale; second Ionian revolt.
479-323	**Classical Age**.
478-477	Formation of the Delian League.
c. 468	Battle of Eurymedon.
464-424	Artaxerxes I.
c. 461-429	Ascendancy of Pericles.
460-445	(First) Peloponnesian War.
c. 459-454	Athenian expedition to Egypt.
c. 449	Peace of Callias.
431-404	Peloponnesian War.
431-421	Archidamian War.
425	Spartans on Sphacteria surrender.
421	Peace of Nicias.
416	Melos crushed.
415-413	Sicilian expedition.
413-404	Decelean (or Ionian) War.
424	Xerxes II.
424-404	Darius II Ochus.

412	Sparta-Persia alliance.
405-367	Dionysius I tyrant of Syracuse.
404	Surrender of Athens; decarchies of Lysander.
404-359	Artaxerxes II Memnon.
401	March of the Ten Thousand; battle of Cunaxa; third Ionian revolt.
400	Spartan army in Asia Minor.
395-386	Corinthian War.
390	Iphicrates' peltasts destroy a Spartan detachment.
386	Peace of Antalcidas (King's Peace).
384-322	Aristotle.
378-371	Sparta at war with Thebes and Athens.
377	Formation of Second Athenian League; Mausolus satrap of Caria.
371	Peace of Callias (King's Peace II); battle of Leuctra.
371-362	Ascendancy of Epaminondas and Thebes.
c. 370	Formation of Aetolian League.
359-338	Artaxerxes III Ochus.
359	Death of Perdiccas II; Philip regent for Amyntas.
358	Philip II king of Macedon; defeats Paeonians and Illyrians, marries Olympias.
357	Philip captures Amphipolis; Rhodes, Chios, Cos and Byzantium revolt from Athens.
356	Birth of Alexander III; Philip defeats Illyrians; Phocians occupy Delphi.

356-346	"Sacred War" against Phocis.
352	Philip destroys Phocian army.
349-348	Philip reduces Chalcidian League.
346	Peace of Philocrates; Philip seizes Thermopylae.
343-335	Aristotle tutor to Alexander.
342-341	Philip completes conquest of Thrace.
340	Philip besieges Byzantium; Athens declares war on Macedon.
339-338	"Sacred War" against Locrian Amphissa.
338	Athens-Thebes alliance; battle of Chaeronea; League of Corinth.
338-336	Arses (Bagoas).
337	League of Corinth declares war on Persia.
336-330	Darius III Codomannus.
336	Macedonian troops in Asia Minor; assassination of Philip; accession of Alexander III (the Great).
334	Battle of the Granicus.
333	Battle of Isus.
331	Battle of Gaugamela (or Arbela).
326	Battle of the Hydaspes.
323	Death of Alexander; conference at Babylon; birth of Alexander IV; Perdiccas regent.
323-30	**Hellenistic Age**.
323-280	**Age of Successors (Diodochi)**
323-322	Lamian War.
321	Assassination of Perdiccas; Antipater regent.
319	Death of Antipater.

317	Execution of Philip Arrhideus.
316	Execution of Olympias.
315-312	Coalition of Successors fights Antigonus I.
c. 310	Execution of Roxane and Alexander IV.
305-304	Siege of Rhodes.
301	Battle of Ipsus; death of Antigonus I.
297	Death of Cassander.
283	Death of Demetrius I and Ptolemy I.
280	Death of Seleucus I; formation of Achaean League.
c. 275	Major expansion of Aetolian League begins.
c. 256	Bactria independent under Diodotus I.
c. 250	Parthia independent.
241	Sicily becomes Roman
223-187	Antiochus III.
221-179	Philip V.
201	Rhodian-Pergamene appeal to Rome.
200-196	Second Macedonian War.
192-189	War between Rome and Antiochus III.
171-167	Third Macedonian War.
175-163	Antiochus IV Epiphanes.
168	End of the Antigonid dynasty.
c. 166-142	Revolt of the Maccabees.
c. 150	Menander's expedition to Patna on the Ganges.
149-148	Fourth Macedonian War.

148	Macedon a Roman province.
146	Greece a Roman province.
64	End of the Seleucid dynasty.
c. 30	Last of the Greek kingdoms in the east overrun.
30	Death of Cleopatra VII; end of the Ptolemaic dynasty.

NOTES

(Endnotes)

1 Translation by Michael Ventris & John Chadwick.
2 Translations by Richmond Lattimore.
3 Translation by A.R. Burn.
4 Translation by F.M. Cornford.
5 Translation by William Arrowsmith.
6 Translation by H.G. Evelyn-White.
7 Translations by Richmond Lattimore.
8 Translation by John M. Robinson.
9 Translation by G.L. Huxley.
10 Translation by John M. Robinson.
11 Translation by William Arrowsmith.
12 Translation by Elizabeth Wyckoff.
13 Translation by H.D.P. Lee.
14 Translation by Robert Fitzgerald.
15 Translations by David Grene.
16 Translation by G.W. Bowersock.
17 Translation by Kurt von Fritz & Ernst Kapp.
18 With the noted exception translations of Thucydides are by Rex Warner.
19 Translation by C.F. Smith.
20 Translations of Herodotus by Aubrey de Sélincourt.
21 Translation by William Arrowsmith.
22 Translation by Jeffrey Henderson.
23 Translation by R.M. Berthold.
24 Translation by Anne Carson.
25 Translation by William Arrowsmith.
26 Translations by William Arrowsmith.
27 Translations by Rex Warner.
28 Translations by George Norlin.
29 Translation by Desmond Lee.

30 Translations by T.A. Sinclair.
31 Translation by R.G. Bury.
32 Translation by Desmond Lee.
33 Translation by Ian Scott-Kilvert.
34 Translation by John Ferguson.

INDEX

69-70, 72-75; in Thucydides, 124-26; in Euripides, 158-60; in Plato, 179-80; in Aristotle, 183; in Stoicism, 226; in Epicureanism, 228

O

Odyssey, see **Homeric epics**
Olympias of Epirus (Macedon), 194, 198, 201, 209, 218
Orphism, *see* **Mystery cults**
Ostracism, 85

P

Panhellenism, 111, 171-73, 198
Parmenides of Elea, 68
Parmenio of Macedon, 194, 198, 201, 202, 203-4, 208; plot against, 208-9
Peisistratus of Athens, 44-45, 88
Peloponnesian League, *see* **Sparta**
Peloponnesian War: causes, 129-33; initial situation and strategy, 135-36; Archidamian War, 136-39; Peace of Nicias 139; Sicilian expedition, 140-41; Decelean (Ionian) War, 141-42
Peloponnesian War (first), 126-28
Peltasts, *see* **Warfare**
Perdiccas of Macedon, 210, 212, 217-18
Pericles of Athens: political reforms, 86-87, 89, 92-93; on the empire, 115-16, 120; Thucydides' attitude towards, 93, 124, 126, 142-43; and (first) Peloponnesian War, 128-29; and Peloponnesian War, 129-32, 136-37
Perioikoi, see **Sparta**
Persian empire: 99-100; invasions of Greece, 101-9; involvement in Peloponnesian War, 141, 143; revolt of Cyrus, 164; involve-

ment with fourth century Greece, 164-65, 166; invaded by Alexander III, 203-8; east occupied, 208-12
Philip II of Macedon: invitation from Isocrates, 172-73; regent, 193-94; army reform, 194-95; uniting Macedon, ; securing Macedon, 195-96; conquering Greece, 196-98; assassination of, 198-90; evaluation of, 199; *see also* **Macedon**
Philip V of Macedon, 220
Philip Arrhidaeus of Macedon, 201, 217-18
Philocrates, peace of, 196
Philosophy, 67-68; *see also* **Sophism, Plato, Aristotle, Cynicism, Skepticism, Stoicism, Epicureanism**
Philotas of Macedon, 209
Phocis: at Themopylae, 105-6; and (first) Peloponnesian War, 127; invaded by Thebes, 165; and Third Sacred War, 196
Physis, see Nomos
Piracy, 4-5
Plataea, battle of, 108
Plato: life, 176-77; deductive thought, 183; metaphysics, 177-78; on the soul, 172; ideal state, 178-82; *Epistles*, 176-77; *Republic*, 179, 183; on women, 181, 185; compared to Aristotle, 183, 186
Polis ("city-state"): emergence of, 24-27; size of, 28; nature of, 29-30, 70; religion of, 55-57; "end" of, 197-98, 220; in the Hellenistic Age, 219, 220, 224
Porus of India, 210-11
Potidaea, 130, 132, 137
Pre-Socratics: 62-64, 67-68; *see also* **Sophism**